AF849934

More Precious than Gold

A Guano Port, Chincha Islands. Mary Robinson Wright. *The Old and the New Peru.* Philadelphia: George Barrie & Sons, 1908.

More Precious than Gold

The Story of the Peruvian Guano Trade

David Hollett

With a Foreword by William M. Mathew

Madison • Teaneck
Fairleigh Dickinson University Press

© 2008 by David Hollett

All rights reserved. Authorization to photocopy items for internal or personal use, or the internal or personal use of specific clients, is granted by the copyright owner, provided that a base fee of $10.00, plus eight cents per page, per copy is paid directly to the Copyright Clearance Center, 222 Rosewood Drive, Danvers, Massachusetts 01923. [978-0-8386-4131-6/08 $10.00 + 8¢ pp, pc.]

Associated University Presses
2010 Eastpark Boulevard
Cranbury, NJ 08512

The paper used in this publication meets the requirements of the American National Standard for Permanence of Paper for Printed Library Materials Z39.48–1984.

Library of Congress Cataloging-in-Publication Data

Hollett, D. (Dave)
More precious than gold : the story of the Peruvian guano trade / David Hollett ; with a foreword by William M. Matthew.
p. cm.
Includes bibliographical references and index.
ISBN 978-0-8386-4131-6 (alk. paper)
1. Guano industry—Peru—History. I. Title.
HD9484.G9P335 2008
338.1'718660985—dc22

2007024678

PRINTED IN THE UNITED STATES OF AMERICA

Contents

Illustrations

Foreword

THE PERUVIAN GUANO TRADE, BASED ON THE RESOURCES OF THE minuscule Chincha Islands, was one of the great commerces of the nineteenth century, elevating Peru to a leading role in Latin American trade and generating by far the largest accumulation of state debts in the continent. This new international prominence, bringing the onetime Spanish silver colony to the notice of farmers and investors in Europe and North America, commenced in the 1840s, and derived fundamentally from the environmental peculiarities of the Chinchas. Geographical determinism combined with illiberal mercantile tradition to give Peru a remarkable triple guano monopoly.

The offshore islands and surrounding chilly ocean had the best conditions in the world, through successive, immense populations of plankton, fish, and birds, for the production of a fertilizer combining high proportions of the two main plant nutrients, nitrogen and phosphorus. The intense aridity of the Peruvian coast, the driest place on earth, meant, moreover, that there was no leaching of nitrogen compounds from the deposits. This natural monopoly in nitrogenous guano was supplemented by a system of digging and loading that was so low cost and primitive in technique that the Peruvian government was able to control the sector as a state monopoly and confine private parties in and around the islands to the ancillary tasks of labor recruitment and shipping. Capitalists, foreign and domestic, found their main rewards within a third contract band of monopoly, whereby they were awarded exclusive rights of sale in specified overseas markets, with attendant opportunities for regular lending, on the security of guano held, to the government in Lima. The largest of these firms was Antony Gibbs & Sons of London.

With their short-term perspectives as mainly caudillo administrations in a highly unstable body politic, Peruvian governments rapidly consumed their earnings, funding an ever-increasing floating and bonded debt, demolishing the internal tax structure, and pampering the armed services. Responding to both pressures and opportunities for price rises, governments and contractors took foolish liberties with consumers that inflicted irreversible damage on the trade, mainly through the stimulation of an "artificial" industry providing cheap specialist manures. Overeager exploitation of the resources, moreover, brought about the departure of the otherwise-replenishing bird population. In the context of a militarized Peruvian polity, the advantages of the triple monopoly proved self-defeating. When guano faded, however, its impact did not fade with it. Money had filtered through to other sectors of the economy and alternative sources of revenue were sought by the state. The political advance of civilismo, the nitrate trade, the War of the Pacific, the astonishing work of railway construction in the Andes, the late-century revival of coastal agriculture, and the continuing and enlarging debilitations of Peru's indebtedness were all to varying degrees consequences of the guano years.

The Chincha Islands form the underlying physical element in this peculiar history. Directly or indirectly, they provide the principal focus for David Hollett's wide ranging and vivid study. Drawing on an abundance of English-language newspapers and British parliamentary reports, and on some recent historical accounts, he describes the tangible, usually harrowing, human reality of the Chincha trade and the other businesses that it spawned. Chinese laborers were brought to the islands by duplicitous means and treated there with great cruelty; Polynesians were sought by barbarous methods to supplement the workforce; foreign sailors received the fertilizer in clouds of lung-damaging ammonia and sailed off on hazardous, protracted voyages around Cape Horn to overseas markets; and contract laborers died in their thousands as guano-financed railways were pushed over the high passes of the cordillera.

In Peru, enterprise in both guano and guano-related industries attracted an assortment of villains. Their activities and, where possible, their biographies are worked graphically into Hollett's narrative. They include the self-styled governor Carlos "Kossuth", Hungarian commander of loading operations on the middle Chincha island in the early 1850s and Domingo Elias, local planter and subsidized provider of coolie labor.

Merchant monopolies were, in fact, so lucrative, and the desire to win fresh contracts (against intensifying indigenous competition) so strong, that opportunistic irregularities appeared to be, for the most part, self-defeating. Secret payments may have been offered, but the main source of success in contract-bidding lay with easy access to foreign money markets and a capacity to lend generously in advance of sales. However, there can be little question that for all the new conquistadors of nineteenth-century Peru, the objective, and often the outcome, was great personal wealth, secured by whatever means best guaranteed success. Peru's physical and human resources were seen as fair game for the foreign marauder. How could it be otherwise when they were so little respected at home?

The curator of natural science at Brooklyn Museum, Robert Cushman Murphy, led an oceanographic expedition to the Peruvian coast in 1919–20 with a view to understanding the fecundity of the offshore waters, subsequently writing the splendid *Bird Islands of Peru* (1925). He had, he recorded, particularly looked forward to visiting the Chincha Islands, for reasons only partly scientific. "Small though the islands are," he wrote, "their name is known in the farthest seaports of the world, and their share in making fortunes and abetting calamities, in debauching men and demoralizing administrations, and in serving as the inanimate cause of greed, cruelty, extravagance, economic ruin and war has given them a historic place quite out of proportion to their size." David Hollett's book gives some idea why an otherwise sober scientist resorted to such extremes of language.

William M. Mathew

Acknowledgments

THE AUTHOR WISHES TO THANK

*Dr. William M. Mathew, for his expert advice, writing a foreword to this book and allowing me to make reference to his published material on nineteenth-century Peru and the guano trade, notably, *The House of Gibbs and the Peruvian Guano Monopoly* published in 1981; *Anthony Gibbs & Sons, The Guano Trade & the Peruvian Government,* chapter IX in *Business Imperialism 1840–1930* edited by D. C. M. Platt; *A Primitive Export Sector: Guano production in nineteenth century Peru,*—Chapter 1X in *Journal of Latin American Studies,* Vol. 9, 1977; and *Peru and the British Guano Market 1840–1870* in *The Economic History Review,* 2nd Series, Vol 23, 1970.

*Professor Lawrence A. Clayton, Head of The Department of History, the University of Alabama, for allowing me to make reference to his publications, namely *W.R. Grace & Co. the Formative Years 1850–1930,* and his introduction to *Merchant Adventurer, The Story of W.R. Grace* by Marquis James.

*Scholarly Resources Inc., Wilmington, Delaware, for allowing me to make reference to two books published by them, namely, *Merchant Adventurer—the Story of W.R. Grace,* by Marquis James, and *Slavery & Abolition in Early Republican Peru* by Professor Peter Blanchard, Department of History, University of Toronto.

*Dr. Rory Miller, Reader in International Business History, University of Liverpool Management School, for his help and advice, and permission to make reference to his published material on Peru and the guano trade, including *The Making of the Grace Contracts, British Bondholders and the Peruvian Government, 1850–1890,* published in *The Journal of Latin American Studies,* Vol. 8, 1976 and Cambridge University Press for granting permission to refer to the aforementioned article by Dr. Miller published in their *Journal.*

*The American Geographical Society, 156 Fifth Avenue, Suite 600, New York, N.Y, for permission to make reference to their publication Peru *from the Air,* (AGS, 1930) by George R. Johnson (and to reproduce illustrations from same, as listed, and a recent article about the Shippee-Johnson expedition, which took the photographs. This article being in the Geographical Review, the learned journal of the AGS, October 1993, 238–51.

*The National Library of Canada, Ottawa, Ontario, Canada, for sending me copy from two nineteenth-century publications, *Anecdotes of a Life on the Ocean* by David Cowans, and *Melbourne and the Chincha Islands* by George Washington Peck.

*Bob Read, my son-in-law, for computer work and general production advice.

*Birkenhead Central Library for obtaining publications and invaluable assistance from the Reference Department staff.

*The Guidhall Library, London for providing me with copy from nineteenth-century documents held by this institution.

*The British Library, Newspaper Library, Colindale Avenue, London, for providing me with copy from nineteenth-century British and foreign newspapers.

*The British Library, London, for obtaining much of the material I required for this work.

*The Public Record Office, Kew, for providing me with nineteenth-century Crew Lists and general shipping records.

*Mr J. H. Ray, for helping me find Captain William Ray's "lost" journal.

*Liverpool University Library for copy obtained from British Parliamentary Papers, *The Times,* as listed, and various nineteenth- and twentieth-century material.

*Liverpool Central Library and Record Office for invaluable assistance in locating and providing me with copy from many publications used in this work.

*My Family, who gave me much support while researching and writing this book. Most importantly, of course, my maternal ancestors and their colleagues at Thomas & John Brocklebanks, Captains Anderson, Ray and Ellery, whose hard lives at sea sparked my interest in maritime research and to whose collective memories I dedicate this book.

Captain Abraham Vaux Wise (1784–1827)
And his sons:
Captain Abraham Vaux Wise (1812–1855)

John Wise, mariner (1814–1837)
Captain George Wise (1817–1857
Captain Joseph Wise (1821–1882)*
Captain Francis Wise (1826–1875)
Captain Sir James Anderson (1824–1893)
Captain William Ray (1839–1926)
Captain William Ellery (1838–1924)

*Author's great-grandfather.

Introduction

PERU IS A LAND THAT REMAINS GEOGRAPHICALLY, SOCIALLY, AND ECONOMICALLY divided into three quite distinct parts; the high Andes; the almost impenetrable jungle area to the east of these mountains; and the long, barren coastal strip that lies between the Andes and the Pacific Ocean. The latter area is where the Conquistadors settled, and it is primarily this area that is the main subject of this book. Francisco Pizarro, an illiterate, but veteran Conquistador, first landed at Tumbez, in northern Peru, with 183 men. By an act of treachery he then captured and executed Atahualpa, and set up Manco as a puppet ruler. Later, on January 6, 1553, Pizarro founded the city of Lima, on the barren coastal strip, as his new capital. The sixteenth century conquistadors came for three reasons: "God, gold and glory," but after the initial "glory" of their conquest they tended to concentrate on gold, rather than God. Direct colonial rule by Spain lasted for almost 300 years, only ending in 1826, when the last Spanish flag was hauled down from the battlements of Real Felipe Fortress.

These long, brutal years of colonial rule had reduced the original population of Peru from seven million to one million, and those indigenous people who did manage to survive to the level of slaves. This Spanish colonial experiment had been one of economic, social, and political decay. Just a few short years after Peru had declared its independence from Spain, however, the attention of some people in Lima began to focus on a potential source of untold wealth, an organic bonanza that subsequently proved to be worth more than all the gold shipped back to Europe in the Spanish treasure galleons. This organic material was guano, the sale of which was to change the history of Peru and all the nations on the Pacific coast of South America. In its greatest concentration guano, the best fertilizer in the world, lay on the Chincha group of islands.

While some men grew rich on the proceeds of the guano trade, the unfortunates who were forced to work the deposits suffered greatly. They were overworked, tortured and lashed by cruel overseers. At first convicts and army deserters were used to dig and load the guano then in 1849 Chinese workers were recruited for this work, usually by crude deception. This marked the beginning of the Chinese Coolie labor system in Peru. Between the years 1849 and 1875 more than 90,000 Chinese workers reached Peru under various "colonization schemes." Thousands died and few ever saw their native land again.

Although guano was in daily use in Peru for centuries it did not occur to anyone to export it until 1840 when Quiros, Allier & Company, a local commercial establishment in Lima, sent a small trial consignment to England. From this venture the value of the product was immediately established. Then, in 1841, Captain Joe Benn, master of the Brocklebank schooner *Bonanza,* brought the first commercial cargo of Chincha Islands guano back to England. The significance of this voyage, in the long, traumatic history of Peru, cannot be underestimated, for this small, 176-ton, Cumbrian vessel was, in fact, acting as the forerunner of a vast international fleet of merchant ships that would soon be sailing to the Chincha Islands. The extent of this trade can be appreciated simply by noting, for example, that during the year of 1857 more than 490,000 tons left the islands, giving employment in that year alone to 620 ships. The lives of the mariners engaged in this Cape Horn South Pacific trade was one of unremitting toil, hardship, and great danger, a subject that receives appropriate coverage in this work.

The income derived by nineteenth-Century Peru from guano sales was for many years on a par with the petro-dollars income of the Gulf States in the twentieth century. However, during the main years of the Peruvian "Guano-Age" the government levied no taxes, relying instead on the massive income derived from the sale of guano to fund state pensions, the armed forces, and the construction of a national railroad system. The cost of wars with Spain and Chile were also funded by the future sales of guano and nitrates, which were continually offered as collateral to obtain foreign loans. Consequently, the republic of Peru remained permanently in debt to foreigners throughout the main part of the nineteenth and the first half of the twentieth century.

During the same period, however, merchants and shipowners made fortunes out of the guano trade and, in particular, the old-established London House of Antony Gibbs who for many years acted as the main government guano contractors. William R. Grace, an Irish landowner of Norman descent, also grew enormously rich on the proceeds of this trade. Grace, however, made his fortune not by selling or shipping guano, but by running a marine store on the main Chincha island, catering for the requirements of the huge fleet of ships permanently moored off the islands waiting to load. After making his fortune, Grace then moved to New York, where he became the first Catholic mayor of the city and then built up a trading and shipping empire that grew powerful enough to dominate the Peruvian economy for decades.

His younger brother Michael's acknowledged masterstroke was undoubtedly the historically significant Grace-Donoughmore Contract of 1890, whereby he practically secured a mortgage on Peru, took over the huge national debt, and received tremendous concessions in return. The Grace Brothers also worked with Henry Meiggs, the American railroad contractor, known as the "Yankee Pizarro," who obtained lucrative contracts from the Peruvian government to develop a national railroad system. Unfortunately, it was Henry Meiggs's fabulous Andean "Railroad in the Clouds" the construction of which cost thousands of lives, that finally bankrupted Peru leaving Michael Grace to pick up the pieces, through the aforementioned financial agreement that he had spent many years negotiating.

The last three chapters of this work record the economic and social condition of Peru in the last years of the nineteenth and the early years of the twentieth century. In this section the many shipping lines that traded with Peru during this period are listed. Mention is also made of the notorious Putamayo Affair, labor relations, and the phenomenal rise of W. R. Grace & Company, known throughout the world as the "Casa Grace." The establishment of Pan-American-Grace Airways, Panagra, in the 1920s, was made possible by the introduction of the United States "Foreign Air Mail Act". Finally, the role of the Brocklebank sailing fleet in the Pacific trade is put into historical perspective, followed by a brief summary of the life and times of their leading mariners.

More Precious than Gold

1

Peru: Land of the Incas

FOR CENTURIES THE NAME OF PERU, LAND OF THE INCAS, WITH THEIR legendary hoards of gold, so coveted by their Spanish conquerors, has stood in the minds of men as a symbol of unbounded wealth. Although Peru may boast of this ancient "golden age," its "Age of Guano" in the nineteenth century was to generate riches way beyond the wildest dreams of Francisco Pizarro and his fellow Spanish conquistadors. The actual name of the country, it should be noted, arose by accident, for it was at first spelled Piru, no doubt from Biru, one of its rivers, but time and use have established it as Peru.[1] The area of this very extensive country at the close of the nineteenth century was variously estimated at between 440,000 and 480,000 square miles or, including certain territories then disputed in the Amazon valley, 677,000 square miles. It is a strange geographically divided land.

Peru is traditionally described in terms of three broad longitudinal regions. First, there is the arid coastal plain bordering the Pacific, a barren and desolate area where little or no rain falls. In the north this plain is typically 20 to 30 miles wide with a maximum width of 90 miles in the Sechuara desert south of Piura.[2] In most of this narrow strip man's foothold is still painfully uncertain, except where rivers move through to the sea, or irrigation from deep wells has made cultivation possible. Midway along this barren coast are the capital, Lima, and its port, Callao. Founded by Pizarro in 1534 to replace lofty Cuzco as capital, Lima nestles in the green Rimac Valley, but a few miles either way, one passes through monotonous and arid country, where at times the wind lifts up great clouds of sand. Not until the clouds, the Ceja de la Costa—"Eyebrow of the Coast,"—thousands of feet up touch the base of the mighty Andes does some moisture bless the land and a few of the hardier shrubs and trees grow perennially.[3]

The geographical factors that make Peru's coast rainless should be noted, for it is this peculiarity that preserved its great guano wealth. Guano, the deposits of millions of seabirds over many centuries, formed an extremely valuable and exportable fertilizer. This was, of course, before the arrival of cheaper chemical fertilizers ended the trade. The Humboldt or Peruvian Current running through the vast Pacific Ocean teems with millions of fish that in turn support the seabirds. This great ocean stream maintains its course for thousands of miles from the icy wastes of the Antarctic in the south to the equator.[4] The continental shelf bordering the coast of Peru is also very narrow. This brings this cold stream so close to the mainland shore as to preclude the occurrence of warm seas or the development of typical "tropical" conditions. Since breezes from a cool sea must pass over lands that are warmed under a tropical sun, no opportunity for precipitation occurs, and neither rainy seasons nor occasional rains may prevail. The significance of this with respect to the famed guano deposits of Peru easily becomes apparent. Guano deposited here beneath a clear dry atmosphere bakes in the sun, and its most valuable components are imprisoned for an indefinite period. Upon these combined factors the economic, social, and political history of Peru itself rested for the greater part of the nineteenth and the first half of the twentieth centuries.[5]

This long, bare coast of Peru stretches for vast distances between the few havens provided by small seaports.[6] Through this barren world of coastal desert and along wide valleys hemmed in by bright red bluffs flow tranquil rivers, thirty of which have sources high enough in the Andes to ensure a continuous flow of precious life-giving water. In these oases formed by the river valleys, algaroba trees and willows, rice, sugar, cotton and cornfields, and fruit and nut orchards spread green carpets. The Mochicas, and probably others well before the time of Christ, began in a modest way the painful and laborious conquest of this somber desert strip. Those ruled by the Incas then labored under the intense heat of the tropical sun to build monumental aqueducts, circling around the upper foothills that brought water to the parched earth and made life possible. Sadly, Pizarro and his gold-crazy fellow conquistadors further reduced the area of cultivation by stripping higher levels of all trees, thus decreasing river flow and mindlessly abandoned all this magnificent effort.[7] Irresponsible behavior did lasting social and ecological damage to the area from which Peru in general, and the indigenous people of this land in particular, have still not recovered.

They were not even able to recolonize the coast completely; consequently, forced Indian labor, followed by Negro slaves, then, during the republic, Chinese coolies', and Japanese and Polynesian workers were brought in—slaves in all but name—to work the large feudal estates and the guano deposits on the Chincha Islands.

This coastal strip, although barren and rainless, enjoys an excellent climate. The mean temperature, for example, at Lima and Callao is between 66 and 78 degrees Fahrenheit, with little variation from these figures throughout the year. The tropical sun is rarely obscured by cloud, but its heat is tempered by southerly breezes, cooled by their passage over the Humboldt Current. This climate is very suitable for Europeans, and it is therefore in this region that the Europeans settled, due in part to the climate but also to the fact that the Pacific Ocean provided a maritime highway to the rest of the world. At the close of the nineteenth century, however, the population of this strip still only stood at 700,000.

The next distinct area is the Cordillera of the Andes itself, the Sierra, consisting principally of two, and in some areas three, main parallel ranges joined, in some areas, by transverse sections.[8] Commonly called the Cordilleras Occidental, Central, and Oriental, these great ranges were created by tectonic activity in which the South American Plate moved over the Nazca Plate.[9] Young in geological terms, the whole area remains highly unstable and subject to frequent and devastating earthquakes. On the western chains are many volcanoes and thermal springs, and in the valleys and on the lofty plateau are the Alpine lakes, which are the sources of the coast rivers and the great inland drainage basin of Titicaca. In the western chain many rugged peaks soar well above the snow line, which varies from about 16,500 feet in the latitude of Lima, to 19,000 feet in the south. Here in the haunt of the condor are to be found herds of swift-footed vicuna, llamas, and wool-bearing alpacas, and last but not least, the indigenous people of the Andes whose ancestors tended similar flocks long before the arrival of the Spanish conquistadors. To the south the land becomes more arid, and the Altiplano becomes a cold, dry, windswept plain. In this region the average altitude is between 10,000 and 11,000 feet. Here life is difficult to say the least, and while the local inhabitants of this inhospitable region have over the centuries adapted themselves to these high-altitude conditions, strangers run the danger of mountain sickness from lack of oxygen in the air and various other complaints peculiar to these regions.[10]

It was among these great peaks that Henry Meiggs, dubbed "The Yankee Pizarro," was to build his celebrated guano-funded "Railroad in the Clouds"—the Callao, Lima, and Oroya line, one of the engineering wonders of the world. Alas, notwithstanding some rudimentary attention being paid to the care of the workers, principally Chileans and Chinese, its construction claimed the lives of 10,000 men, long before it was finished. They went down like flies with verruga, a fever, usually fatal, which burst out in frightful pus and ate away throat, mouth, and nose of the poor sufferers. A disease peculiar to the Rimac Valley, along which the line ran, although less fatal than the so-called Oroya fever, it took a heavy toll. This complaint produced bloody warts, and even before these appeared, the system would be greatly depressed, for the warts tended to bleed profusely, and men working on the line often reported back to their base with their boots filled with blood. The Soroche, or altitude sickness, also took a very heavy toll, the progress of this work being hindered considerably on that part lying along the higher elevations.[11]

Beyond the high Andes lies the Montana, the eastern slopes of this majestic range, and the Amazon plain, which spreads out from this elevated land, covered by a heavy and impenetrable growth of tropical rain forest. Here are to be found countless thousands of plant and animal species, which include the jaguar, tapir, and capybara, and several species of monkeys. Of special note is the wide and colorful variety of bird and fish life. Here also troop millions of devastating ants, huge serpents, enormous hairy spiders, and oversized toads. All the rivers and streams in this endless jungle flow to the east, fed by the perpetual snows of the high Andes, still at this point over two thousand miles from their Atlantic destination. The mighty Amazon and the Ucayali, for instance, are navigable for a thousand miles, even before they reach the frontier of Brazil. These great streams, and scores of others, flow slowly between enormous jungle walls, for even when several thousand miles up the Amazon, the surrounding land is only some 350 feet above sea level.

This eastern region, over which the rain falls incessantly for twelve months in the year, is literally filled with swamps, rivers, and impenetrable forests and accounts for nearly a third of all the land area of Peru. Here the equatorial heat, humidity, and other factors combine to produce a "Green Hell." It is here where deadly diseases carried by swarms of mosquitoes, sand flies, and other voracious insects make life precarious for settlers, who are liable to fall prey to typhoid, malaria, beriberi, leprosy, and an endless variety of horrible skin ailments. Only particularly strong Europeans can exist here, for not only is the area unhealthy, but despite its strange fascination, those new to the area are often seized with an overwhelming desire to escape!

In the few towns that exist here, such as Saposoa, Moyobamba, and Yurimaguas, residents tend to drag out a boring and lethargic existence made weary by the humidity, the blazing tropical sun, and the endless rains, a place where everything tends to rust or rot within a very short period of time. Years ago this eastern department exported a few tropical products such as rubber, timber, coffee, fruits, and cotton, but these had be taken over 2,000 miles down the Amazon before they could even reach the Atlantic or, to a lesser extent, taken over the Andes to Lima or Callao. So isolated was this area from the rest of Peru in the nineteenth century—prior to the age of air travel—that a particular strain was put on the Peruvian administration. For instance, when President Pierola wanted to put down a revolt in this jungle region, the only practical way he could do it was to send a warship through the Straits of Magellan and up the Amazon, a voyage of some 8,000 miles in all. To the conquistadors and nineteenth-century Europeans settled on the coastal strip, the "Green Hell" of eastern Peru was a land of mystery and danger, almost entirely disconnected from the rest of the nation.

The conquistadors overran all of the vast area known as Peru, the coastal strip, the Andes, and the eastern jungles, but these intrepid adventurers never really conquered more than the barren coastal area. A trip into the high Andes was and still is dangerous for Europeans, with the ever-present danger of an attack of Saroche or altitude sickness, and ills too numerous to mention threatened those who attempted to settle in the jungle area. By the same token, some highlanders adapted to these heights who came down to the coast often fell prey to tuberculosis or pneumonia. In 1934 Professor Sievers calculated that the Sierra accounted for 63 percent of Peru's total area, the eastern jungles 28 percent, and the coastal strip 9 percent. The coastal population, largely isolated from the rest of Peru until well into the twentieth century, was where most of the Europeans settled. Their outlook remained colonial, feudal, and Catholic.[12] Even by 1961 only about 2 percent of Peru's total land area was under cultivation, and this vast area remained the homeland of just 12 million people, and most of these were people of Indian, Spanish, or local descent.

During his election campaigns in 1962 and 1963, President Belaunde pointed out that the history of Peru was one of unremitting toil against a hostile environment. It was, however, also a land blessed with many riches: minerals in the Andes, oil and gas below the deserts and forests, and coastal waters teeming with fish, together with a varied climate that made it possible to grow almost any type of crop. However, he conceded, it was also a land that consisted almost entirely of desert, mountain, and jungle, and the exploitation of these many assets required an extraordinary amount of effort. Many of the mines were situated at altitudes of 15,000 feet, and roads to reach them had to be built along the sides of precipices, or taken through solid rock, to reach their destination. In the eastern jungle areas road making was rendered extremely difficult because of the constant rains and the deep swamps that had to be crossed.[13] Lima and the port of Callao are now modern cities, but the life of the Indians remains trapped in the past, their lives as hard now as when the Incas ruled over them, long before the arrival of their Spanish conquerors.[14]

Throughout the early pre-Hispanic period, the people of Peru were almost totally isolated from each other by the varied topography of the country. It would appear, though, that at least three times a unifying culture spread across the Andes, reaching down into the eastern forests and across the coastal strip. However, precisely how long humans had actually lived in this part of the world remains a matter of dispute, with some historians claiming signs of human occupation in South America going back 25,000 years, when emigration from the Orient and Polynesia began. Academics now look to Easter Island, far off the coast of Chile, for evidence to support this view, where huge carved statues supposedly record a very early eastward migration.[15] However, as the origin of these statues remains something of a mystery, not too much reliance can be placed on this theory. According to the traditional history of this mysterious island, it was first settled by King Hotu Matua. Fifty-seven generations of kings then succeeded him, from which it is estimated that Matua and his people only reached this remote place around AD 450.[16]

Other writers state, perhaps more objectively, that there is archaeological evidence to support claims that man has indeed lived in Peru for at least 12,000 years, and possibly 10,000 years more, a Stone Age people, the very first Peruvians, roaming the country in small hunting groups. If this is correct, they must have been contemporaries of several animals long extinct, notably the great woolly mammoth. Evidence of some modest agricultural activity dating from about 4000 BC exists, which was followed by more formal and organized farming. About 1800 BC pottery made its appearance in the coastal settlements, but substantial evidence of human settlement in the humid eastern forests dates only from the introduction of durable pottery about 1000 BC.[17] It was also at this point in time that the Chavin culture spread across the region, probably from the northern ceremonial site of Chavin de Huantar, high up beyond the Maritime Cordillera. These mysterious people are held responsible for carving rocks into Maya-like glyphs of jaguars, dragon-shaped monsters, serpents, and other symbolic figures.

The Chavin people came down from the Andes and settled on the coast at Cupisnique, and perhaps elsewhere, from which point their influence spread among other peoples living on the coastal strip. By 100 BC and down to AD 500, the Mochicas and other coastal groups were producing notable ceramics and metalwork. After AD 600 the Huari civilization, based at the site of the same name near-modern Ayacucho, dominated most parts of the central Andean region. Finally, the Inca Empire developed, which subsequently came to control all of the territory from northern Ecuador to central Chile.

The rise of the Inca civilization was notable and to an appreciable extent overlooked by Europeans because, unlike the civilizations of the Middle East, it was not central to the development of Occidental culture. Also to be noted is the fact that unlike other mainstream cultures, such as those of India and China, historically and commercially linked to later European developments, the empire of the Incas had none of their advantages. These great Oriental civilizations were based on the highly productive valleys of great rivers. In contrast to this the Incas built their civilization in a territory that would seem to be totally unsuited to the rise of a sophisticated society.[18] There was, however, a negative as well as a positive side to this early civilization that throws much light on all subsequent Peruvian social developments, particularly as they relate to the conquest of the Inca nation by the Spanish and the use of migrant labor in the nineteenth century.

This great empire flourished, as far as can be ascertained, from the time of the first Inca, Manco Capac, who founded the dynasty at the beginning of the eleventh century down to the arrival of Pizarro and the overthrow of Atahuallpa in 1532. This empire of the Incas, at the time of the conquest, had its main centers at Cuzco and Quito, which were connected by the famous Inca roads, the principal ones running for over 1,100 miles, which were traversed by a system of runners maintained by the Inca rulers. There were, in fact, two main roads—one along the high Altiplano and summits of the Andes and the other along the barren coastal strip. Quite amazingly, the extension of Inca political control over a vast area, extending from central Chile in the south to northern Ecuador, was accomplished by a remarkably small ruling class. In fact, the name "Inca" only applied to this ruling elite, who formed a close-knit band of administrators—loyal to the emperor himself—the Sapa Inca.[19]

Alas, the beginnings of Inca history are shrouded in mystery. However, the main fable is that the Inca was the child of the Sun, which celestial body, noting that the Andes were inhabited by savage tribes, living more like animals than men, obliged humanity by sending a son and daughter to instruct these poor unfortunates. The son was called "Inca," and the daughter was both his sister and his wife. Despite the obvious genetic dangers of such an incestuous arrangement, the line of the Incas was, until their demise at the time of the Spanish conquest, perpetuated by the marriage of the Inca with his own sister. The Sun apparently left his offspring on an island in lake Titicaca, leaving with them a scepter of gold, with specific instructions to journey northward with the scepter and to advise the people as they went of their unusual origin and mission. Suitably impressed with this dramatic story, the people worshipped the strangers as true children of the Sun and obeyed them as sovereigns, following them in great numbers. Further instructions by the Sun told them that at whatever point the scepter should sink into the ground, a city was to be established, which happened when they reached the valley of Cuzco, where the golden object buried itself in the ground and sank from view. Thus the imperial city of that name was established and the Inca dedication to gold, symbol of the Sun, revealed.[20]

This kingdom was divided into four parts, each great province being placed under a governor who ruled over the people with the assistance of one or more councils for the different departments. These powerful governors spent at least a part of their time in Cuzco, the capital or navel of the Peruvian monarchy, where they formed a sort of council of state to the Inca. The nation itself was actually managed by making every tenth man supervisor of the rest, who was required by strict laws to see that each enjoyed their rights, but also to bring any offenders to justice. To keep these minor officials on their toes the Inca thoughtfully decreed that in the case of neglect, the supervisor would suffer the same penalty that would have been incurred by the guilty party. Needless to say, with this law hanging over their heads, one can well understand why these functionaries did not often neglect their duties. The laws, in fact, were few but exceedingly severe. The crimes of adultery, theft, and murder were all capital offenses, as was any form of blasphemy against the Sun, and the malediction of the Inca, and indeed all offenses of the same complexion, were also punished by death. To burn a bridge was death, but rebellion against the Inca, the "Child of the Sun," was considered to be the greatest crime of all. A rebellious city or province was laid waste and its inhabitants exterminated.[21]

Moving up from the basic organizational unit of ten, the people were still further divided into bodies of fifty, one hundred, five hundred, and a thousand, with officers of appropriate rank placed over each unit. Last, the whole empire was split into departments of 10,000 inhabitants, with a governor over each from the Inca nobility. Their relatively sophisticated legal system was based on judges holding their authority directly from the Crown. However, the fiscal regulations of the Incas and their laws respecting property were the most remarkable feature of their empire. The entire territory was divided into three parts, one for the Sun, another for the Incas, and the last for the people. The lands assigned to the Sun furnished an income to support the vast number of priests, their temples, and the costly ceremony of Peruvian worship. Those reserved for the Inca went to support the royal state and the government. The remainder of the land was divided in equal shares among the people. Further, every Peruvian man was required to marry at a certain age, and when he did, a dwelling was assigned to him with sufficient land for his own maintenance and that of his wife, with an additional portion being granted for every child. The division of the soil was renewed every year and increased or diminished according to the number in the family.

In accordance with strict rules, the lands of the Sun had to be attended to first. Next, they were obliged to till the lands of the old, the sick, the widow, and the orphan, and of soldiers engaged in service; in short, of all that part of the community who from age, sickness, or other genuine causes were unable to cultivate their own plot. The people were then allowed to work their own land, but social tradition and customs, many dating from pre-Inca times, encouraged them to assist their neighbors when any circumstance might demand it. Last, they cultivated the lands of the Inca.[22] The Incas also gave great priority to the extending of arable land, and to accomplish this the Andenes were made, these being terraces upon the steep hillsides, the soil being kept in place by retaining walls on the lower side and excavated on the upper. On the barren coastal strip, Inca engineers also organized the construction of irrigation channels to enable water to be conducted from rivers for distances of many miles.[23] In fact, agricultural methods were relatively advanced. Of particular note is the fact that the value of guano was well understood. Adequate use was made of this fertilizer from the guano islands, and it should be noted that the death penalty awaited anyone who approached or disturbed the birds.[24] The Inca rulers also took steps to care for the people during times of shortage. Huge warehouses were built throughout the empire in which the surplus produce of Inca and church lands was stored for distribution in case of famine. Wool, utensils of copper, gold, and silver were also stored in these great warehouses. After the conquest, the invaders were to find, loot, and live on these stores for a long period without effort.

Under Inca rule it is clear that subjects lived under what might be termed a "benevolent dictatorship" under which rule the needs of all were taken into account. However, there was another feature of this system that should not be overlooked. Communal tradition permitted the Incas to assemble great aggregations of manpower for public works—the construction of irrigation channels, roads, temples and palaces, which still amaze tourists who visit them today. For instance, it is estimated that building the Cuzco fortress required the labor of twenty thousand men over a period of fifty years. Massive stones, some thirty-eight by eighteen by six feet, were brought from quarries twelve to forty-five miles distance, without mechanical assistance or beasts of burden, across rivers and ravines and all manner of hazardous terrain. The stones were then precision worked so that they could be put in place, so that a knife blade could not be wedged between them.[25] One assumes there were no "beasts of burden"—that is, apart from the Peruvian Indians, who must have suffered greatly while engaged in such monumental works. It is also inconceivable that a great deal of coercion was not required by the Incas in order to force their subjects to complete such projects.

Also on the negative side for the Peruvian subject was the fact that there was no way he could better his condition. Born as a beast of burden, chained to the land, the quarries, or the mines, he had to remain so for life. Every aspect of his life, down to the smallest detail of daily living, was governed by strict laws, and although benevolent in intent, these offered little or no prospect of escape. He was cared for, but his life was that of a prisoner, with no control whatsoever over his own life. The great laws of human progress were not for him. As he was born so he was to die. The only exceptions to this general rule were a few lucky peasants who became small office-holders in their village, and others who managed to join the ranks of the artisans. Nevertheless, the vast majority remained chained to a life of hard manual labor. As the noted historian William Hickling Prescott put it, "The Peruvian, laboring all his life for others, might be compared to the convict in a treadmill, going the same dull round of incessant toil, with the consciousness that however profitable the results to the state, they were nothing to him."[26]

The attitude of the Inca elite toward the people was also extremely condescending. "Science was not intended for the people; but for those of generous blood. Persons of low degree are only puffed up by it, and rendered vain and arrogant. Neither should such meddle with the affairs of government; for this would bring high office into disrepute, and cause detriment to the state." Such was the revealing maxim, often repeated, of Tupac Inca Yupanqui, the Peruvian sovereign who came to power in AD 1439. The aristocratic elite crudely exploited their people, taking from them in tribute two-thirds of all they produced. On the other hand, it watched over the people with paternalistic concern. They were, in fact, regarded as mere children, incapable of acting or thinking for themselves, whose sole purpose in life was to serve and obey their rulers. Such were the humiliating conditions of the people under the Incas.[27]

Apart from the peasantry and the nobility there was also another very small class of people in Inca society. These were the Yanacuna, people who had been taken away from their villages when young to become house-servants of the nobility or, if they proved to be particularly talented, assigned to serve in the royal household. Essentially they were little more than slaves. As was the case in the Roman Empire, intelligent men of this class occasionally, perhaps very occasionally, had the chance to break through the rigid Peruvian social structure and achieve high office in the state, a chance that never came to the Peruvian peasant chained to the land in some remote village far from the "corridors of power."

Women, as might be expected, did not count for very much in Inca society. In the villages a wife was expected to cook, spin, bear children, and work in the fields. Children were considered a great asset, for, as noted, the size of the peasants' yearly allocation of land was based on the number of children in a family. Accordingly, a peasant woman would be valued most for the number of children she bore. However, then, as now, beauty was at a premium, consequently the most attractive young girls in the village would often be taken away by nobles to serve as their concubines. Attractive young women would also be taken away and obliged to serve as "Virgins of the Sun"—an order of nuns bound by vows of perpetual chastity who were responsible for making the robes of the priests and serving in various ways in the Temples of the Sun.[28]

In schools established to educate the Inca elite, young men studied the laws and principles of government, in which many of them were destined to participate. They were also initiated in the complex rites of their religion, which those who were to assume the role of priests would require. They were taught to speak elegantly and become acquainted with the mysteries of the *quipas,* which was the complex Peruvian means of recording ideas and transmitting them to future generations. The quipa was, in fact, a cord about two feet long, composed of different colored threads twisted together, from which smaller threads were suspended in a fringe. The different colored threads were tied into knots, the word quipa, in fact, signifying a knot. The various knots and colors sometimes stood for abstract ideas, but they were also used with great accuracy for arithmetical purposes. By the use of these devices, the government was provided with a mass of statistical data, but they could not represent the manifold ideas and images that are expressed by writing. To relate and record the history of the empire, functionaries with particularly good memories were selected, their responsibility being to chronicle the great deeds of the reigning Inca or his illustrious ancestors. Here the quipas could be used by the chronicler to arrange the incidents with method and to refresh his memory. Clearly, though, these devices were a poor substitute for our own alphabet and were even below the crude picture writing of the Aztecs.[29]

It might have been expected that the Incas, who claimed to be the Children of the Sun, would have made astronomy one of their central interests, but this was not the case. However, on reflection, when one considers that death was the penalty for "blasphemy" against the Sun, and radical theories concerning the nature of the universe would have been considered in this light, perhaps this shortcoming is not altogether surprising. They did, though, manage to divide the year into twelve lunar months and also had "weeks," but of what length—seven, nine, or ten days—is not certain. By these periods, however, the Peruvians regulated their complex religious rites and ceremonies, and prescribed the nature of their agricultural labors. They also had some knowledge of one or two constellations and watched the motions of the planet Venus, to which they dedicated their altars. These meager details constitute almost the sum total of what has come down to us of Inca astronomy.

The ancient Peruvian rulers were, among other things, decidedly imperialistic, each Inca ruler being under a standing obligation to extend the boundaries of his far-flung empire. They achieved their expansionist aims by a combination of military skill and cunning diplomacy. Once in the field, the Inca generals deliberately did not push their foe too hard. In fact, at every stage of a particular war, it was made clear that they were open to propositions of peace, this "generosity," as might be expected, being more in their own rather than their enemies' interests. "We must spare our enemies," one of the Peruvian princes is quoted as saying, "or it will be our loss, since they and all that belongs to them must soon be ours." It was a wise maxim, founded equally on benevolence and prudence. Invariably the Incas won their battles with their less-organized neighbors. Then, the first thing the Inca did after the reduction of another nation was to introduce the worship of the Sun. Temples were quickly erected, then priests installed, who preached to the conquered people, explaining the mysteries of their faith and dazzling them with great ceremonials.

The next step was to take a careful census, and then a division of the conquered nation was made. Land was then allocated for cultivation on the principals adopted throughout their own kingdom with the traditional two-thirds of all produce being taken from the peasant occupier to support the ruling elite and their priestly entourage. In case the religious rites, thoughtfully designed to justify all of this wholesale robbery, had not been as effective as might have been desired, troops would also be stationed at strategic points throughout the newly acquired territory to suppress any possible resistance. In practice though, little organized opposition was ever offered by those they conquered. To cement their ever-expanding empire into one cultural and political unit, the Incas also determined to make one language universal throughout their domain, this being Quichua, the language of the court. Teachers were provided in the towns and villages throughout the land and instruction then given to all. At the same time, it was made abundantly clear that no one would be able to hold office or profit in any way if they remained unable to master this new language. By this means, while each province retained its own language, a universal means of communication was introduced throughout the ever-expanding area of

Peru. This was the state of things on the arrival of the Spanish conquistadors.[30] Inca society therefore had its positive and negative aspects, its greatest defects clearly being overcentralization of power in the hands of the Inca and that all individualism had been stifled, factors that the Spanish conquistador Pizarro was quick to spot and take advantage of. To conclude this summary, according to Enock, writing in 1908, "The Inca social regime may be summed up as a species of Socialism, yet under the rule of an absolute but beneficent monarch."[31]

Nevertheless, notwithstanding its shortcoming under Inca rule, absolute destitution did not exist. The sick and the old were also provided for. Against the system, as noted, personal initiative was discouraged, or not developed, as it is in the West today. It was consequently a static autocratic society, incapable of further social, scientific, or political development. However, in the opening decades of the sixteenth century, the days of the Inca Empire were decidedly numbered. Huayna Capac, the eleventh Inca emperor, conquered Ecuador and established his residence at Quito. His death there around 1525 produced a disastrous schism within the far-flung Inca Empire, which was by then dangerously overextended.

Huayna Capac's son and presumed heir, Huáscar, promptly claimed the throne from his palace in Cuzco. However, this claim was challenged by Atahuallpa, another of the emperor's sons. Atahuallpa lived with his father at Quito. Throwing aside the prudence of their forefathers, the two half-brothers were soon at each other's throats with their nation divided in a bloody civil war that lasted until 1531. Atahuallpa eventually defeated the armies of Huáscar and installed himself as the sovereign of a reunited empire. But Atahuallpa's reign was destined to be a short one. Rumors of a large ship upon the coast and of white-faced bearded men had been brought by Indians to Atahuallpa. The isolation of the nations of South America was drawing to a close, and soon the ruthless and oppressive shadow of Spain was to be thrown athwart the Andes. Ruthless individualism and greed were to replace the oppression of the Incas, culminating in the almost genocidal destruction of whole sections of the indigenous people.

2

The Conquest: Gold, God, and Glory

THE ASCENDANCY OF SPAIN AS A WORLD POWER BEGAN WITH THE marriage of Ferdinand of Aragon and Isabella of Castile in 1471, which was followed by the establishment of the Inquisition in 1481 by the Dominican monk Torquemada. In 1492 the surrender of Abu Abdallah marked the end of the Moorish kingdom of Granada. The whole of the Spanish peninsula, except Portugal and Navarre, then united into one kingdom, thus laying the foundations of the Spanish Empire in the sixteenth century. It was also in 1492 that Columbus made his first voyage and discovered the West Indies. Working with Columbus was an Italian explorer by the name of Amerigo Vespucci. Born at Florence in 1451, Vespucci became a provision contractor and provisioned one or two of the voyages of Columbus. When he was fifty years old he organized a voyage to the New World by the same route as Columbus. Sailing under the commander Hojeda, he explored the coasts of Venezuela. His name, Amerigo (America), was then given to the two continents, through the erroneous belief, fostered by the letters he wrote, that he had reached and discovered the mainland in 1497, the year before Columbus. Spain's empire in the New World now began to grow rapidly, with Jamaica being occupied in 1509, Colombia (South America) in 1510, Cuba in 1511, and Florida in 1512, while from 1519–21 Cortés was occupied in the conquest of Mexico, which had been governed by the Aztec monarch Montezuma.

It was, however, Vasco Núñez de Balboa, not Hernán Cortés, who was the first European to see the Pacific. Born at Xeres, Spain, in 1475, when he was still a young man he crossed the Atlantic. At first he lived in Santa Domingo, but he then went to Darien—the name formerly applied to the narrow strip of land joining Central and South America, subsequently called the Isthmus of Panama. Appointed governor of this new territory Balboa set out to explore his domain. It was, in fact, on September 25, 1513, from a mountaintop in Darien, that he first caught sight of the great Pacific Ocean; and, significantly, with Balboa at this time was the illegitimate and illiterate son of a Spanish army officer by the name of Francisco Pizarro. Just four days later Balboa and his followers were wading in this great South Sea, as they called it at the time. Brandishing sword and banner, they then modestly took possession of the greatest ocean on the surface of the globe in the name of Christianity and his Catholic Majesty. All of which, in the best tradition of imperial invaders, tended to ignore the legitimate claims of the indigenous peoples and the inconvenient fact that most of Oceania had already been settled for thousands of years by the Polynesian people.

Alas, Indian chiefs then advised Balboa of the mysterious land of Peru, which lay to the south, where there was gold in fabulous quantities and new lands to be conquered. As fate would have it, though, Balboa lost his position in 1514. Three years later he was beheaded by the bloody new governor, Pedro Arias de Avila; otherwise his bones, rather than those of Pizarro, might now be resting in state in Lima, as the legendary conqueror of Peru. However, the honor of being the first European to actually sail into the Pacific was to go to a Portuguese sailor, albeit in the service of Spain, prior to the arrival of Pizarro and his brothers in Peru. Fernão de Magalhães, or as we know him under his Anglicized name, Ferdinand Magellan, was born about 1470. The son of a noble Portuguese family, he was brought up in the court of King John II of Portugal.

It was during those exciting years at the close of the fifteenth century, when the enthusiasm for new discovery was at the highest, that Vasco da Gama sailed and succeeded. Portugal had half the world given to her by the famous bull of Pope Alexander—and Catholic Spain the other half. Kings and nation alike were eager for new conquests. The young Ferdinand was trained for service with the fleet as well as for the army. His first spell of active service was in the fleet sent out by King John in 1505, under Francisco de Almeida, for the reduction of the islands in the East Indies discovered by Portugal. He then assisted in the conquest of Malacca, and by his prudence and courage saved the expedition from a dangerous native conspiracy. Magellan then obtained the command of a separate expedition, with Serrano, his friend, commanding another. They then gained information, new to Europe, concerning the fabulous wealth of the Spice Islands—"rich in cloves and Nutmegs"—and their exact position. This information was the basis on which, when the time came, Magellan built the plans of his great historic expedition. Unfortunately, at this point in time an argument arose between Portugal and Spain relating to the papal bull that had so generously divided the world between Spain and Portugal. Unfortunately, agreement could not be reached as to whose half-section of the planet the Spice Islands lay in!

From the faraway Spice Islands Magellan then returned to Portugal and settled down for about a year on his estates, but to a man of his temperament, inaction was impossible. He therefore volunteered to serve with the Duke of Braganza in his expedition against the Moroccans, and it was in fighting them that he received a lance wound that made him limp for the rest of his life. He was then accused of trading illegally with the Moors, and of returning to Lisbon without receiving official leave to do so. Slighted over a matter of salary and expenses, to make matters worse, he was then told by his sovereign, Manuel—"a man of niggardly disposition, and suspicious of his servants"—that his lameness was a pretense! Outraged by this indignity Magellan asked the king if he was free to take his services elsewhere and received no discouragement from doing so. Accordingly, he renounced his allegiance to the Crown of Portugal, and after consulting with Ruy Faleiro, an eccentric character who was both astronomer and astrologer, he decided to abandon his allegiance to Portugal and try his luck in Spain.

Thus, at the age of thirty-seven, we find the black-bearded Magellan and Faleiro laying before Charles V of Spain their scheme to reach the Spice Islands by the western route. By this they meant around the southern end, if southern end there happened to be, of that vast new continent discovered by Columbus, but named after Amerigo Vespucci. This was in fact simply a renewal of the plan of Columbus, but with the distinct advantage of twenty-five years of experience and discovery. An agreement was eventually drawn up, whereby Charles promised to fit out five ships, with two years' provisioning, under the command of Magellan as captain-general and Faleiro as joint leader. It was also agreed that both men were to receive a twentieth of the profits arising from their discoveries, a fifth of the profits of this first expedition, and, if they discovered more than six islands, a fifteenth of the profits of trade from any two they chose to name. With these remarkable incentives placed before the adventurers, on March 22, 1518, a contract was drawn up and duly signed by all concerned. Sadly, though, the already unstable Faleiro went completely crazy just before the expedition got under way and was not able to continue.

On Tuesday September 20, 1519, a fleet of five small vessels, the *Trinidad, Santa Antonio, Concepcion, Victoria,* and *Santiago,* manned by 237 men of many different nationalities, set sail from Seville upon what was then the most momentous voyage of discovery ever made, the first voyage around the world. Magellan, with commendable foresight, made the *Trinidad* his flagship. His reasoning was sound, for although she was not the largest ship in the fleet, she did not leak as badly as the others did. She was of 110 tons burthen, about the size of a Thames barge. Fortunately, now aboard the flagship was a certain Italian gentleman with the unforgettable name of Antonio Pigafetta, who had managed to persuade Magellan to let him join the expedition. He accurately recorded their adventures for posterity, and his writings now provide us with the fullest account of the expedition of all those that have come down to us.

Because Magellan was Portuguese, and this was a Spanish expedition, he inevitably had his detractors and this notable misfortune: the second vessel was placed under the command of Juan de Carthagena, who had been appointed, in consequence of the jealousies about Magellan, as an "inspector," a kind of guard to ensure that Magellan did not exceed his authority and acted throughout in the best interests of his adopted country. An appointment that was bound to lead to friction, Magellan—probably correctly—regarded him as nothing more than a meddling spy. Before the fleet left the Cape Verde Islands, one account tells us that Carthagena claimed the right to know what the king's orders were. He then refused to salute the admiral, and at a conference on the flagship with the other commanders, he tried his hand at a few more insults, but he had mistaken his man. Magellan striding forward grabbed him by the lapels of his coat and roaring "You are my prisoner" promptly clapped him in irons and handed him over to Mendoza of the *Victoria* to be kept in custody.

On November 29, the coast of Brazil was sighted, and following it south the fleet arrived in the Bay of Santa Lucia (now Rio de Janeiro) on December 13. Here they remained for two weeks, reveling in the fresh fruit and the welcome change of diet from the standard ship's rations. On the day after Christmas the small fleet sailed southward again, and in February 1520, they reached the fifty-mile-wide mouth of the Rio de la Plata, which they explored, in the mistaken belief that it might be the straits he was seeking. After a fortnight they found fresh water everywhere, and in consequence realized that it was the mouth of a great river and nothing more.

1. Fernando Magellan. *Harpers New Monthly Magazine* (European Edition) June–November 1890. Vol. XX.

They continued southward, nosing into every likely looking estuary that might turn out to be the elusive strait, until they discovered the Bay of San Julian, and here Magellan determined to winter. Here, alas, trouble broke out. The disaffection of Carthagena, and what must be called his party, started as soon as the instructions were given for wintering so far from home. They declared that provisions were not adequate, and the mutiny began. However, Magellan's skill and experience enabled him to deal with the situation. Mendoza, one of the ringleaders, was killed, then his body taken ashore, drawn, and quartered. Juan de Carthagena and a mutinous priest were sentenced to be marooned, and before the fleet set sail, they were put ashore with some biscuits and a few bottles of wine. Needless to say, they were never heard of again.

In the middle of October 1520, Magellan led his little fleet from the harbor and continued the voyage, and although they met baffling headwinds, they continued southward until, a few days later, they found themselves near land, a cape was sighted, and an opening like a bay. Magellan had found his long-hoped-for strait at last. He promptly sent in two ships, the *Santa Antonio* and the *Concepcion,* to find if there was a passage through, and everyone was delighted when they eventually returned, with all guns blazing, to indicate a strait. However, there were still mutinous feelings among the officers and crews; consequently, the *Santo Antonio,* his largest ship, then seized the opportunity to slip away and make off for Spain. For more than five weeks the three remaining ships threaded their way through the intricate maze of winding channels, completely unaware at the time that the masses of land to the south of them were merely islands, and that a relatively short distance beyond them was the clear open sea, beyond the point we now know as Cape Horn.

They now began to run short of food, and many of the crew begged to be taken home, but Magellan swore that even if they had to eat the leather of the ship's yards, he would continue and complete his mission. A few days later the lookout heard, coming from over the islands on the port side, "the beating and roaring of the sea, as though upon some farther shore." Full of joy on this day, November 28, 1520, over sixteen months after leaving Seville, they entered the Southern Ocean. They actually believed they had found a passage between South America and the Great Southern Continent, and one that Spain could defend and close at a score of points, thus giving their imperialistic nation a monopoly in all subsequent trading developments.

Unsuspecting of the enormous width of the new ocean, and with only a few provisions left, they sailed on to the north, helped by the northerly current, which bore them, like every other explorer until Captain James Cook, toward the tropics and the coast of Peru, the mysterious land of the Incas. For its freedom from storms, the ocean received from Magellan the name of the Pacific Ocean, which it has ever since retained. And it was this name that gradually blotted out the name of the "South Sea," which had been given to it by Balboa and the other Spaniards who first discovered it by looking southward from the Isthmus of Panama on September 25, 1513. The days of independent isolation for Peru were now drawing to a close.

However, before they reached the coast of Peru, Magellan turned his ships to the west-north-west and headed across the vast expanse of the Pacific Ocean. Reduced to eating rats and rotten biscuits, the men soon fell sick with scurvy, and at least nineteen of them died. At last, on March 6, 1521, they came to some inhabited islands, where they restocked with badly needed provisions. The three ships then sailed on to the Philippines. The king of one of the islands appeared to be willing to convert to Christianity, but his willingness to submit to Spain provoked a rebellion. Magellan went ashore, got involved in the dispute, and was killed. The expedition, now much weakened, then resumed its voyage, but with only 115 men remaining out of the 237 who had left Seville, and this reduced number being insufficient to work the three ships, the *Concepcion* was destroyed. The two surviving ships then sailed to Borneo, and from there on to the Moluccas, the "Spice Islands" of their dead leader's desires. Here they loaded the *Trinidad* and *Victoria* with spices and prepared to set sail, but at the very last moment the *Trinidad* sprang a serious leak and had to be abandoned. Eventually, after more adventures, the *Victoria* rounded the Cape of Storms, made her way up the Atlantic, and arrived at Seville, concluding a voyage that had lasted three years. The *Victoria* made world history as the first ship to circumnavigate the world.

Magellan had now crossed the Pacific and ended his days on the Philippines, but the dispute between Spain and Portugal over the fate of the Spice Islands continued, with the latter eventually retaining them. The Spaniards had also settled Panama when Balboa crossed the isthmus with Pizarro in 1513. Andagoya had also made voyages down the coast in 1522, toward the region that Balboa had named Peru, and it was against this historical background that Francisco Pizarro, the man destined to be the conqueror of the Inca nation, eventually set out on his first expedition in 1524.

The celebrated conquistador, Francisco Pizarro, was an interesting character whose origins, upbringing, and attitudes were to have an overwhelming impact on the development of Peru. The actual date of his birth is uncertain, but it is probable he was born at some point between 1471 and 1478, at Trujillo, on the high, bleak tableland of Extremadura, as was his fellow conquistador Hernán Cortés. He was an illegitimate child, the son of Gonzalo Pizarro, a colonel of infantry who had served with some distinction in the Italian campaigns and in the wars of Navarre. His mother, Francisca Gonzales, was a peasant girl from the town of Truxillo. Few hard facts are known about his early life, but historians do agreed that young Pizarro received little care from either of his parents. His main occupation was that of a swineherd, and he was neither taught to read nor write. As the son of a high-ranking army officer, a person of some social standing, one can well imagine that Francisco was far from satisfied with his own lowly position in Spanish society. Inevitably, as he grew older, he listened to the tales, then widely circulating, of opportunities that existed for bold young men in the New World.

At the beginning of the sixteenth century most young and ambitious Spaniards were, in fact, obsessed with one idea—that of crossing the seas to the Americas, those newly discovered lands of romance, and above all, golden treasure. In fact, so great was the rush to leave that the principal Spanish cities actually became depopulated. Seville, the main port of embarkation, was at one point so stripped of its male inhabitants that an observer stated that it presented the appearance of a "city of women." Francisco, not surprisingly, shared in this popular enthusiasm, as Spain clearly had given him little and had little to offer him. Consequently, he availed himself of the first opportunity to abandon his pigs and to seek his fortune on the opposite shores of the Atlantic. No doubt already a somewhat embittered young man, he was later described by those who knew him well as withdrawn, taciturn, vengeful, and suspicious. He was also a very hard, courageous man, intelligent, although unscrupulous, a combination of characteristics, negative and positive, that were later to serve him well in his chosen role—that of a ruthless conquistador. It was this character—shaped on the austere plateau of Extremadura by parental desertion and hard manual labor—that was to leave its mark on the Peruvian nation for many long centuries.

The first we hear of Pizarro in the New World is at Hispaniola in 1510, where he took part in an expedition under the legendary cavalier, Alonso de Ojeda. Interestingly, Hernán Cortés, whose mother was a Pizarro and related to the father of Francisco, was then in St. Domingo and prepared to accompany Ojeda's expedition but was prevented from doing so by an injury. So far as Pizarro is concerned, he shared in the disastrous fortunes of Ojeda's colony but managed to obtain the confidence of his commander, to the extent that he, a humble lieutenant, was left in charge of the settlement when the latter went to obtain supplies. It was after leaving this colony in a small vessel that we find him associated with Balboa, the discoverer of the Pacific, and cooperating with him in establishing the settlement at Darien. He was to have the glory of accompanying Balboa, in his terrible march across the mountains, and therefore of being among the small party that first saw the Southern Ocean and going down to the shore, waving aloft the banner of the Virgin Mary. They then scooped up the water to ascertain if it was salt or fresh. Little did Balboa know at this point in time that he would soon lose his post to a new governor, Pedrarias, then, in turn, Pedro Arias de Avila, who would have him arrested on trumped-up charges and beheaded, and that his arresting officer would be none other than Francisco Pizarro!

In 1515 Pizarro was selected, with another officer named Morales, by Governor Pedrarias to cross the isthmus and trade with the natives on the shores of the Pacific. While there, and when he was busily engaged in collecting his booty of gold and pearls from the local islands, his eye ranged along the shadowy line of coast. Soon he got the idea of attempting to conquer the mysterious lands that lay far to the south beyond the great mountains. The seat of government then moved across the isthmus to Panama, and Pizarro moved to this new center with Pedrarias. Pizarro then distinguished himself on various expeditions but only managed to secure a small amount of gold and a tract of rather unhealthy land near the capital for himself. Such was Pizarro's situation in 1522 when Andagoya returned from a mission in the south of Panama. He brought back detailed accounts of the vast empire of the Incas, which indicated that it was a land of opulence, gold, and grandeur, all of which, coinciding with the achievements of Cortés, gave a new impulse to the spirit of "adventure"—or—to be more objective—avarice. It was under these circumstances that Pizarro formed the idea of emulating his celebrated relative and mounted an expedition to conquer another nation, Peru. Ostensibly for the greater good of Spain, and in the interests of the Catholic Church, in reality the prospect of gold and conquest provided the real motivation.

However, lacking the funds to mount his own expedition, Pizarro had to seek support from others, and he obtained this from two individuals, one of them being Diego de Almagro, a soldier of fortune who, like Pizarro, was a foundling. The other was Hernando de Luque, the vicar at Panama who had formerly filled the office of schoolmaster in the cathedral at Darien. Luque seems to have been a well-educated man and one with considerable influence in the small community and, most importantly, one who had control of funds, which made his participation in the proposed venture essential. It was agreed between the three adventurers that all would contribute to the cost of the proposed venture, but that Luque would have to find most of the funds required. The consent of the governor was then obtained, and two small vessels were purchased. They then assembled just over a hundred men, and about the middle of November 1524, Pizarro weighed anchor and took his departure from the little port of Chicama, Panama. Almagro was to follow in a second vessel, as soon as it could be fitted out. It was, in fact, the rainy season and a most unsuitable time of the year to select such a voyage, when navigation to the south was invariably impeded by contrary winds, and tempests swept over the coast. Undeterred by these considerations, however, Pizarro pressed on. After touching at the Isle of Pearls, he headed across the Gulf of St. Michael, steering due south for the Puerto de Piñas, a headland in the province of Biruquete that marked the limit of Andagoya's voyage.

They then sailed up the river Biru and explored the swampy land in the area with great difficulty. Cutting their way through the undergrowth, they eventually reached hilly land where the ground was so rough that it cut their feet. The heat was oppressive, and to make matters even worse, they were encumbered with heavy mail. They ran short of food, and one by one they fell from exhaustion. Demoralized, they returned to their ship and dropped down the river and continued to sail south, down the coast. They were then lashed by a terrible tropical storm that lasted for ten days, and to add to their calamities, their supplies of food began to fail. They returned to a place where they had previously taken in supplies of wood and water, then once more explored the forests. However, the rain rarely slackened, and they made little headway.

The men now began to complain bitterly, and Pizarro eventually had to agree to send the ship back to the Isle of Pearls, under the command of an officer by the name of Montenegro, to obtain more provisions. Half the company went with Montenegro, the others remaining with Pizarro. A further attempt was then made by Pizarro and his men to explore the area and find Indians, but without success. They were now reduced to living off shellfish and berries, and men began to die for want of decent food. The weeks went by, and still there was no sight of the ship that was to bring back food to the adventurers. Their situation was now deteriorating, as more than twenty men had died, and the survivors seemed on the point of following them. It was at this point that they actually did discover a small Indian village in the forest, where they managed to get a limited amount of food. Importantly though, it was in this place that Pizarro obtained fairly conclusive evidence of the wealth that lay farther to the south. First, he noted that the natives wore heavy gold ornaments, the bait that had lured him to forsake his estate in Panama for the trials of the tropical rain forests. He also gathered confirmation of reports he had often heard about a rich and mighty monarch—the Child of the Sun, whose gold-rich dominions lay to the south, many days' march, beyond the great mountains.

At length, after more than six weeks, Montenegro returned with the ship laden with supplies, accounting for his delay by bad weather and constant headwinds. Revived by good food, they re-embarked and set sail once more, continuing to explore, in great detail, the coastal lands to the south. Eventually they landed at a place where the forests were less dense, but then became involved in a battle with the local people. The Spanish fought valiantly, but many of their party were seriously injured. To add to their troubles, their ship was now in a crippled state, so with much reluctance, Pizarro decided to return to Panama and make a full report to Governor Pedrarias, trusting that enough had been done to vindicate the importance of the enterprise and justify a further expedition.

While all of this was going on, Almagro had been busily employed back in Panama, fitting out the second ship of this ill-fated expedition. He had in fact sailed down the coast soon after Pizarro had left, steering in the track of his comrade, but failed to establish contact with him. Almagro then landed but ended up in a battle with the local natives, in which he lost the sight of one eye. Despite this injury, he continued down the coast, calling at several places where he managed to trade for a considerable amount of gold. Still concerned about the fate of Pizarro, Almagro then decided to return to Chicama, Panama, where the two adventurers soon had the satisfaction of embracing each other. Almagro had actually returned with far more gold than his confederate had. Like Pizarro, he had also collected more confirmation of the existence of the fabulously rich Inca Empire. It was then agreed that Pizarro would remain on the west coast, and that Almagro would pass over to Panama and lay the case for support for a further expedition before the governor. So ended the first attempt by the Spanish to discover the land of the Incas.

On arrival at Panama, Almagro found that Governor Pedrarias had many problems on his mind and was not keen to support another expedition. However, the sagacious ecclesiastic Hernando de Luque came to the rescue and eventually obtained the required backing. But Pedrarias made it clear to Luque that he was not impressed with Pizarro, whom he blamed for the loss of so many lives, and therefore only agreed to endorse a further expedition on condition that it was led with Almagro being in equal command with Pizarro. This arrangement sowed the seed of permanent distrust between the two adventurers.

Notwithstanding the above complication, a notable contract was then produced. It began by invoking—in a most solemn and dignified manner—the names of the Holy Trinity and the Blessed Virgin, prior to getting down to the really serious business, which clearly was how the spoils of conquest were to be apportioned. First, it was agreed that these good Christians would have full authority to discover and subdue the land of Peru. All treasures of every kind—gold, silver, and precious stones—that they could steal from the conquered people were to be divided equally between the commanders and the wily ecclesiastic Luque, who was once again putting up most of the money required. In the event of failure the two captains were bound to reimburse Luque for his advances, all the property they possessed being held as collateral to ensure collection. After the document had been signed on March 10, 1526, Father Luque administered the sacrament to give greater efficacy to the compact. Such was the nature of this document that carved out and partitioned among three obscure individuals the entire empire of the Incas. The religious tone of the document is not the least remarkable feature of it, when we contrast this with the actual intent of the parties to it. In the name of the Prince of Peace they were ratifying a contract of which plunder, pillage, and bloodshed were to be the central objectives.

This second expedition eventually made its departure from Panama, under the direction of the experienced navigator Bartholomew Ruiz. Although they reached much farther south and obtained even more confirmation of a land in the interior rich with gold, they met with such hardship that it was eventually impossible to continue, at least without further supplies and support. It was therefore agreed that Almagro would go back to Panama to obtain all that was required, while Pizarro once more remained on the coast. Alas, the authorities in Panama were not supportive, regarding Pizarro's refusal to abandon the expedition as suicidal. However, some support was eventually mustered, and provisions and men were sent south to assist the obstinate adventurer, though only on condition that Pizarro had to return within six months and report himself at Panama, whatever might be the results of the expedition. More tales of the incredible wealth of the Incas then began to reach the ears of Pizarro and Almagro. This induced them to press on until they reached the ninth degree of southern latitude, and then, in response to the urging of their crews, they turned north once more and made for Panama.

At Panama, Pizarro and his fellow adventurers received a good public welcome, but the new governor, Pedro de los Rios, refused to back a further venture. Disheartened by this, Luque suggested the only expedient by which they could hope for success was to apply to the Crown itself. Accordingly, Pizarro went to Castile and gave a glowing account of his work to the king. Suitably impressed, and excited by the stories of gold, silver, and other riches that could easily be acquired by conquest, the adventurer got the backing he required. He was also promoted and granted powers to rule over all the lands he intended to discover. Animated with zeal, Pizarro returned to Panama with reinforcements that included a considerable number of his own close relatives. These were his three younger half-brothers Juan, Gonzalo, and Hernando, all by different mothers, and all of whom were, needless to say, just as unscrupulous and hard-bitten as Francisco. They also took with them Pedro Pizarro, a young cousin. Hernando was the only legitimate and literate member of the "viper's brood." After mass and sacrament on St. John's day, January 1531, the Pizarro clan, with three ships, 180 men and 37 horses, sailed forth once more from Panama, bound for the ill-fated kingdom of the Incas.[1]

They beat a way south to St. Mathew's Bay, Ecuador, where they landed. Starting as they meant to continue, they fell on a local town, sword in hand, which they looted and plundered. One of the ships was then sent back to Panama with their ill-gotten gains. Pressing on to the south, they arrived at Talgarala, at which place Pizarro and Valverde founded the first Spanish city in Peru—San Miguel, where lands and the reluctant, enslaved Indians were allotted to those who chose to remain, "it being evident," remarked Xerez, "that the colonists could not support themselves without the services of the Indians, and ecclesiastics and leaders agreed that repartimiento of the natives would serve the cause of religion and greatly further their spiritual welfare." In this manner was established the coastal base for the audacious conquest of the vast Inca Empire, an empire that was, very fortunately for the Pizarro brothers and their fellow conquistadors, then divided in a bloody civil war.[2] In fact, the ruthless, illegitimate son of the previous Inca king, Atahuallpa, was soon to put to death with the most refined tortures, as well as every single one of the female line of the royal family, in the presence of his half-brother Huáscar, the real heir to the throne. All these developments took place in 1532, the year that marked the arrival of the conquistadors, events that no doubt made the conquest itself possible.[3]

Pizarro soon heard that the seat of the empire of the Incas was not on the coast but beyond the rocky fastness of the Maritime Cordillera. Therefore, on September 24, 1532, he began his memorable march to Cajamarca, high in the Andes. With just a handful of supporters, Pizarro was intent on confronting the great Inca prince, Atahuallpa. One can be critical about Pizarro's aims, objectives, and methods, but not about his audacity and courage, particularly as he soon heard that Atahuallpa had no less than fifty thousand soldiers with him. In fact, rather less than this number were with the prince, the remainder having been sent to make war against his enemy. However, as Pizarro must have been well aware, the Spaniards were still hopelessly outnumbered.

Contact was eventually established with Atahuallpa who, through vanity, was unable to appreciate just how vulnerable he was. Confident that no harm could come to him, with thousands of troops with him and more near to hand, he agreed to come and meet Pizarro. At the appointed time, the great Atahuallpa, the last of the Inca chiefs, arrived with a retinue of 5,000 lightly armed soldiers, carried in great style on a golden litter, adorned with plumes of colored feathers and plates of gold and silver. It was then that Friar Vincent Valverde—at the instigation of Pizarro—with a Bible in one hand and a cross in the other, accompanied by an interpreter, advanced and addressed the Inca, while Pizarro and his band remained hidden behind a wall. The Inca was then exhorted to render tribute to Spain, the pontiff, and the God of the Christians, by whose mandate and in whose service they were acting. A Bible was then given to Atahuallpa, who promptly threw it away. The cunning friar, clearly acting in accordance with an agreed strategy, then called out in a loud voice, "Christians, I call upon you to avenge this insult to the faith." Atahuallpa then stood up in his litter, addressing his soldiers and ordering them to be prepared. What *he* had not been prepared for was the sheer audacity of Pizarro and his men and the danger of being taken hostage. Pizarro grasped his sword and dagger, and with just four men rushed forward and seized Atahuallpa. The trumpets sounded, the guns fired, and the Spaniards rushed forward, and within a short space of time killed 2,000 Indians without a single Spaniard falling. Two thousand more Indians then meekly surrendered. The captured prince was treated well but confined with his women and attendants.

In this strategy it seems likely that Pizarro had drawn on the experiences of his relative, Hernán Cortés, the conqueror of Mexico. Pizarro had neatly decapitated the overcentralized, autocratic rule of the Inca nation with a single, bold, audacious stroke. While the all-powerful monarch remained in the hands of the Spaniards, Atahuallpa's subordinates could offer little resistance. Atahuallpa, then fearing for his life, proposed to buy his freedom with enough gold and silver to fill a large room twice over. Not surprisingly, this generous offer was accepted, Pizarro no doubt merely seeing this as nothing more than an easy way to collect the riches he desired. One must assume, however, that even at this stage, he had not the least intention of keeping to the deal by ever freeing the Inca prince. When the Inca complied with his half of the bargain, Pizarro predictably did indeed fail to honor his pledge. Having got himself into this situation by treachery, his options were now extremely limited. Clearly, if he had freed the prince, Atahuallpa would almost certainlya have organized his forces to attack the Spanish. On the other hand, if they kept him prisoner, it would seem likely that sooner or later the Inca generals would attempt a rescue of their god-king. After receiving dubious information that a large Inca force was preparing to attack Cajamarca, Pizarro accused the prince of treacherously ordering the assault. The Inca was hastily condemned to death. The murder of Atahuallpa remains one of the worst stains upon the pages of Spain's notably dark history in the New World.

A brother of Atahuallpa, Tupac, was then selected by Pizarro as a puppet successor to the Inca throne, by which means it was hoped to ensure obedience from the armies in the field; but Tupac died soon after this arrangement was concluded. Some resistance was then mounted, but the Spanish survived them. Manco Inca, the next legitimate brother of Huáscar, was cunningly inaugurated with great ceremony by Pizarro as a ploy to undermine support for Atahuallpa's generals. The tactic worked; the Spanish then made great efforts to consolidate their gains. About this time, 1534, Hernando Pizarro took ships back to Spain, bearing the vast treasure that had been acquired. Arriving on July 9 in the *Santa Maria de Campo,* he was, not surprisingly, very well received. The king, in particular, was absolutely delighted with his share of the loot, which consisted of gold in bars, plates, vases, and enormous pots, all made of the same precious metal. To show his appreciation for services rendered to the Spanish state, the pope, and God, Hernando's brother, the conquistador, was created a marquis, and the aforementioned, outstanding Christian, Friar Vincent Valverde, was named bishop of Cuzco.

Pizarro then selected a site on the coast near the banks of the river Rimac and established the new capital city of Lima, the first stone of the cathedral laid by him in January 1535. The following year Manco raised the standard of revolt against Spanish dominion, but after a long and bloody struggle the Indian resistance was broken. Pizarro then feuded with his partner, Diego de Almagro, over the division of the newly acquired empire. In 1538, the armies of the two leaders met in combat at Las Salinas, and Pizarro's forces were victorious. Almagro was executed, and his followers stripped of many prerogatives. Three years later though, malcontents, under Juan de la Rada, ruined adherents of the faction of Almagro, conspired to murder Francisco Pizarro. His house was invaded on June 26, 1541, and, after receiving a wound in the throat, the aged warrior fell to the floor and, making the sign of the cross expired. So ended the most remarkable life of Francisco Pizarro, the illiterate swineherd who had, by a combination of courage and duplicity, constancy and brutality, conquered a great but oppressive empire, and all with a mere handful of supporters. He was a Spaniard of his time, and as such merely operating within the traditional parameters of Spanish expansionist policy, that of endeavoring to destroy any society it came in contact with and arbitrarily imposing its own regime on the conquered.

Soon after Valverde was nominated bishop of Cuzco, he received the papal sanction to enter into his duties of office, and a place was selected for the cathedral of his diocese, facing the plaza where he had played such a prominent role in the massacre of 2,000 Indians. A spacious monastery subsequently rose on the ruins of the House of the Sun, an altar was raised on the spot where the Incas had worshipped the Sun, and Christian churches and monasteries gradually supplanted the ancient edifices, on which point William Hickling Prescott now tells us that "The Fathers of St. Dominica, the

Brethren of the Order of Mercy, and other missionaries, now busied themselves with the good work of conversion. We have seen that Pizarro was required by the Crown to bring out a certain number of these holy men in his own vessels; and every succeeding vessel brought an additional reinforcement of ecclesiastics. They were not all like the Bishop of Cuzco, with hearts so seared by fanaticism as to be closed against sympathy with the unfortunate natives. Many of them were men of singular humility, who followed in the track of the conqueror to scatter the seeds of spiritual truth, as they saw it, and with disinterested zeal devoted themselves to the propagation of the gospel. Thus did their pious labors prove them to be the true soldiers of the Cross, and showed that the objects so ostentatiously avowed of carrying its banner among the heathen nations was not an empty vaunt."

Prescott continued in a similar vein, pointing out that efforts to "Christianize" the heathen was an honorable characteristic of the Spanish conquests, and that other adventurers who had occupied the New World had very little regard for religion and were therefore not very keen on spreading it among the "savages." In fact, from first to last, Spanish missionaries had shown a keen interest in the spiritual welfare of the natives. In particular, Prescott had a good word for Las Casas, who, he correctly noted, had gathered his Indians into communities for their welfare and protection. Many, Prescott pointed out, had also spoken out against the cruelty of the conquerors and the colonists. And indeed, who can doubt the sincerity of such men.[4] One wonders, though, how the real message of Christ, the "Prince of Peace," can ever be spread by those who are, in reality, merely an integral part of a national and religious entity, intent on robbing and exploiting those it expresses deep spiritual concern for. In particular, Prescott does not draw attention to that most notable feature of Spanish imperialism—slavery—and the remarkable role that the priest he praises, Bartolomé de Las Casas, played in the establishment of this social evil.

The slave trade from Africa was actually introduced by the Spanish conquistadors, who, on taking possession of many islands in the West Indies, forced the native Caribs to work the mines of Hispaniola. The labor was cruel, dangerous, and exhausting, and the Caribs suffered and died, and almost became extinct. Faced with this situation, in 1511 Ferdinand V of Spain granted a patent to allow four thousand African slaves to be taken every year into Hispaniola, Cuba, Jamaica, and Puerto Rico. Ironically though, it was the eminent Spanish divine, Bartolomé de Las Casas, who was the prime mover in all of this. He was born at Seville in the year 1474, and at the age of nineteen accompanied his father to the West Indies. At this time Rodrigo Albuquerque ruled in Hispaniola, which the Spanish still regarded as their principal colony. Albuquerque, like Pizarro, his counterpart in Peru, was a violent and greedy man under whose rule the native Indians were worked to the point of exhaustion and finally subjected to such brutal treatment that they were almost exterminated. To their eternal credit the Catholic missionaries did stand in opposition to the enslavement of the Indians. (Chattel slavery in the Spanish colonies was to virtually disappear by the end of the fifteenth century, but the substitute system of repartimiento, or forced labor, was to be just as evil, and the abuses it aroused from the conquistadors no less vicious.)

With great courage Las Casas remonstrated with Albuquerque upon his and the colonist's treatment of the Indians, but found that he was not the least bit sympathetic to such humanitarian considerations. Still deeply concerned about the welfare of the Indians, Las Casas eventually hit on the idea that would save them, this being the introduction of stronger laborers into the islands. The "laborers" he actually had in mind were stronger enslaved Africans. This plan was put before the Council in Spain, and although strongly resisted by Cardinal Ximenes, who rightly considered it wrong that an innocent people should be condemned to perpetual slavery to save another, the measure was carried by a majority of voices and Charles granted a patent to allow the trade to begin.

Las Casas defended his extraordinary position by arguing arithmetically, pointing out that as one strong Negro would perform the labor of four weaker Indians, the substitute would effect a fourfold diminution of human suffering! Thus the notorious slave trade originated from the best of motives by Bartolomé de Las Casas, bishop of Chiapa, a tender and devout man, attempting, by his own form of logic, to mitigate the suffering of the natives of the West Indies.[5] This development, following in the wake of the Spanish conquistadors, was to have the most devastating impact on Africa and the Americas. For the next three hundred years, slavery, the crude exploitation of the Indians, then, in turn, Chinese and Polynesian indentured labor, was to shape the history of Peru, the Roman Catholic Church giving a veneer of religious respectability to an essentially sick, brutal, and oppressive colonial regime.

3

From Colony to Guano Republic

FROM THE OUTSET, AND IN KEEPING WITH GENERAL IMPERIALISTIC tradition, the Spanish Empire did endeavor to justify its questionable policies, arguing that all actions had to be based on sound religious principle. At the request of King Ferdinand, the crown jurist, Rubious, examined the rights of Spaniards in the Indies, and he took as his starting point the rights of the natives. His "human and liberal spirit," wrote a modern Mexican scholar, "was to fructify in the theory and law of Spain." And so it was that the Spanish court—after being responsible for unleashing the conquistadors on the land of the Incas—then began to show concern for the natives of Peru. Nevertheless, this royal tradition was to remain constant. For the king, the Indians were his subjects, no less than the Spaniards, and therefore men whom he felt obliged to protect—albeit against the excesses of his own predatory settlers.[1] Appropriate laws and acts designed to protect the native people of the Americas, consistent with Christian teachings, were ultimately put in place. Humanitarian theories and well-meaning laws passed in distant Spain, however, was one thing, but implementing them against the perceived interests of the conquistadors was to prove exceptionally difficult. In practice, the Spanish settlers, like the Incas before them, were destined to use native institutions to serve their own purposes, but in a less responsible and extremely brutal manner.

Alarmed at reports emanating from Peru, the emperor eventually took action, and on March 4, 1543, the first Spanish viceroy, Don Blasco Núñez Vela, arrived in the country, armed with full powers to impose upon the colonists the "New Laws of the Indies," which had recently been promulgated. These well-meaning laws had indeed been drafted in order to protect the Indians against the depredations of the colonists and were aimed in particular against the system of encomienda, whereby the victorious conquistadors had carved out for themselves vast feudal estates and had virtually enslaved the local people.[2] As might be expected, the colonists were not the least bit interested in religious theory, humanitarian laws, and the well-being of the Peruvians. These adventurers argued that they had not risked their lives and, in many instances, their fortunes, merely to become peasants in the distant land of Peru. Furthermore, it was certainly not in the tradition of the Spanish aristocrat to soil his own hands with menial work. Those settlers of a more humble origin, men who had, in many cases, been nothing more than simple, illiterate peasants in Spain, adopted a similar line, thus making the virtual enslavement of the Indians inevitable, if they were to successfully exploit the conquered land. The settlers felt the locals belonged to them, like the land, by right of conquest. On the other hand, these pioneers had no objections to priests and friars converting the Indians to the true Catholic faith, which they conceded had been one of the aims of the conquest. However, in return for the "blessing" of having the Christian message of brotherly love imposed upon them, it was felt proper that the Indians should repay their "debt" by working, as slaves, for their new Spanish masters.[3]

Hard as it was on the Indians, however, the encomienda system of land distribution carried with it no right to the actual ownership of the land, and thus it did not really satisfy the long-term ambitions of the conquistadors, with their newly won high social positions as nobles and gentlemen. Nevertheless, Spain did introduce this system as a means of protecting the Indians. Supposedly, the grantees were acting directly for the king and were thus obligated to protect and "Christianize" the Indians on their estates. But in practice all this system did was create a new class of feudal lords similar to those the king was trying to weaken in Spain. In 1542, after a long and bitter struggle, and before Vela arrived, new laws had been introduced, "for the good treatment and preservation of the Indians." The granting of further encomienda was then stopped, and the inheritance of those already given restricted the obligations that the Indians owed to their Spanish masters, to cash payments, and in other ways attempted to inhibit the crude exploitation of the Indians. This was done by the Crown, which compromised on the critical issue of inheritance. After three lives—those of the original grantee, his son, and grandson—the tribute obligation of the Indians reverted to the king.

The rule of Blasco Núñez Vela was to be a short one. Soon after his arrival a large portion of the colonists, with Gonzalo Pizarro as their leader, formed a revolution and established a base at Cuzco. At this juncture the Royal Audience, a court of justice nominated from Spain, arrived in Lima. Disagreements soon arose between this body and Vela, who proved incapable of dealing with the situation and was thus placed under restraint. Cepeda, the senior judge of the Royal Audience, then took control, and soon after this Gonzalo Pizarro emerged as the governor of Peru. Blasco Núñez Vela, who had embarked on a ship for Panama, then landed at Tumbez and advanced to Quito, where he managed to organize a force of five hundred men. Gonzalo Pizarro and Carbajal followed close upon him; a battle was fought on June 18, 1546; the viceroy was killed and the rebellion was triumphant. Under the brief rule of Gonzalo Pizarro, some revival of agriculture took place, and the development of gold and silver mining was established. Pizarro was advised to consolidate his gains by proclaiming independence and making himself the king of Peru, but he hesitated. However, on hearing about these alarming developments, Spain declared that the rebels had to be crushed.

The emperor sent out as peacemaker the astute ecclesiastic, Pedro de la Gasca. This inquisitor was capable but pitiless, cruel, and cunning. A letter was then sent to Pizarro, granting forgiveness, provided he submitted to the authority of the inquisitor, which offer the governor rejected. A battle was then fought, which, with forces loyal to Pizarro under the leadership of Gonzalo, won. Gasca then organized more support and marched toward Cuzco, being joined by Valdivia from Chile and the Inca Paulla. Desertion and disorganization then undermined Gonzalo's army to the extent that he eventually had no option other than to ride across the plain and surrender. A court-martial was held, and Gonzalo and his officers were all sentenced to death. In January 1550 Gasca entered Cuzco, where he committed various barbarities upon prisoners and colonists and, sated with blood, returned to Lima. In the same month this notable ecclesiastic sailed for Panama, leaving confusion behind him and the government in the hands of the Royal Audience.

The second viceroy was Antonia de Mendoza, an experienced administrator from Mexico. He carried out the royal order prohibiting enforced labor among the natives, for the book written by Bishop Las Casas in 1538 had aroused the Spanish emperor to the necessity of treating the Peruvians fairly. Through these actions Mendoza entered the pages of history as "The Good Viceroy," but his reign was extremely short-lived. Discontent became rife over the whole country. A rebellion then broke out, headed by Francisco Giron at Cuzco.

This rising was soon crushed and Giron captured. He was sentenced to death, and his head nailed on a board in Lima, to join those of Gonzalo Pizarro and Carbajal. These heads remained on display for ten long years, until, in the dead of night, these gruesome remains were secretly taken down and buried in the cloister of a convent. Such were the circumstances attending the establishment of Christian civilization in the land of the Incas.[4] Numerous viceroys then came and went their way. Meanwhile, the suffering of the native Peruvians continued unabated.

Apart from other considerations, the encomienda system had, in fact, proved to be an inadequate source of labor, even before steps were taken to undermine it. By the middle years of the sixteenth century, Peru had fewer than five hundred encomenderos, but the Spanish desire for Indian labor was insatiable. To meet this demand the Crown was persuaded to resurrect and refine the "mita" draft of the Inca rulers. The introduction of this law obliged most male Peruvians to labor as required by the state. By law these unfortunates were supposed to be paid a fair wage, sufficient to buy the necessities of life, and their taxes. These men were employed on various projects, the most dreaded of which was mining. This system of forced labor kept several mines in operation, but the largest and most notorious of these establishments was at Potasi, the source of almost ninety percent of the silver extracted from the Andean mountains. At first the Peruvian laborers were obliged to work twelve hours per day, five days each week. After a two-week shift, they were allowed to rest for fourteen days. However, as the shafts became deeper, and the lodes poorer, more and more work was extracted from these unfortunate men, slaves in all but name. Entering the mines on a Monday, they were forced to remain below ground until the following Saturday. Working alternate shifts, they had to mine 2,500 pounds of ore a day, load it into 100-pound bags, and carry it up ladders to the surface, sometimes a climb of 750 feet.[5]

At the opposite end of the social scale in this brave New World were the pious Spaniards who enjoyed all the real privileges, while others toiled for them. Next in this oppressive pecking order came the Creoles—Spaniards born in the New World, followed by those of mixed race, who enjoyed only scant rights and opportunities. At the bottom of this structure came the conquered and oppressed Indians, carrying all on their broad shoulders, as those of Spanish, or even part-Spanish descent, considered any form of manual labor to be beneath their dignity. Dragged off in chains to work the aforementioned mines, they were also used on the haciendas as mere pack animals. The mortality was alarming, for within a century of the conquest, the vast native population had been reduced to less than two million souls. Writing about these times, Cieza de Leon, in his *Guerra de las Salinas,* quoted by Beals, tells us of "the great evils and violence." He continued, "the Indians had to carry loads, chained to each other by their necks: and as they had to cross deep sands and their loads increased, and the sun was big and there was no tree to give them shade, nor spring to get water, the poor Indians grew exhausted; and instead of being allowed to rest, were given hearty beatings, called lazy pigs so maltreated many fell on the ground and in order not to have to stop to unfasten the chain to get them loose, their heads were cut off with little fear of God." Continuing his story, Beals then wrote, "Once in those valleys there were great numbers of people and because of the evil treatment they have received from governments and past captains, they have been reduced so much that now many of those valleys are uninhabited and so deserted there is nothing to be seen but ruined buildings and the sepulchres of the dead and the rivers that flow through those valleys."

Phillip II's royal cedula to the Peruvian archbishop (May 27, 1582) recited even worse abuses. "In some parts a third are missing, they are treated worse than slaves, bought and sold, murdered by flogging, women die and break under their heavy loads, and give birth in the fields, bitten by poisonous insects many hang themselves, others starve themselves to death and others take poisonous herbs . . . mothers kill their new born babes, to free them from toil. Said Indians have a great hate for the word Christian."[6]

In one village a man called Francisco de Chavez killed all the Indian babies and women were raped at will. For "sport" Indians were regularly hunted down with bloodhounds and often had their hair tied to horses' tails, then dragged around until they were severely injured—or dead. What cruelty and exploitation did not accomplish was completed by contagious diseases, which swept through Peru in 1546, 1589, 1597, 1700, and 1719, decimating the native Peruvian population. The Indians had lost their lands and the limited freedoms and rights they had once enjoyed under Inca rule, being reduced to a condition of slavery and human degradation. Based on this mineral wealth produced by gross exploitation and despotic rule, Lima, the glittering outpost of European and "Christian" civilization, became ever more courtly, wealthy, and hypocritically pious!

Other ethnic groups were to partially replace the declining Indian population of Peru, notably black Africans, some of whom actually accompanied the conquistadors to Peru, assisted in the subjugation of the Indians, and, in the nineteenth century, were to act as overseers of Chinese laborers on the Chincha Islands. By 1550 the colony had as many Negroes as whites, which disturbed the colonial administration and prompted the implementation of discriminatory legislation. A census taken in the early 1790s indicated that the total population of the colony stood at almost 1,100,000. Of this number 58 percent were Indians, 12 percent, whites, 7 percent Negroes, and those of mixed-race, 22 percent. One estimate indicates that the Spaniards imported 95,000 black African slaves into Peru during the colonial period. Many of these slaves labored on the vast coastal estates, where they were subjected to the cruel treatment common to plantation workers throughout the New World. Many also worked in Lima where they were employed as domestic servants and artisans.[7]

Meanwhile, the Spanish conquests of Mexico, Chile, and Peru yielded great stores of treasure, first to the individual conquistadors and, when the colonial governments were properly organized, to Spain. The incoming treasures, had they been wisely used, could have provided Philip II of Spain (1527–98) with a navy capable of crushing the English and Dutch fleets, but this was not to be the case. Owing to bad administration, the treasury at Madrid was often in dire straits, and German bankers, like the Welsers and Fuggers, managed to exploit the situation, recouping themselves from the treasures brought in by the Spanish galleons.[8] Despite these shortcomings, Spanish trade with the Americas was well organized, albeit to the advantage of Spain.[9] Less well organized was the actual defense of the inward-bound treasure fleets. Though well guarded, they were easy prey because their place and time of sailing were nearly always known. To protect these ships adequately on the high seas was virtually impossible, and it was Drake who showed his strategic ability in 1577 when he assured Queen Elizabeth that the best way to undermine Spain was in the Indies.[10]

Spain was to receive some well—merited punishment during the time of Drake, for English ships were now in the Pacific, and a stream of freebooters from 1577 onward harassed the ports of Peru and Chile, a period leading up to that crushing blow to the mother country—the loss of the Armada in 1588, when Philip II of Spain sent 130 ships out from Cádiz to conquer England, but was defeated. Following this humiliation, Sir Richard Hawkins, only son of Sir

John Hawkins, continued the family tradition by raiding Spanish ships. He arrived off the coast of Peru in 1594, but was captured, mainly through the efforts of the Marquis of Canete, son of a former viceroy of Peru.[11] During the last decades of the sixteenth century, bullion imports into Spain from the New World were at their maximum but began to decline steeply in the seventeenth century. From 1590–1600 imports, calculated in sterling, reached the enormous figures of over one million pounds for the government and about three million pounds for private citizens. During the next decade, the total dropped to three and one quarter million. The following decade saw the figures reduced to three million and by the middle of the century the imports had fallen to less than half that figure.

The decline was due to various factors, but the main one was undoubtedly the exhaustion of the best mines, which meant that far less productive ones had to be worked. Smuggling of precious metals also became more extensive and better organized. The efforts of Dutch, French, and English pirates, such as John Hawkins, then accounted for some losses, though not as large a one as tradition suggests. Also, as the population of the colonies increased, they retained more bullion for their own use, and as their local industries developed, they imported fewer goods from Spain, consequently paying her less in bullion. The effects of bullion imports on the people and policy of Spain were incalculable. Above all, though, it was responsible for stirring the popular imagination, which led to a huge and socially damaging emigration. The pick of the population were sailing away, for by 1574 it was estimated that 32,000 Spanish households were in the New World, which implies a total Spanish emigrant population of nearly 150,000 even at this early date. Such considerations were to inspire Bismarck in the nineteenth century to note that colonies might cause his own country "to send her best blood across the seas."[12] Certainly, the general decline of Spain as an imperial entity, dating from this period, was one of the prime factors leading to English capital dominating the Peruvian economy in the nineteenth century.

Following the debacle of the Spanish Armada, more and more demands were made on Peru by Spain for money, and excessive tributes were demanded from the indigenous people and colonists, which resulted in an insurrection at Quito. These exorbitant demands put a continual drain on Peruvian and Mexican treasures and resources, all in order to allow the mother country to continue her extraordinary home and foreign policy, that had ruined her, a policy that had its pernicious effect upon her colonies. From the end of the sixteenth century until the early part of the nineteenth when the rule of Spain was thrown off, Peru was governed by successive viceroys, the total number of these, including those who only bore the title of governor, and dating from Pizarro, was forty-four. The vice-regency of Peru became the most important in Spanish America, and Lima virtually the capital of Spain's dominions in South America.[13]

For the two and a half centuries, when viceroy followed viceroy, Peru was locked in a feudal, dictatorial time warp. Their power was almost omnipotent, and, ironically, all these autocratic viceroys were holy men. They were received under arcs of solid silver; they traveled with twenty four lackeys, twenty four pages, three footmen, and six outriders in boots and spurs, all in red, silver, and blue livery. Artillery salutes, troop reviews, and bullfighting honored these simple and devout men of the Church. The court was sumptuous and formal.[14] From the sixteenth century onward the education of the people was in the hands of the priests, and it was in general accord with the methods of the Inquisition, whose mission was the destruction of all freedom of thought. In 1573 the first auto-da-fé took place, and from that period the benumbing and desolating ecclesiastical dominion continued throughout the following centuries of Spanish colonial rule.

Away from the pomp and splendor of Lima, the crude exploitation of the Indians continued unabated, which the following statistics and facts demonstrate adequately. The aforementioned mines of Potasi were supplied with laborers from the nearest provinces, by enforcing a mita of a seventh of the male population. In 1573 this mita consisted of 11,199 Indians, in 1620 of 4,249, and in 1678 of 1,674, a decrease that reflected the rapid depopulation of the country. At the latter date, when the authorities at Potasi failed to receive a sufficient number of laborers by the ordinary mita, they resorted to kidnapping people in their homes and carried them away to forced labor in the mines. Potasi thus became an exhausting drain on the surrounding country.

The mines of Huancavelica supplied the quicksilver necessary for extracting the silver of Potasi from its ores and also desolated the ten adjoining provinces. In 1645 the mita, or seventh part of the adult male population, amounted to 620, and in 1678 to only 354 Indians. Service in these mines was so dreaded that mothers were reduced to maiming the arms and legs of their children in order to save them from the horrors of Potasi and Huancavelica. Men who were taken for this service were rarely seen by their loved ones again, and while the men were working in the mines, the wives of these unfortunates were obliged to till the land and also raise their children as best they could. At the end of their labors each day these women would often be seen, hand in hand, returning from the fields, singing melancholy songs and lamenting the cruel fate of their husbands and brothers—doomed to slave in the bowels of the earth until they dropped dead from exhaustion.

Many who were not rounded up for service in the mines were dragged away to labor in the factories, producing coarse woolen and cotton cloths. In these places conditions were little better than the mines. If the owners of these establishments could not find the particular men they required, the gangs they employed to obtain their labor would take their children, wives, and nearest neighbors, rob them of all they possessed, and frequently violate the women and young girls. The masters in these establishments would then force their victims to get deeply into debt, thus obtaining an excuse to keep them in perpetual slavery. In many of these places there were Indians who had not been outside the walls for forty years or more. Children as young as six would be dragged from their homes and taken to these places, where they would be forced to work hard at twisting woolen and cotton threads and flogged cruelly if they relaxed in their labors.

The Indians, however, did not endure their fate without courageous attempts at resistance. In 1666 there was a great revolt at the Laycacota mine, then the Juan Santos revolt in the Chanchamayo in 1742. It is essential that we should not forget the courageous Spaniards and Indians in Peru who raised their voices against the lawless cruelty of those in office who were so blatantly abusing their power. Among these was Don Ventura Santalices, the governor of La Paz, who devoted his time and fortune to the cause of the oppressed Indians and was appointed to the Council of the Indies. Sadly though, he was rewarded for his efforts by being poisoned on his arrival in Spain.

Another defender of the Indians met with a similar fate, this being Blas Tupac Amarú, a descendant of the Incas. Like Santalices, he too was summoned to Spain, where he obtained promises of many concessions, but he was assassinated at sea during the return voyage. Many Christian friars and priests also spoke out in favor of the Indians, as did the more powerful members of Peruvian society. The names of just some of these defenders of the Indians deserve to be recorded: Don Manuel Arroya, Don Ignacio Castro, Don Augustin de Gurruchategui, and Don Francisco Campos, bishop of La Paz. Needless to say, the efforts of these brave men bore no fruit, and in 1780 the corregidor of Chayanta placed even more burdens on the long-suffering Indians. This was the final straw that broke the camel's back—an Indian chief, named Tomas Catari, set the example of revolt; thousands flocked to his standard and those of his brothers Damaso and Nicolas. In a few months the whole of Upper Peru (modern-day Bolivia) was in revolt.

In the following year José Gabriel Condorcanqui, who took the Inca name of Tupac Amarú, raised the standard of revolt; thus the last desperate struggle for liberty was actually started by a member of the ruling elite.[15] Amarú was, in fact, a mestizo, a man of property and a trusted local magistrate. In calling the Indians to arms against the burden of tribute and the abuses of the mita system, he proclaimed himself a loyal subject—indeed, a viceroy—of the king, and only the enemy of corrupt and brutal tax-gatherers. General del Valle, who commanded the troops employed to put down Tupac Amarú's rebellion, was even driven to complain about the avarice of the corregidors in recovering their claims on the Indians. This was illustrated by the fact that when he tried to recruit their Indian workers to pacify the country, they made it clear that they would rather see the defeat of the king's troops than send away a single Indian who might owe them a yard of cloth![16] Many native Peruvians supported the great uprising of Tupac Amarú, which lasted for two years and was only suppressed with great difficulty and bloodshed by regular troops. Sadly though, others were as alarmed by the course of events as were the officials themselves. Many played their part—from conviction or fear—in operations against Amarú, and made no protest when the rising was over, or against the frightful manner of his and his relatives' executions.[17]

In the annals of barbarism there is probably not to be found a record of wickedness so revolting as the one concerning the persecution and torture of Tupac Amarú, and his family and supporters, following their defeat in the spring of 1781. The Spanish victor, General del Valle, promptly hung sixty-seven Indian prisoners at Tinta, whose heads he then stuck on poles by the roadside. Amarú and his close relatives were then captured. On May 15, 1781, the visitador Areche pronounced a lengthy sentence, in which he declared that it was necessary to hasten its execution to demonstrate to the natives that it was not impossible to execute an heir of the Inca of Peru. Just three days later, on Friday, May 18, 1781, the great square at Cuzco was surrounded by Spanish and Negro troops, and ten prisoners emerged from the church of the Jesuits to face torture and death. One of these was Tupac Amarú, who had earlier in the morning been visited by Areche and urged to betray all the accomplices in his rebellion. With courage, and great dignity, the Inca turned to face the oppressor of his people and contemptuously threw back his immortal response: "You and I are the only conspirators: you for having oppressed the country with exaction's which were unendurable, and I for having wished to free the people from such tyranny."

The Inca's companions in misfortune were his wife Micaela; his sons Hipólita and Fernando; his brother-in-law Antonio Bastidas; his uncle Francisco Tupac Amarú, Tomasa Condemaita, José Verdejo, and Andres Castelo, captains in the Inca's army; and the executioner Oblitas. Verdejo, Castelo, Oblitas, and Bastidas were hung at once. The rest were heavily chained, placed in bags, and dragged into the square. Francisco, Hipólito Tupac Amarú, and Tomasa Condemaita then had their tongues cut out and were garroted by an iron screw. Micaela, the wife of the Inca, then had her tongue cut out and, in the presence of her husband, the screw was placed around her neck; but she suffered dreadfully because her neck was so small the screw failed to strangle her. The fiendish executioners then placed ropes around her neck and pulled in different ways at the same time, kicking her in the stomach and chest until she was mercifully released from this torment by death.

The great Inca was then taken into the center of the square, his chains taken off, and his tongue cut out. He was thrown to the ground; ropes secured to four horses were then fastened to his ankles and wrists, and the horses made to drag in different directions. The great man's body was thus raised in the air. His youngest son, Fernando, an innocent child of ten years who had been forced to witness this disgusting massacre of his relatives, then uttered a heart-rending shriek, the sound of which continued to ring in the ears of those who heard it to their dying day. One also senses that young Fernando's cry of horror and anguish still echoes, down to this day, across the barren windswept Altiplano and among the high peaks of the Cordilleras.

In addition to all this, the Inca's houses were demolished. All documents relating to his descent were burned and representations of

Quichua dramas forbidden. All the musical instruments of the Indians were then destroyed and all signs of mourning for the Inca forbidden All the Indians were then forced to give up their national costumes and dress henceforth in the Spanish style, and the use of the Quicha language was totally forbidden. After the aforementioned hideous tortures and murders, the victims' heads, bodies, and limbs were sent to different towns of Peru in order to strike terror into the hearts of the Indians, but this had the opposite effect and goaded them to fury. During the following year the authorities conducted a war of extermination, in which 80,000 people fell victim to the vengeance of the Spanish troops, and, sad to say, many native Peruvians served in this brutal army.[18]

"It would be difficult," said Dean Funes, "to find in the history of revolutions one more justifiable and less fortunate than that of Tupac Amarú. America had, in those days, become the theatre of the most widespread tyranny; but the Indians of Peru were those on whose necks the yoke weighed heaviest. Mitas and Repartos, were, in Peru, the deadly plague of Spanish invention, which devoured the human race."[19]

In writing about Peru, however, it is easy to be carried away by self-righteous indignation against the Spanish rulers, but if we look honestly at the colonial structures established by other European nations, it will be difficult to say who really has the right to cast the first stone. The aboriginal people in Tasmania were almost exterminated and their numbers greatly reduced in mainland Australia by the British. The indigenous people of North America were, undoubtedly, oppressed by the European immigrants. Then the North Americans, soon after they won their independence from Britain, began to exploit and oppress other nations, notably, in Latin America. However, the Spanish colonies cannot be directly compared with these relatively modern settlers, the vast majority of whom emigrated, in the late nineteenth and early twentieth centuries, for most came with the intention of working to support themselves as farmers or artisans, not in order to join the ranks of a non-working aristocratic elite.

The Spanish, on the other hand, emigrated primarily as a master race with the clear intention of avoiding any form of manual labor whatsoever. However, at the close of the eighteenth century, events in Europe were soon to influence politics and social attitudes throughout the world. On March 7, 1793, France declared war on Spain, her troops, and intellectuals, carrying with them dangerous notions of liberty, equality, and fraternity. Liberal and even revolutionary ideas began to be nourished in the Peruvian centers of learning, with clandestine meetings taking place in Lima and Arequipa.[20]

By the revolting affairs surrounding the execution of Tupac Amarú, Spain was also clearly working toward her demise in South America. Nevertheless, some reforms were made in the treatment of the Indians after the above-mentioned horrors, and considerable scientific, geographical, and literary advances made under the viceroys Jauregui, de la Croix, Taboada, and others, including, in particular, Don Francisco Gil during the years 1780 to 1800. During this period the coast was surveyed, a nautical school established, and statistics compiled. Another great leap forward then took place in September 1813, when news of the abolition of the Inquisition in Spain reached Lima. The people took to the streets, and in this great progressive uprising, the Holy Office, its archives, prisons, and instruments of torture, were destroyed amid scenes of tremendous relief and rejoicing.

Britain had now become the dominant world power, and politics in this imperial nation were being influenced—to an ever-increasing extent—by the Abolitionist Movement, led by William Wilberforce. The abolitionists first strove for the abolition of the slave trade, which Wilberforce carried through Parliament in 1807, all of which was to directly influence Spain and attitudes to labor in her colonies.[21] The immediate objective of the British abolitionists was that of ending the transatlantic slave trade. Because of Britain's naval supremacy the task was assigned to the Royal Navy. Britain also bore the chief financial burdens. In 1817, when Castlereagh induced Spain to sign a separate treaty abolishing the slave trade in Spanish vessels everywhere after May 30, 1820, Britain had to pay £400,000 as compensation for the recent capture of Spanish slave ships. The other once-great Catholic imperial power, Portugal, drove an even harder bargain with Britain. Portugal, and her colony Brazil, were the chief slave-trafficking states in the early nineteenth century, and in a treaty of 1817, she required the remission of a balance of a loan of £600,000, and also the payment of £300,000, for the renunciation of the trade.[22]

The main point to note, however, was that the decrepitude of Spain was revealed to the colonists of South America, first by the invasion of Napoleon and then by Britain dictating policy to Spain and Portugal on the crucial issue of the period—abolition. Spain was clearly no longer the power it once was, and the colonists did not delay long in organizing native administrations—Caracas on April 19, 1810, Chile on September 18, 1810 and Buenos Aires in 1813—showing by their declarations that the inevitable was happening. For a while Peru remained loyal to the Crown of Spain, but the cry of independence was raised in August 1814 by a number of prominent Peruvians, when feeling generally became unanimous for throwing off the Spanish yoke.[23]

Here we should pause to reflect on the condition of Peru just prior to the first attempt by this colony to gain independence from Spain. The population of the Inca Empire at the time of the Spanish conquest in 1532 is commonly estimated to have been around 12,000,000, although not all these people lived within the boundaries of modern Peru. Nevertheless, it is clear that Peru was the most densely settled area in pre-Hispanic South America. During the first century of Spanish domination, the Indian population declined by almost 80 percent due to overwork, malnutrition, and the introduction of such diseases as smallpox and measles. The first accurate census (1791) showed the impact of Hispanic dominance over the native people: the population had declined to slightly more than 1,000,000, which included Europeans, people of mixed ancestry, and black slaves. After independence the population was to increase gradually, but it was to take more than three hundred years to replace the population lost in the first century of Spanish rule. The Spanish had built hundreds of churches, indoctrinated the Indians, and spread the Roman Catholic faith, but in doing so had destroyed millions more than they had "converted." Such was the state of this nation, striving for independence from Spain in the opening decades of the nineteenth century.[24]

In 1814, General Ramirez marched against the forces striking out for independence. The patriots, led by the elderly Pumacagua, retreated over the high Cordilleras from Arequipa. The rebel leader then wrote to Ramirez asking him for whom he was fighting, for Ferdinand VII of Spain had just been sold to the French. Ramirez refused to enter into a dialogue. A battle followed in which the Peruvians were defeated and large numbers killed. However, other operations soon took place on land and sea. A Spanish squadron was defeated in May 1814 by Captain William Brown, a capable British seaman commanding revolutionary vessels from Argentina. An organized rising was planned at Lima, but was frustrated by the arrival of veteran troops from Spain. Bolivia and Chile had been reconquered and Peru was brought under subjection; Buenos Aires alone remained in freedom. In July 1816 Pezuela entered Lima as the Spanish viceroy. This was merely the calm before the storm, for external developments were soon to sweep away the rule of imperial Spain.

The liberation of Peru, and indeed all of Latin America, can be said to stem from two men: Jose de San Martin in the south and Simón Bolívar in the north. In 1816 Bolívar landed again in Venezuela, and in a series of brilliant campaigns made himself master of a vast area that later emerged as Venezuela, Ecuador, and Colombia. San Martin, a son of the governor of Paraguay, educated in Spain and with friendships in England, entered the Spanish army, but left for Buenos Aires to take part in the liberation of his country. He was appointed to a post by the Argentine government, but when Chile called for help from Argentina, San Martin organized an army of four thousand men and with his artillery and supplies made one of the most heroic marches in the annals of military history. Crossing the great snow-covered heights of the Cordilleras in 1817, San Martin entered the capital of Santiago, and the Spanish forces were defeated. Thus encircled, with Bolívar in the north and San Martin in the south, time was running out for Peru as the last remaining bastion of Spanish power in the Americas.

The fact that Peru had not generated another internal rising since 1814 was a reflection on the fact that Lima was the old center of the centralized, imperial government under which many of the rich peninsular landowners enjoyed special privileges granted by the Crown. For these aristocrats, whose wealth was continually increased by the forced labor of Indian and Negro slaves, life was pleasant, and that they should respond less enthusiastically than others in South America for revolution is not surprising. The brutal campaigns of the illiterate conquistadors conveniently forgotten, the capital city of Lima had, among other things, become something of a magnet to Spanish nobility, having attracted during the colonial period no fewer that one grand duke, fifty-eight marquesses, forty-five counts, and knights too numerous to mention. Lima was a sick city of rich snobbish consumers riding on the backs of Indian slaves who, by contrast, were locked up at night in ghettos, in a ward across the river Rimac that was known as the Cercado. Also riding on the backs of the downtrodden, albeit less ostentatiously, were another class of nonproducers. As late as 1841, according to Manuel González de la Rosa, Lima still had an ecclesiastic, monk or nun, for every four and a half family groups. The perceived interests of many in the wealthy privileged classes, the Church, and the ecclesiastics clearly lay in supporting the status quo.[25]

Despite this situation, it was inevitable that Peru should be liberated from Spanish rule, however lukewarm or hostile some factions might be. San Martin got there first. After having installed an independent Chilean regime under Bernardo O'Higgins, the new government enlisted the services of Lord Thomas Cochrane, a former British naval officer who was given the task of organizing the Chilean navy. With much relish, and an improvised fleet, Cochrane soon started to attack Spanish shipping in the Pacific, and within a short space of time he had also succeeded in forcing the Spanish navy to seek refuge under the huge guns at the Peruvian port of Callao. The vital sea link between Peru and the mother country had been broken. In August 1820 Cochrane's fleet sailed for Peru manned by 1,600 sailors and carrying San Martin's 4,500 soldiers. They faced overwhelming odds, for the viceroy of Peru had 23,000 troops under his command. In addition to his troops San Martin had taken with him a "secret weapon" in the form of a printing press, with which he hoped to produce appropriate literature to revolutionize the Peruvians. In the event of this strategy succeeding, he had also brought with him sufficient arms and ammunition to equip no fewer than 15,000 recruits.

On September 8, 1820, San Martin landed at the southern port of Pisco, where he advised the people that their hour of deliverance from Spain was due to arrive, adding that any slave who joined his army of liberation would be granted immediate freedom from bondage. During the following months, he took steps to recruit as many Peruvians to his side as possible, making a notable breakthrough in these efforts in December when the Marquis de Torre Tagle declared for San Martin. The general also took steps to avoid a major confrontation will the much stronger royalist forces. Meanwhile Cochrane's blockade of the port of Callao, and Lima, the capital it served, was having a devastating impact on the royalist forces. Imports of food and supplies were cut off; the well-to-do citizens of Lima became increasingly hostile. Outbreaks of fever were also decimating the ranks of General José de la Serna, San Martin's opponent. In June 1821 Serna therefore made the decision to split his forces in half; one part he marched to the Sierra, while the remainder were sent to bolster defenses at Callao. Two weeks later San Martin triumphantly entered Lima and proclaimed Peru free and independent. Being a Royalist himself, though, he pointedly did not declare that Peru was a free and independent republic!

San Martin was of the opinion that the interests of the newly independent nations of Latin America would best be served by the installation of local constitutional monarchies. As might be expected, this stand met with the warm approval of his prominent supporter, the aristocratic Marquis de Torre Tagle, but San Martin was unable to placate the pro-republican elements, for they held firmly to the view that republicanism offered a greater degree of freedom. Having upset the Peruvian left wing, San Martin wasted no time in alienating those to the right of the political spectrum. A week after San Martin's declaration of independence, the leading citizens of Lima named the foreign general "Protector of Peru," with dictatorial powers to rule and bring the civil war to a speedy and satisfactory conclusion. He showed his appreciation for this support by immediately taking measures against those who had elected him and this by increasing taxes, forcing loans from wealthy citizens, granting exclusive import rights to many foreign merchants, and, to cap it all, instituting several anticlerical reforms.

In September 1821 the Royalists made an attempt to break San Martin's siege of Callao, but this daring attempt failed. A few days later the starving royalist troops in Callao fort surrendered, but this was a hollow victory, for the problems facing the foreign dictator were mounting. First, a somewhat embarrassing cash-flow problem meant that he was unable to pay his Chilean and Argentine troops or Cochrane's sailors. The British officer dealt with this challenging situation by seizing the Peruvian treasury, which had been entrusted to his care, and promptly sailed away to Peru. This exacerbated problems with the unpaid troops who, quite understandably, increased their demands to be sent home. Their exasperated officers also made an unsuccessful attempt to overthrow San Martin in October 1821. Having lost his navy, and made enemies of the Royalists, the republicans, the Church, the Spanish merchants at Lima and Callao, and his army, San Martin was not exactly in a very strong position to continue the war. Nevertheless, a born optimist, he then asked Chile and Argentine to send him reinforcements, which requests were refused. With few options left, he then turned to Bolivar for assistance.

Simón Bolívar was born at Caracas on July 24, 1783. He was educated in Spain and inherited a considerable fortune. On his return to Venezuela he soon became active among those who were working to free the continent from Spanish rule, and he was a leader in a rising at Caracas in 1810. In 1813, after a victory over the Spaniards, he was proclaimed dictator of Venezuela, but was soon driven away and took refuge in the West Indies. However, he returned to the struggle and proclaimed a larger republic, which he called Colombia. Independence of this new state was formally recognized in 1821, when Bolívar was installed as the first president. San Martin and Simón Bolíivar met at the Ecuadorian port of Quaquil in July 1822. They spent three days discussing many issues, but the main topics were the use of Bolívar's troops in Peru, national boundaries, and the structure and constitution of the states that would replace the old Spanish colonies. Bolívar stood for republicanism, albeit of a rather royalist variety, while San Martin, as might be expected, argued for setting up local monarchies.

However, at the time when this famous meeting was held, Bolívar had still not overcome all royalist opposition in Ecuador, and was therefore reluctant to resolve the principal issue—that of sending troops south to Peru—until his position was more secure. Bolívar wanted no part in helping to place San Martin on a Peruvian throne, so refused to accept his ostensibly generous offer to serve as his subordinate. This situation led San Martin to the inevitable conclusion that only his own departure from Peru would persuade Bolívar to send his troops to the south. Accordingly, San Martin arrived back in Peru in September 1822, resigned his position, and handed over his authority to the Peruvian Congress that had just been established. In May, the following year, 3,000 Colombian troops arrived in Peru under the command of Bolívar's protégé, General Antonio José de Sucre. After various battles against the remaining Royalists were fought and won, Bolívar himself arrived in Peru where he received a triumphant welcome when he entered Lima on September 1, 1823.

Bolívar became absolute dictator in 1824 and, with General Sucre and the combined forces of Colombian and Peruvian troops, continued to defend the independence of the country against the Royalist forces. Bolívar then made an advance on Cuzco, the last great stronghold of Spanish power in Peru. The patriots numbered almost six thousand men; the Royalists counted somewhat more than nine thousand. On December 9, 1824, the two armies faced each other at the hacienda of Ayacucho. The Royalists were utterly routed; nearly fifteen hundred were slain; the viceroy, his generals, officers, and army captured. The battle of Ayacucho delivered a deathblow to Spanish rule in South America, but a few die-hard Royalists continued the struggle in Bolivia, where it required a further six months to suppress the Spaniards. However, the royalist stalwarts, trapped in the fort at Callao, stuck it out until January 1826, by which time 66 percent of the heroic but misguided defenders had starved to death. Thus Spanish rule in Peru, and indeed all of South America, came to an end after three hundred years.[26] The positive and negative qualities of the Iberian people and Christianity had, however, by this time been indelibly stamped on the inhabitants of this vast continent for all time.

Following the historic battle of Ayacucho, Simón Bolívar made a triumphal tour of the country and was received as its deliverer. Upper Peru was established as a separate country, named after Bolívar. Sucres became the first president in October 1826. In August 1827, Lamar became president. Various internal disturbances occurred, and in February 1835, Salaverry proclaimed himself master of Peru. Following closely upon these events was a war with Bolivia, the president of that country, Santa Cruz, taking the field against Salaverry. The operations took place principally in the neighborhood of Cuzco and Arequipa, but Lima fell prey to anarchy during the absence of the president in the interior. In this campaign Santa Cruz and the Bolivians triumphed, and Salaverry and his officers were shot at Arequipa in February 1836. Santa Cruz entered Lima as protector and continued the administration of the confederation of Peru and Bolivia, the formation of which had been the object of his campaign. It is now that we come to that crucial point in time, when the exploitation of guano, notably from the Chincha Islands, enters the pages of Peruvian history as the dominant economic, social, and political factor.

After the arrival of the conquistador Francisco Pizarro in the 1530s, agriculture declined, as the Spaniards enforced the mita and concentrated economic activity on the extraction and exportation of gold and silver. However, it is thought that some loading and internal use of this valuable fertilizer continued, albeit on a small scale, throughout the 300 years of Spanish rule. In the 1820s, at least 1,700 tons a year were being sold in Peru, which brought in a handsome profit for the merchants involved. On the establishment of the republic, the importance of this commodity was officially recognized. On July 23, 1830, the government decreed the abolition of all duties and charges on guano brought into the country from the islands, declaring guano to be "an article very useful and necessary for the development and prosperity of agriculture. It was now, in fact, considered to be one of the most important branches of industry of the Peruvian nation."[27] The republican government was also increasingly aware that very valuable nitrate deposits existed on the coastal deserts of Atacama and Tarapacá, these deserts being part of the aforementioned vast region, the long, sterile, and rainless territory between the Cordillera of the Andes and the Pacific coast of South America. Bare of vegetation, apart from the fertile, irrigated river valleys, this territory had previously been considered of little economic value.

Unfortunately for Peru, her powerful neighbor to the south was also becoming increasingly aware of the aforementioned riches, missed by the gold-crazy conquistadors and all their avaricious successors for so long. Chile also feared the formation of the Peruvian-Colombian Confederation. Upon various pretexts, therefore, Chile declared war with Peru in November 1836, but previous to the declaration, a Chilean officer seized a Peruvian fleet of three vessels that were lying unmanned in the harbor of Callao. In September 1837, the Chilean general Blanco Encalada was dispatched from Valparaiso with eight men-of-war and twenty transports and, landing at Islay, near Mollendo, with over three thousand troops, advanced on Arequipa. However, this expedition was cut off and defeated by the Peruvians, after which a treaty of peace and commerce was signed. But the Chileans refused to keep to the terms of this treaty, and a further expedition of six thousand men was sent north. This substantial army landed at Ancon and marched on Lima. Led by Castilla, Gamarra, and La Fuente, a great battle was fought, at which the defenders were defeated. Santa Cruz entered Lima in November 1838. Early the following year, the invaders were pursued and a battle was fought at Yungay. However, the forces of the Peru-Colombian Confederation were utterly routed. The Battle of Yungay dissolved the Confederation, and the Chileans departed. Gamarra then entered Lima as provisional president, and a new constitution was introduced in November 1839. Gamarra then declared himself chief, with the title of "Restorer."

Vivanco then rose up against Gamarra. In January 1841, the "Regenerator" formally took up his position. Alas, in the now firmly established tradition of Latin America, his rule was a short one. Meanwhile, Santa Cruz, who had earlier escaped from Peru in a British ship, following the battle of Yungay, conducted intrigues in Bolivia with the hope of recovering his former power. Noting this activity, Peru then made war with Bolivia, and some initial gains were made. However, the Peruvian forces were defeated in November 1841, when peace was diplomatically arranged. For a period, the ambitions of various generals and civil leaders then caused civil war to prevail in the country. Such was the state of Peru in 1841 when this South American nation first began to develop its lucrative international guano industry. It was to generate riches beyond the wildest dreams of the conquistadors, albeit for the fortunate few, and result in untold misery and suffering for the many unfortunate workers, imported to work these deposits on the barren, isolated, and soul-destroying Chincha Islands.

4
Dawn of a New Age

BY 1840 PERU'S EXTERNAL DEBT, CONTRACTED DURING HER LONG AND bitter struggle with Spain, continued to mount rapidly. The nation was virtually bankrupt and unable to repay her foreign creditors or even meet the ever-mounting interest charges on sums outstanding. Independence had been bought at a very heavy price. Mineral production had also declined by the 1840s, and the provisioning of troops had depleted the nation's livestock. To make matters worse, due to church objections to moneylending, Peru had not developed her own banking system. Her economy was increasingly coming under the control of foreign merchants and bankers, and the nation was becoming an object of international ridicule. It was when the nation was in this rather sorry state that individual merchants began to develop the lucrative international guano trade, primarily from the Chincha Islands. Within a decade Peru was to become virtually dependent on this one product.

As always, native Peruvians and other ethnic minority groups were soon to pay the price for this bonanza. The first guano contractors entrapped peasants from certain Andean regions as cheap labor to mine the deposits. Ammonia fumes, released from the guano during excavation, shriveled the skin of these unfortunate men and blinded some of them. The fate of Chinese and Polynesian workers, later brought out to replace much local labor, was to be even worse, most dying, as will be seen, from inhuman working conditions and torture.[1]

The Chincha Islands are three in number, known as the North, Middle, and South Islands, and are situated in longitude 79 degrees west, and latitude 13.5 degrees south. They lie about ninety miles south of Callao, the port of Lima, capital of Peru. The largest of the group is the North Island, which is just under a mile in length and half a mile in breadth at the widest part. The only value of these islands that are, in fact, little more than barren rocks, consists in the enormous deposits of guano that had accumulated there for thousands of years. The value of this deposit was well known to the ancient Peruvians, and in order to ensure a continuous supply, the Incas issued an edict many centuries ago prohibiting the destruction of the birds.[2] Natural forces combined on the coast of Peru to preserve the riches so highly valued by the ancients. The Humboldt Current, supplemented by the rise of cold bottom waters, maintains its course for thousands of miles, from icy Antarctic latitudes to the equator. Due to this, cold ocean waters bathe a tropical shore. Thus, when the winds blow over the cool Peruvian Current, then touch the lands warmed by a tropical sun, expansion or rarefaction occurs, rainfall is prevented, and the atmosphere is dry.

The significance of this, with respect to the guano deposits of Peru, easily becomes apparent. In places where seabirds nest in ordinary wet climates, the nitrates of the guano give rise to ammonia and are wasted by evaporation or seepage. However, in Peru, year after year, guano is laid down beneath a clear, dry atmosphere, the deposit bakes in the sun, and its most valuable components are imprisoned for an indefinite period. Guano is primarily the deposit of fish-eating birds, but into which may be incorporated, in greater or lesser proportion, a variety of other substances, such as the eggs and bodies of birds and the bodies of sea lions. It may be found mixed with gravel and sand in very small proportion or sometimes to an extent, rendering it unprofitable to extract.

Great beds of guano have been formed upon islands of the Caribbean Sea, upon Ichaboe and Possession Island, off the coast of southwest Africa, and other islands of the southern and far Pacific. These guanos, however, were invariably not up to the standard of the Peruvian product, for in Peru conditions for the natural production and preservation of this material are virtually perfect.[3] Nevertheless, many of these deposits were also to be exploited in the nineteenth century, the ensuing "Guano Treasure Hunt" being engendered by the establishment of the industry in Peru in 1840. Although the main Peruvian guano deposits were to be found on the Chincha group of islands, there were other places where substantial deposits were found on headlands and other islands off this long stretch of coast, that is, from Paita, at 5 degrees south, to the southernmost limit of present Peruvian territory, at 18 degrees south—a distance of about 1,300 miles.

However, chief among the Peruvian guano locations that were to be exploited, following the Chincha Islands, were the Ballestas

Islands, the islands of Guanape and Macabi, and the larger Lobos Islands. Of the two groups, de Afuera and de Tierra, Pabellon de Pica, now beyond the territory of Peru, were also important at one point in time. Among those places of secondary importance were the Islas Santa Fronton, Palominos, Asia, Santa Rosa, Vieja, and Cerro Azul. From year to year, as the industry developed, the scene of activity was to shift from island to island, as the deposits accumulated or became exhausted, but the Chinchas, Ballestas, and Lobos islands were rarely abandoned for a full twelve-month period while the trade lasted. None of these islands are very large or any real distance from the mainland. The nearest islet, in fact, was so close to the shore that when its deposits were exploited, it was possible to do this by means of an aerial trolley, linking it to the mainland, while most of the other islands are not more than twelve miles from the coast.

The only group at all remote is the Lobos de Afuera group, which are about thirty-three nautical miles off the mainland. The largest of this group is Lobos de Tierra, with its length of nearly six miles and a width varying from one-sixth of a mile to two miles. The Lobos de Afuera Islands, combined, are slightly smaller. The islands of Ballestas, close to the Chinchas and like them, are composed of three principal units, each approximately equal to the smallest of the Chinchas. They are more rugged, and access can only be gained by climbing from the water, as they are without beaches except at the bases of great cliffs.

Briefly, to indicate the economic significance of the guano trade, it should be noted that a quantity of more than 10,000,000 tons of first-class guano was extracted from the Chincha Islands between 1851 and 1872. Such an amount of guano of the higher grades, then exclusively used, would have had a value, in 1913, of about three-quarters of a billion dollars.[4] The guano-producing birds were the innocent agents in what was to develop into a vast global trade. The primary requisite for the abundant bird life that produced the guano was the existence of a plentiful supply of food, and the guano birds found this off the coast of Peru in the vast shoals of small fish that swarm in the cold Peruvian Current.

Not all species of birds found in this area were of equal importance to the guano industry. Indeed, two species virtually supported the industry, these being the big Gray Pelican (Alcatraz), and the White-headed Gannet (Piquero). Three species of cormorant are also numerous on the mainland coast and islands of Peru. Only one of these, however, was of particular economic significance in the guano trade, this being the White-breasted Cormorant, which the native Peruvians named the Guanay, meaning "the guano bird." Guanays, in fact, occur on the Peruvian coast from near the northern to the extreme southern boundary, but their main base is the double group of islands opposite Pisco, in the south, the Chinchas, and the Ballestas.

The scientist, Robert Coker, visited the Ballestas in the early years of the twentieth century, when the deposits were still being worked, albeit on a much more modest scale. He marked out an area of 5,500 square yards within which he counted nearly 14,000 nests. At the same time, he calculated that a pair of guanays, with their offspring, produced nearly one dollar and fifty cents' worth of guano each year, besides leaving their progeny to continue the service in future years. From this it was calculated that each pair of breeding birds had a commercial value of fifteen dollars. At the same time, on the south island in the Chincha group, it was estimated that deposits accumulated at the rate of about 4.5 inches per annum, or nearly 300 pounds per square yard. In total, this amounted to 5,000 tons a year, on this one island. From all this it is easy to appreciate just how much guano had accumulated over many thousands of years, when the large-scale exploitation of guano commenced in 1840.[5] There is clear evidence that guano was taken from the northernmost Chincha island by the Incas. Indeed, the irrigated river valleys, running through the barren coastal strip of Peru, could never have been brought to a high state of productivity by the Incas without this fertilizer. Accounts of the Inca period, in fact, clearly describe the widespread use of guano fertilizer in the terraced fields that supported a population of probably more than ten million people.[6]

In 1873 Hutchinson noted that stone idols and water pots had been found buried deep down in the Chincha guano deposits. "How many thousands of years may have passed, in a case like this it is nonsense to talk of hundreds since that stone idol was made and worshipped before it got by design or accident in a position that the daily droppings of birds and seals covered it to a depth of sixty-two feet?" He continued, "How many decades have elapsed between this evidence of the stone-age, and the period of the wooden idol discovered at a depth of thirty-two feet, or with twenty-seven feet intervening?"[7]

Other writers state that the earliest human exploitation of guano deposits on the Chincha Islands, for which evidence exists, was by the Mochica people, probably sometime between the first and fifth century AD. It should also be noted that the true value of these guano-producing birds was clearly recognized by the Incas, who took measures to protect the birds by banning their destruction, or even visits to the islands, during the crucial breeding season. These wise, but autocratic rulers also allocated guano-bearing islands, or a part of an island, to a particular province, which then had the sole right to distribute it to their farmers.[8]

However, after the arrival of Pizarro and his fellow conquistadors, agriculture was neglected, when thousands of native Peruvians were forced to enter the aforementioned gold and silver mines to cater to the Spaniards' insatiable lust for precious metals. The indications, though, are that some relatively modest extraction and distribution of guano continued throughout the entire colonial period with perhaps a dozen small ships loading at the various islands each year during the seventeenth and eighteenth centuries.[9]

The introduction of guano into European farming was mainly due to the famous German scientist, Baron Friedrich Heinrich Alexander von Humboldt, after whom the Peruvian Current was named. Born in Berlin on September 14, 1769, he was the son of aristocratic parents.[10] He was educated at home by private tutors and then went to the University of Göttingen to study science. In 1798 he teamed up with the botanist Aimee Bonplan, and together they based their plans for a proposed exploratory and scientific expedition on a promise of French governmental backing. Unfortunately, at the last minute this offer of support was withdrawn. Then, by chance, in March 1799, Humboldt secured an introduction to King Carlos IV of Spain and Queen Maria Luisa, who he promptly impressed with his excellent knowledge of Spanish. They were even more impressed with his plans to explore the Latin American countries then under Spanish rule. Humboldt and Bonplan, who by then were planning their own expedition to South America, then received practical support from the Spanish monarch who issued special passports to them that were not commonly available to non-Spanish citizens. These impressive documents, bearing the royal seal, required the king's subjects in the Spanish colonies to give the two travelers any assistance they might require.

On June 5, 1799, Humboldt and Bonplan sailed from Coruna on their celebrated voyage of discovery that was to take them to Peru and many other places. Humboldt's scientific discoveries, made during his great American expedition, were subsequently to fill thirty-

2. Baron Friedrich Heinrich Alexander von Humboldt at the age of 33 in 1802. James Orton. *From the Andes to the Amazon.* New York: Harpers, 1876.

two books: sixteen volumes on botany, four on astronomy and geophysical data, two on zoology and comparative anatomy, and ten devoted to an account of the journey itself and the geography of the many places visited. It was while the expedition was making a short stay in Peru in 1802 that he noted, with great interest, the high value placed on the amalgam of bird droppings known as guano, and therefore took samples back to Europe.[11] These samples obtained by Humboldt were examined in France in 1806; then in 1813 this material was evaluated by the celebrated English chemist, Sir Humphry Davy, who wrote, "from its composition it [guano] might be supposed to be a very powerful manure."[12]

From Gore's Liverpool Directory, Hutchinson found that South American guano was first imported into Liverpool by the brig *Heroine* from Valparaiso, consigned to Messrs. W. J. Myers and Company, and it arrived on July 23, 1836. It was, however, only a sample of thirty bags, which was given away to various parties for experiment.[13] According to Mathew, it was Carlos Barroilet and Aguiles who asked Horace Bland, an English merchant resident in Valparaiso, to pass on some samples of guano to his Liverpool associate, William Myers, and that all of this took place around 1837–38. This date would seem to be confirmed by a small item that subsequently appeared in the *Times* from which it will be noted this first, noncommercial sample came from Bolivia, not Peru: "By Mr W. J. Myers of Liverpool, in 1839, to whom we are indebted for the introduction into England of this valuable manure; on which the character of the Peruvian guano arose was Bolivian, not Peruvian."[14] Britain was to receive its first commercial shipment of Peruvian guano in 1841, and within a few years the great guano boom was on. Only six years later, in 1847, guano was to become Peru's most important export and continued to dominate Peruvian economic and political life until 1878.[15]

To put the dawn of the Peruvian guano age into historical perspective, we should note that it had only been on December 27, 1831, that Her Majesty's ship *Beagle* had sailed into these waters. This ten-gun brig, under the command of Captain Fitzroy, RN, had sailed from Devonport, taking Charles Darwin, as naturalist, on this famous voyage of discovery. The stated object of the expedition was to sail south to complete the survey of Patagonia and Tierra del Fuego started by Captain King in 1826 before sailing north to survey the shores of Chile, Peru, and some islands in the Pacific. The voyage lasted several years, the most significant end result of this venture being the publication of Darwin's celebrated book, *The Origin of Species,* a work that was to shake the ideological foundations of the world's nations and, in particular, those of the pious Catholic states such as Peru![16] Meanwhile, also coinciding with the establishment of the Peruvian guano trade, the development of steam power began to conquer the Pacific, which was to have a more immediate commercial and social impact on the west coast states of Latin America.

One of the first steamers to trade along the Pacific coast of South America was a small vessel named the *Telicia,* this being in 1825, six years before Fitzroy and Darwin arrived off the coast of South America. She was owned and commanded by a Spaniard who, for reasons that are not very clear, went under the Russian name of Mitrovich. Alas, this venture proved to be a sad failure, chiefly due to the scarcity of fuel. Frustrated and in despair, the unfortunate captain then brought his pioneering venture to a dramatic conclusion by firing his pistol into a barrel of gunpowder, thus managing to blow up his vessel in Guayaquil harbor, killing himself and all on board, except for one man.

The next person to attempt to establish steamship communications along the Pacific coast was an American citizen, Mr. William Wheelwright, born at Newburyport, Massachusetts in 1798, the son of Ebenezer and Anna Coombs Wheelwright. His father was at first a sea captain. He attended Phillips Academy, Andover, and at the age of sixteen shipped as a cabin boy to the West Indies and after three years of adventure commanded a Newburyport barque to Rio. In 1823 the *Rising Empire,* under his command, ran ashore in the Rio de la Plata. Depressed by the accident, he refused to return home and shipped as a supercargo on a vessel bound for Valparaiso. In 1824 he became the United States consul at Guayaquil, where he was serving when Captain Mitrovich blew himself up in the harbor. He remained in Guayaquil for five years, and in addition to his consular duties there started to trade successfully on his own account.

In 1835 Wheelwright started to seek the permission of the west coast nations for such a line. Finding that American capital was not available, he went to England to raise funds.[17] He eventually got the backing of Sir Clements R. Markham, the celebrated historian cited in this work, P. C. Scarlett, and others, and on February 17, 1840, a British charter for the Pacific Steam Navigation Company was obtained, together with a small subsidy for the mails. The firm at first had its offices in London, but was to move to Liverpool in 1846.[18]

Wheelwright became chief superintendent of the company, and late in 1840 he took the twin 700–ton steamships, *Chile* and *Peru* through the Straits of Magellan to enthusiastic receptions at Valparaiso and Callao, the first terminals of the line. Soon, however, a Liverpool registered Brocklebank sailing ship, the aptly named *Bonanza,* was to set sail for the Chincha Islands. She was the forerunner of a vast fleet of merchant ships that would be setting sail for these islands.[19]

It was in 1840 that Quiros, Allier, & Company, a Peruvian commercial house in Lima, determined to send a commercial consignment of guano to England. Then having great faith in the success of their venture, they proposed to the Peruvian government to purchase from them the deposits on the three Chincha Islands. An agreement for the sale was actually made, according to the London press, for $200,000.[20] However, upon the establishment of the republic, many of the economically dominant Spanish upper class had left Peru, taking with them a large percentage of the nation's capital. Therefore, when Quiros started in the guano export business, he was, not surprisingly, obliged to enter into an arrangement with William Joseph Myers & Company of Liverpool, who supplied some of the capital and management that such a venture required.[21] Mathew provides further information about this interesting deal:

> The sum of 40,000 pesos was to be paid at once to the Government, 10,000 more at the end of the first year, and a further 10,000 at the end of the second. Less than a month later, on December 4, 1840, the duration of the monopoly was extended by an extra three years, on the understanding that at the start of this period a further 15,000 pesos would be given to the Government, with another 15,000 coming 18 months later. On December 17, it was decreed that the trading rights applied to all the deposits in existence, along the coast of Peru, whether they be on the islands or not. All these arrangements were made in Quiros's name, and his alone. The Gamarra regime was charging 90,000 pesos, or £18,000, for trading rights extending over almost a decade. Of the 40,000 pesos that were required immediately, 38,000 were taken in the form of depreciating Debt Certificates that Allier had been holding and which were accepted at face value. The initial cash payment received by the Government, therefore, amounted to no more that 1,500 pesos, or about £300. Figures such as these suggest that the Government was in a state of almost total ignorance as to guano's potential profitability as an export commodity.[22]

The first commercial consignment of guano came back to England on the *Bonanza,* a vessel owned by the older established and more substantial firm of Thomas & John Brocklebank. It would seem likely that the main contractors also entered into appropriate subsidiary arrangements with this company and probably others. Few records remain regarding William Joseph Myers, but what we do know is that he died on August 24, 1871, at his home Lezayre House, Seaforth, near Liverpool, leaving a relatively modest fortune of under £7,000.[23] On the other hand, the Brocklebank enterprise had been established by the founder, Captain Daniel Brocklebank, in 1770, and by 1840 had already been trading for seventy years.[24]

The first vessel this enterprise traded on the west coast of South America was the 154-ton brig *Ariel III,* in 1820, under the command of Captain Cragg. Captain Cragg also traded their eight-gun barque, *Crown,* built at Whitehaven in 1821, to Valparaiso, Lima, and Guayaquil, from the date of her launch until 1824. Other Brocklebank vessels also worked as Cape Horn South Pacific traders, prior to the establishment of the guano trade. These were as follows: *Globe I; Swallow II; Andes,* from 1823–33, by Captain King; *Manchester* and *Courier I,* a small schooner of just 142 tons register; *Oberon, Gleaner, Irt, Esk,* and *Avoca.* There was also the aforementioned *Bonanza,* which was first traded around the Horn to Valparaiso in 1831 by Captain Storrs. In addition there was also the *Rimac, Globe II, Dryad IV, Horsborough, Swallow III,* and the *Kestrel,* which all began trading to the west coast in 1840, the year when the international guano trade began.[25] As the involvement of the Brocklebank enterprise in this trade was, however, long-term, and several of their masters left written accounts of their life at sea, more detailed coverage is given of this famous enterprise in a later chapter.

The *Bonanza* arrived at Callao from Liverpool with a general cargo on January 1, 1841. She remained in port for three weeks, until she left on the 22, of the month, bound for the Chincha Islands, in ballast. She reported back to Callao for final clearance, something all ships were then obliged to do, with guano, on February 14, where she remained until March 11, when she set sail for Liverpool with a cargo then described by acting consul Sealey as "Native Produce"—presumably guano—and other items. The following is a complete list of all the British vessels that loaded guano at the Chincha Islands in 1841, the first year of the international guano trade. Some of the dates given are when their arrival was recorded at Callao others when leaving Callao bound for the Chinchas. As will be noted, a large proportion of these vessels, whose ownership can be readily identified, were Liverpool owned and registered:

Name of vessel	To/from Chinchas	Tons	Crew	Owner #
Bonanza	22 January	176	10	Brocklebank, Liverpool
Europa	03 March	224	11	Bruce, Peterhead
Rimac	05 March	214	13	Brocklebank, Liverpool
Royal Tar	13 March	338	22	
Forager	15 March	249	15	Soames, Liverpool
Maypo	02 April	173	10	Brocklebank, Liverpool
Heroine	28 April	270	15	Myers, Liverpool (?)
Mary Worrall	19 May	—	—	Worrall, Liverpool
Nautilus	17 July	300	15	
Haidee	17 July	335	16	
Atkinson	19 July	306	14	(Gthds) Newcastle
Columbia	07 August	276	15	
Actoen	08 August	569	18	
Ann Bridson	28 August	600	20	W. Prouse, Liverpool
Dorothea	20 September	305	12	Laidman, Liverpool
Elizabeth Radcliffe	06 October	222	—	
Oberon	13 October	150	10	Brocklebank, Liverpool
Kestrel	20 October	232	12	Brocklebank, Liverpool
Earl of Lonsdale	25 October	359	14	J. Piele, Whitehaven
Vitula	22 November	296	14	Rimtoul, Liverpool
Phillipps	25 November	242	—	
Minstrel Boy	26 November	244	13	R. Harley, London
Dyson	26 November	276	14	Tyrer & Company[26]

The records submitted by acting consul Sealey for 1841 also show that many of the British ships that arrived at Callao during this year came directly from Liverpool and on occasion from London or other ports in the United Kingdom. Also worth noting is the fact that the majority of these ships had been trading at other west coast ports, such as Huanchaco, Guayaquil, Iquique, Valparaiso, Islay, Payta, or Panama, prior to putting in at Callao. The cargoes these ships carried out included general merchandise cotton, saltpeter, salt, specie, wheat, oil, and tallow. Vessels that had called at the Chinchas prior to getting clearance at Callao had their cargoes classed as "huano." The following details, showing the total arrival of ships at Callao during 1841, also give us an interesting insight into the maritime commerce of Peru at this point in time.

Ships arrived at Callao, year ending December 31, 1841

Nation	No. of Vessels	Tonnage	No. of crew
Peruvian	258	26,758	2,078
British	68	21,953	1,181
United States	45	14,198	1,194
Chilean	45	5,801	383
French	27	6,376	380
Sardinian	13	3,262	161
Spanish	10	2,537	155
Hamburguese	10	1,803	117
Mexican	8	772	86
Equatorian	7	1,070	91
Granadian	3	243	21
Central American	2	506	26
Danish	1	380	17
Totals	497	85,659	5,890[27]

When the first guano contract was awarded to Don Francisco Quiros, this had been strictly in accordance with Peruvian governmental policy of the period, working to encourage new commercial and industrial undertakings by awarding the respective entrepreneurs with exclusive rights for domestic manufacture or sale. With him in this venture were Carlos Barroilhet, a man of obscure origin; Aquiles Allier, described by Wilson as a "French-Peruvian Stock Jobber"; the French firm of Dutez & Company; and the Liverpool house of William Myers & Company.[28] Therefore, when the government accepted the first Quiros proposal in the aforementioned contract, signed November 10, 1840, they clearly did not appreciate the significance of the deal, seeing it as merely a license for one more run-of-the-mill business enterprise. Unfortunately for Quiros, though, in November 1841, the already mentioned British ship *Dyson* arrived at Callao, carrying a load of coal and, more significantly, news that guano had been selling in London at the very high price of £24–£28 per ton. On hearing this the government promptly canceled the first contract, under which they had only been receiving 5 percent, of the gross proceedings, and drew up a new one, by which the government was to receive 64 percent of the profits after costs. This was to run for one year, with an option of another four.

The contract was put out to tender, but they only received one bid, this being from Quiros, who was therefore back in the guano business but under far less favorable terms. Here, though, Mathew, citing Bonilla, has pointed out that "there was an apparent reluctance to grant privileges of this sort to foreigners, and that a direct concession for the working of the guano deposits (to foreigners) would have aroused public hostility." In such circumstances a respectable Peruvian front man was required. Francisco de Quiros, a man of local prominence who also had some useful money to hand, was selected.[29]

As noted, the British partners of Quiros, Allier & Company in this enterprise were Myers-Bland of Liverpool. This development did much to please the Peruvian bondholder's claims on the state, when the British chargé d'affaires, Sir Belford Hinton Wilson, managed to secure from the Peruvian government a pledge that half its pending guano revenues would go to service its ever-mounting foreign debts. This contract was signed, but no money was actually paid into the Bank of England to meet the debts. A third contract that that was even more favorable to the Peruvian government was then drawn up. Significantly, however, it was made with a combination of firms that included the old contractors, Quiros & Allier, and the Lima branches of two foreign enterprises, Puimirol, Poumaroux & Company of France, and Gibbs, Crawley & Company of England. From this combined enterprise the government managed to obtain a large advance of 487,000 pesos to meet pressing demands.

From the date when this contract was signed at the beginning of 1842 until their last contract expired at the end of 1861, the English firm of Antony Gibbs & Sons became the single most important mercantile party in the huge Peruvian guano trade. There were, in fact, two houses of Gibbs involved in this trade: Antony Gibbs & Sons of London and their subsidiary enterprise, Gibbs Crawley & Company of Lima, which was established in 1822.[30] This enterprise was one of the most important European merchant houses in Peru, and indeed, in Latin America. The Gibbs family enterprises have a long and exotic history, which should be noted here. The original Gibbs business house was established at Exeter in 1778, but even by this early date, the family had been commercially active around this port for two hundred years. Antony Gibbs, the founder of the firm and of the London house, in 1808, was in fact born there in 1756, the son of a wealthy local landowner.

In 1774 young Antony Gibbs was placed as an apprentice to a Mr. Brook, a merchant in the city who specialized in the export of woolen cloth to Spain. On the completion of his apprenticeship in 1778, he obtained some capital from his father and set up his own small woolen manufacturing business. Taking his lead from Brook, he also became involved in the textile trade with southern Europe. Unfortunately, this was a serious mistake, for Exeter's old established serge trade with Italy and Spain began to decline rapidly in the 1780s. In 1789, young Antony Gibbs, then just twenty-two years old, found himself bankrupt, and, as Devon had nothing more to offer him, he packed his bags and made his way to Madrid where he lived and worked as a commercial agent, selling British goods in Spain and Portugal. When his financial position improved, he began trading on his own account and then with a partner, Juan Pomar. However, war was on the horizon. On October 21, 1805, Nelson destroyed the fleets of Spain and France off Cape Trafalgar. It was this conflict between Britain and Spain, and the imposition of an embargo on all British property, that forced young Gibbs to make his way to Lisbon. He then arranged for his own and his principals' stocks in Spain to be held by a Spanish firm, which gave him time to find a way of disposing of these assets. Local buyers were not interested; consequently his attention was drawn to Spanish South America.

The goods concerned were, nominally, in Spanish ownership, and could only leave the country in a Spanish ship. However, such a proposed venture was complicated by the fact that the British Royal Navy was blockading Spanish ports, and it was therefore certain that any such ship would be seized as a prize of war. Fortunately, Antony Gibbs was a man with connections in high places, for his brother, Sir Vicary Gibbs, was then the solicitor general. Through him he managed to obtain a license guaranteeing safe passage for a specified ship, out of Spain, on a round voyage from Spain to Callao and back to England. The ship chartered for this notable voyage was the *Hermosa Mexicana*. She set sail on consignment to Antonio Baras of Lima on December 24, 1806. This venture, although beset by problems, marked the start of the Gibbs enterprises in Peru. Antony Gibbs made his last trip to Spain in 1807, and in the following year was appointed as one of four commissioners to deal with Portuguese property sent to England during the conflict. This position obliged him to live in London.[31] A few days after he had heard of the arrival of the *Hermosa Mexicana* at Vigo, Antony wrote from London to his friend James O'Connor of Madrid on November 21, 1807, in the following terms:

> I have at length wound up most of my concerns in Spain to my satisfaction, and have now established a House in this place with my eldest son under the firm of Antony Gibbs & Son, who will have the pleasure of sending your House a circular in due time. Through the connections I have in Spain, and through the interest of my brother here [Sir Vicary], who now fills the place of Attorney-General in our Ministry, I have good hopes that we shall soon do business of considerable consequence, and, though I did not intend writing to you till we send our circular, I avail myself of this opportunity by a neutral vessel. If I should ever have it in my power to be of any service to you or your House it will always give me pleasure to open connections with people whom I so much esteem.[32]

The letter is interesting, as it shows that at the time he considered his London house as being brought into existence primarily by the return of the *Hermosa Mexicana.* It was not quite that simple, though, for it was not until December 1808 that his financial position actually cleared and enabled him to launch this venture, in partnership with his eldest son George Henry. The firm was then known as Antony Gibbs & Son. His second son, William, joined the business in 1813, the style of the house becoming Antony Gibbs & Sons, as it was to remain for the next 135 years. From this relatively modest beginning, the firm was to expand and trade under various styles throughout the world. At Liverpool the Gibbs-Bright partnership was set up in 1825, where they traded as merchants from offices at 22 Water Street. George Henry Gibbs, the founder's son, with Robert Bright of Bristol subsequently became directors of the Great Western Steamship Company and acted in Liverpool as agents for this notable enterprise.

The firm also established the Eagle Line of Australian sailing packets, the flagship of the line being the Brunel-designed *Great Britain.* At one point they operated a joint service to Australia with the Black Ball Line, established by the legendary James Baines and Henry Hucks Gibbs, the first son of George Henry Gibbs.[33] He became Lord Aldenham, and among the many partners in this enterprise were the Honorary Vicary Gibbs, son of Henry Hucks Gibbs, and Lord Cullen of Ashburn, the grandson of George Henry Gibbs.[34]

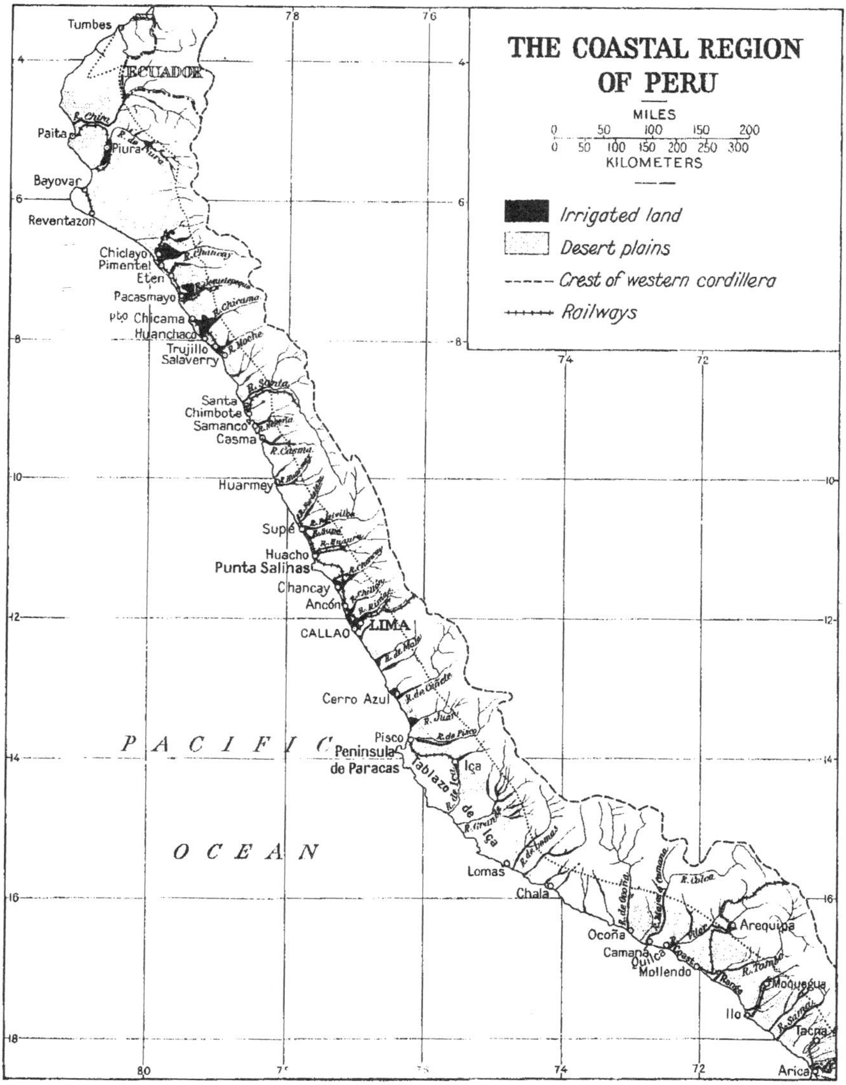

3. Peru from the air, the coastal region of Peru. This map shows the irrigated coastal valleys of Peru. It is along this coastline that the great fish-bearing current named after Humboldt flows. Lieutenant George Robbins Johnson. *Peru from the Air.* Reproduced by courtesy of the American Geographical Society.

The history of the firm in Peru dates from 1820, when the firm engaged John Moens. Provided with Antony Gibbs & Sons' power of attorney, he sailed in the *Baltic* in June 1820 via Madeira and Cape Horn and arrived at Valparaiso on November 15. English firms had established themselves there and at Santiago as soon as Spanish rule in Chile was overthrown. Although Britain did not give immediate recognition to the newly established, independent republics, business was still being conducted between Chile and Peru. During the previous eight years, Spain had sent sixteen expeditions to South America with over 40,000 veteran troops, and had spent 75 million dollars to suppress the revolutions. The financial requirements of the situation therefore obliged the viceroy at Lima to tolerate a degree of trade with Britain. By 1818 British merchant ships were entering the port of Callao and selling their cargoes with no steps being taken to stop them. The following year the situation was given formal recognition when Callao was officially opened to British trade and a limited number of British merchants were allowed to settle there.

At Valparaiso Moens soon made friends with Captain Sherriff of HMS *Andromanche* and on December 10, 1821, sailed with him for Callao, which was then blockaded by the Chileans, arriving off that port on December 20. By mistake one of the guns of the port opened fire, but an apology was soon presented for this error. However, the ship was regarded with some suspicion because it was supposed in Lima that the English and the Americans had given help to Lord Thomas Cochrane, the British commander of the Chilean navy. To make matters worse, Sherriff had Lady Cochrane on board as a passenger, though she was going home in the ship and had only come to take leave of her husband. Clearly, Moens had not arrived in Lima with the intention of opening an office for Antony Gibbs & Sons at a very auspicious moment. San Martin was then at Ancon, just fifteen miles north of Callao, and his troops that had been landed at Pisco were marching inland behind Lima. They were, in fact, on the point of joining with the main patriot army at Huara so that Lima only had a small tract of country left to call its own.

Because of the rather delicate political situation, Moens was not at first allowed to go ashore. After fourteen days, however, and with the influence of some of Antony Gibbs & Sons' Spanish correspondents in Lima permission was given and he arrived in Lima, on January 4, 1821, although on landing he was in danger of losing his life at the hands of the people of Callao. He then called on Viceroy

Pezuela, by whom he was well received, but was advised by him not to show himself in the streets.[35] He wasted no time in getting down to business in Lima. Then, as Gibbs & Sons also had many royalist friends and clients in Arequipa in June, he made his way there. Here he was very well treated and dined with the royalist group. "I wonder much," he wrote, "when Englishmen have brought them to the present pass," meaning, of course, the English officers in the Chilean army and navy. Moens arrived back in Lima on June 28, 1821. A few days later on July 6, the viceroy evacuated the "City of the Kings of Peru." San Martin entered the city on the 12th and was made protector. The independence of Peru was proclaimed on the 28th. Notwithstanding this profound change in the political situation, Moens then shipped $150,000 in silver and gold bars to Antony Gibbs & Sons on behalf of his Spanish royalist friends in HMS *Conway*. In spite of this, the protector acted magnanimously toward Moens, who wrote, "He gives a ball once weekly in the Palace and has given me a constant ticket. A few other English are only occasionally invited."

On September 21st Callao finally surrendered to the patriots, and on the 25th sixty ships (most of them loaded with wheat from Chile) waiting at Ancon were allowed to move to Callao and discharge. Many English ships arrived at the port in the same month. Foreigners were then permitted to set up business, but could only act directly as consignees, as Moens did, by paying 5 percent extra duty on imports; otherwise they had to employ a Peruvian citizen in that capacity. Following this development there was a large influx of Englishmen into Lima. Moens continued to accept work from his royalist friends. In November he shipped about $130,000 in bullion and specie, and some produce, in HMS *Superb* to Antony Gibbs & Sons. This was done on account of some Spaniards. The following month he shipped a further $40,000 for them in HMS *Creole*.[36] The ability of Moens, acting on behalf of Gibbs & Sons, to use ships of the Royal Navy as merchant vessels is notable and must have rested entirely on the fact that the principal's brother was Sir Vicary Gibbs, the attorney general!

The house of Gibbs Crawley, Moens & Company was formally set up in Lima on January 1, 1822. (Charles Crawley, it should be noted, was a nephew of Antony Gibbs, and had held a partnership in the London firm since 1814, but was only to spend four years on the west coast, from 1829–33.) Besides issuing circulars to advertise the firm, in December 1821 Antony Gibbs & Sons sent Charles Crawley to the north of England and to Scotland to bring the Lima house to the notice of manufacturers and to establish agents who would procure consignments for shipment to them. In March 1822, they began to employ, on a similar errand on the Continent, Samuel Bright, who, when he left Antony Gibbs & Sons' office in 1821 had gone abroad to gain business experience, prior to settling down in Liverpool and establishing the aforementioned House of Gibbs, Bright & Company.[37] As might be expected, Moens's sympathies with the Spanish Royalists at a difficult time soon brought him into difficulties with the patriots at Lima. In March 1822 he was in prison for three weeks, falsely accused of sending off some of the Spanish silver in one of HM ships without paying the duty. However, his friends supported him and disproved the charges by papers held in the Custom House.

Moens continued to manage the Gibbs house at Lima in its earliest days, but although he was popular and respected, his business practices and clerical ability left something to be desired (at least according to the Gibbs family). On the other hand, his constant pleas for additional well-trained clerical support staff to be sent out from London were consistently ignored. Eventually, however, Moens went to London. However, the firm agreed to let him return to Peru, but with his partnership interest reduced from 25 percent to 10 percent from July 1, 1824, and with his name omitted from the style of the firm, which from the same date became Gibbs Crawley & Company.[38] Moens finally left the firm in 1829, leaving a Mr. John Hayne as senior partner. Hayne was to remain with the Lima house for the next twenty-two years, working with the following partners/managers: Charles R. Pffucker, 1828–47; Hugh Torrance, 1829–32; Henry Witt, 1830–42; Henry Reincke, 1832–39; Samuel Went, 1833–57; Frederick A. Eck, 1836–52; George Rodger, 1836–39; Thomas Gray, 1841–56; George Garland, 1842–51; and Hermann Schwartz, 1844–57.[39]

"In the last full accounting year of the pre-guano period," Mathew states, "Gibbs Crawley made a profit of $80,462, or roughly £16,000. Credit items came to $134,313, with income from commission business yielding $80,404 or 60 percent of the total."[40] On May 1, 1847, the Lima house was restyled William Gibbs & Company, under which title it was to trade until it became Gibbs & Company in 1880. However, it was on July 10, 1847, that the firm reported they had managed to obtain a contract for the sale of 40,000 tons of guano. Also involved in this deal were Quiros Allier & Company, Montane, and Myers & Company. The selling area excluded the United States, and they were obliged to make an immediate advance to the government of 700,000 pesos. The Peruvian government, shipowners, agents, and many others were to benefit from this trade. Sadly, though, it was a business that rested on the crude exploitation of thousands of unfortunate men, doomed to a miserable existence, working the guano deposits on the bleak, isolated bird islands of Peru. However, before this trade could develop, the product had to be promoted, particularly in Europe.

5

Guano: The Product and the Politics

THE EXTENSIVE TRADE IN GUANO THAT WAS SOON TO DEVELOP, PARticularly between Peru and Britain, rested historically on the Treaty of Amity, Commerce, and Navigation, between the Dominions of His Britannic Majesty, and the states of the Peru-Bolivian Confederation. Signed at Lima on June 5, 1837, by Belford Hinton Wilson, HM consul general in Peru, and Don Lorenzo Bazo, Peruvian inspector general of finance, this formidable document recognized that an extensive commercial intercourse had been established for some time between the two nations. Article I of this agreement stated "There shall be perpetual Amity between the dominions and Subjects of His Majesty the King of the United Kingdom of Great Britain and Ireland, His Heirs and Successors, and the Peruvian Confederation, and its Citizens." Article II guaranteed that the subjects of the two countries would have the liberty to come with their ships and cargoes to all ports in either country, and Article IV ensured that restrictive duties would not be placed on importers by either side. Article VIII decreed that "All merchants, commanders of ships, and others shall have the liberty to manage their own affairs themselves, or to commit them to the management of whomsoever they please, as broker," and so on. Article XIV was particularly notable when related to working conditions on the Chincha Islands. It read, in full: "The Government of the Peru-Bolivian Confederation engages to co-operate with His Britannic Majesty for the total abolition of the Slave Trade and to prohibit all persons inhabiting within the Territories of the Peru-Bolivian Confederation, or subject to their jurisdiction, in the most effectual manner, and by the most solemn laws, from taking any share in such trade."[1]

On the signing of the celebrated guano contracts, Messrs. Myers and Gibbs were then faced with the formidable task of selling 120,000 tons of guano in Britain and Europe before the close of 1846. To make matters more difficult, the market was depressed, and the product still needed a considerable amount of promotion, all of which cost money. At first Britain was virtually the only market in which guano could be sold. Myers was of the opinion that this business was one of price and price only. In August 1842, Gibbs and Myers reached an understanding based on current market returns. This was that for lots of five tons and under, the price was to be £15; for amounts between five and twenty four tons, £14; for quantities in excess of twenty four tons, £13; and for whole cargoes, £12. This proved to be overoptimistic and had to be reduced considerably in January 1843 to a more economically realistic scale, running from £12 for 1–15 tons, to £10 for thirty tons or more. No mention at all was made of a rate for the disposal of an entire cargo.[2]

The capital required to promote and operate this newly established industry was considerable, and well beyond the means of the proud, independent, but impoverished state of Peru. This was particularly so when one considers that much private working capital had recently been taken out of the country by rapidly departing Royalists, aided, to an appreciable extent, by Moens, the commendably zealous, but politically shortsighted, junior partner of Gibbs & Company. Expensive equipment and loading facilities were required to work the Chincha deposits, pay wages, and make advance payments to the government. Furthermore, capital was required to meet shipping, storage, and day-to-day expenses—and for a considerable period—before any payments would be received. Above all though, expensive efforts would have to be made to bring the excellent qualities of the product to the attention of farmers in the United Kingdom. The product, however, was a good one, the value of guano as manure being mainly dependent upon it containing two substances, about which, a British government report of the period on the product noted that:

> 1. Phosphate of lime; and 2. Compounds of ammonia (or animal matters which will furnish them to the soil during their decomposition). The two other ingredients of guano are of minor importance. Commercially, ammonia is many times more valuable than phosphate of lime; consequently the guano that furnishes most of this ingredient will fetch the highest price in the market. The recently deposited guano is that which contains the highest proportion of ammonia or its elements. By exposure to rain and atmospheric influences, the ammonia is gradually dissipated and removed, and the phosphate of lime is then the prevailing ingredient. If, however, the guano has not been subject to rain, it will retain the greater part of its original value, although it may have been

accumulating for ages, as in the immense deposits on the Chincha Islands, off the coast of Peru.[3]

Gibbs & Company were to be involved with the Peruvian government, from the signing of the first Gibbs Myers contract in 1842 until their last exclusive contract, which expired at the close of 1861. Over these two decades the house of Gibbs became the single most important establishment in Peru's largest trade, and behind this old, established enterprise was the enormous capital resources of the city of London. Although the Peruvian government was clearly dictating far more than just the fine print of their joint guano agreements, the relationship between this Latin American government and an enterprise representing the tremendous power of British capitalism was close and delicately balanced. Certainly, both parties had a mutual interest in the success of the venture. Nevertheless, despite these considerations, it is clear that the Peruvian government was most definitely in the controlling position over a branch of industry that was to dominate the economic and political affairs of their nation for decades.

Apart from these considerations about power and control, one thing is quite clear. The House of Gibbs was soon to become exceptionally rich on the proceeds of their trade in guano, this despite the fact that the Peruvian government was, during the same crucial period, to command the bulk of its considerable income from the sale of this single, mundane product. Thus, by the close of the nineteenth century, Messrs. Antony Gibbs were disporting themselves, with charm and regal elegance, in the elevated world of merchant banking. At the same time they were doing their utmost to distance themselves from the rather distasteful fact that, as a wit of the day put it, they had made their money "by selling turds of foreign birds." While the Gibbs family were emerging as merchant princes in London, administrators in Lima were only just managing to stagger from one financial crisis to another. The root causes of this problem included poor administration and the funding of a vast unproductive army and bureaucracy out of the considerable proceeds of guano. However, many Peruvians at the time tried to shift attention away from the failings of their own government by conveniently, but unrealistically, blaming Antony Gibbs & Company for this sorry state of affairs. The many arguments brought forward by Mathew to counter these allegations are given below.

Between 1856 and 1861 a rash of books and pamphlets appeared in Peru and Europe denouncing Gibbs for misconduct in the trade and willful ruination of Peruvian wealth. Authors like Carlos Barroilhet, Luis Mesones, and José Casimiro Ulloa used their pens as swords to cut into the gross flesh of the English capitalists and force their withdrawal from the trade in 1861. Gibbs' participation in guano exporting, commented Barroilhet, had been "a complete disaster for Peru, a public calamity." Mesones described the consignment system as "vicious," involving as it did exorbitant charges and grave damage to the national treasury. According to Ulloa, they wielded "the greatest despotism that a person or family could exercise over a nation." Unfortunately, as Mathew has been at pains to point out, when countering recent accounts of the trade by Peruvian scholars (Levin in particular) these allegations actually bear little relationship to historical reality. In the first place, the conclusions have not been backed up by reference to the records of traders such as Gibbs. Second, there has been a dearth of information on vital matters, such as intermediate costs and market prices. "We cannot be certain that contemporary observers who were so critical of Gibbs were objective and disinterested parties: guano was a very live political issue, and the possible transference from Gibbs was a matter of the greatest economic moment for powerful elements of the Peruvian bourgeoisie."[4]

In the meantime, though, in the early 1840s, the product had to be promoted and sold before either side could argue over the merits or demerits of their joint marketing agreements. Here the British press came to the rescue in the summer of 1841 when the *Times,* quoting from the *Liverpool Times,* gave much welcome coverage to this notable fertilizer, then in such urgent need of publicity:

> A specimen of guano, or the dung of the guano, a South American sea bird, was shown at the agricultural meeting last week, by Mr Shirring. It is likely to become a considerable article of commerce, as it is found in great quantities on the rocky coasts of the Pacific, and is said to be the most powerful and concentrated of all manure's. Applied at the rate of about 2 cwt an acre, it produces very fine crops of turnips and grasses, and is particularly suited for the light lands on which these crops are usually reared. The wonderful effects of sea fowl's dung are mentioned by Sir Humphry Davy in his *Agricultural Chymistry.* Together with nitrate of soda, which is obtained from the same quarter of the world, it is likely to have a great effect on English agriculture. Some of the farmers who were at the meeting last week spoke in the highest terms of the effects of nitrate of soda, particularly on their wheat crops.—*Liverpool Times.*[5]

More publicity soon followed, which, no doubt, played a significant role in lifting guano imports into the United Kingdom from just

2,062 tons in 1841 to 14,123 tons the following year, although due allowance has to be made for the fact that the trade only started in 1841, and many ships only loaded for the first time in the second half of the year, meaning that cargoes would not actually be placed on the market until 1842. Notwithstanding this consideration, it is interesting to note that in 1843 imports dropped to 1,589 tons, but rose to 16,475 tons in 1844.[6] In February 1843 the *Liverpool Mercury* gave extensive coverage to the outstanding merits of the celebrated Peruvian manure called guano.

The editor opened by stating that his paper considered it a duty to call the attention of their readers—especially those engaged in agricultural pursuits—to any discovery that would enable them to produce larger crops, at less cost, than they had hitherto been able to achieve. "Science," the writer enthused, "is rapidly unfolding from her mysterious stores new facts which bear a very intimate connection with many of the most important arts of life. Husbandry, more particularly, has of late derived from chemical and geological science much valuable assistance, recent discoveries having proved the vast importance of a proper and systematic plan of manuring, adapted to the peculiar quality of the soil. In pursuance, then, of the desire we always cherish, of urging upon the notice of the British farmer any new lights that may break forth affecting his profession. We now extract from the *British Farmer's Magazine* (a most valuable periodical) a mass of information, respecting the new manure, guano, which they will do well to read and ponder on."

The writer continued by stating that he was pleased to see that very extensive sales of guano had already been made, and that it was rapidly making its way into the overworked soils of England—and the results were nothing short of magical. It was, the paper noted, not more than eighteen months since this subject had been brought to the attention of the public when, for the first time, Lord Stanley had named it at a meeting of the Royal Agricultural Society in Liverpool in July 1841. France was also excited about the new manure, readers being assured that the French Board of Agriculture and Science, having directed their attention to the value of guano, reported favorably on the item. All in all it was felt that guano was the cheapest and best manure available, and one that cost less per acre to apply. It also promoted heavy yields and enabled growers to get their crops to market earlier, and thus enable themselves to get the highest prices that were generally obtained at the commencement of the harvest.

The *British Farmer's Magazine,* quoted by the *Mercury,* felt that guano was the most permanent fertilizer ever discovered, and at the going rate offered excellent value for the money. However, the writer for this respected paper was concerned that the "London Speculators" might get hold of the present stock, monopolize the guano trade, and raise the price to double its present rate as they had done with nitrate of soda, "Three years back; when it might be adulterated, as nitrate of soda was at that time." The writer was obviously not aware of the fact when he put pen to paper that the guano trade was already under the monopoly control of just two merchant houses working closely together, one from Liverpool and one from the City of London. "I would recommend," he continued, "every farmer to get it though a respectable agent in Liverpool, who will see that he gets the genuine guano direct from the Queen's bonded store, (as imported from Peru) then he will have no fear of his crops failing, if properly put into the soil." Guano, he felt, was very well suited to the humid climate of Great Britain, and especially Ireland, "as by its peculiar chemical and attractive 'ammoniacal concretes and properties' it feeds the growing plant faster."

He felt that without this guano the ancient Peruvians could not have raised crops to feed the 15,000,000 people that once inhabited Chile and Peru. In fact, it was so strong that all one had to do to get excellent results was to put it around a plant with finger and thumb, like pinches of snuff. It was the best compound in nature ready for the English farmer. He had to concede, however, that naturalists disagreed as to the origin of guano formation, but what was known was that in the soft portions of the deposits (on the rainless Chincha Islands) "all sorts of animals burrow in it like rabbits, thus living and dying in the guano." However, the results from guano were very satisfactory for all crops, and a more or less quantity could be put on any field, according to the kind of produce required.[6] Among the many fascinating testimonials quoted in this long article are the following:

> Guano—We are happy to hear from our agricultural and horticultural friends that this new manure, which was tried in our neighbourhood last year, for the first time, with such favorable results, has again proved itself to be one of the most valuable manure's ever introduced either for field or garden crops. It has been used to a considerable extent in this country, both in dry and liquid state, and in every instance, when properly applied, has answered well for crops of every kind. It has also been proved to be a lasting manure, for very good crops have been obtained

without any manure whatever from land where guano was applied and yielded good crops last year. Our farmers and gardeners have no doubt much to learn with regards to the proper quantity to be used of this new manure: but as a great many experiments have this year been made with it, we may expect this point will soon be settled.

Guano has been applied in this neighborhood on wheat and other grain crops, and on grasslands as a top-dressing, at the rate of 2 cwt. per statute acre, with most excellent effect. For turnips, 4 cwt. have been used to the acre, and given good crops; and from 4 cwt. to 6 cwt. to potatoes, with like success. In the gardens and nursery grounds guano has been applied in a liquid state and in that manner has surpassed every manure yet discovered. Its effects on young fruit and forest trees are wonderful; also upon hot-house and green-house plants of every description; even the most exotic heaths, to which manure of every kind has been considered injurious, seem to flourish in a manner beyond precedent, when watered with it. About 4lbs to 12 gallons of water is enough for hot-house and green-house plants: the water should stand 24 hours before use, and when drawn off, 24 gallons more may be put to the same guano, and the guano is good for the land afterwards."[7]

Sir: In one of my fields I made an experiment with guano this year. The test was very unfavourable for the guano, as the field was in a very bad state of cultivation. In consequence of the land never having been drained, it was very wet. From this cause, the crop of turnips failed entirely on it in 1841. (Being a very wet season.) The field is near the wall of the Kirkdale Gaol, and has a cold, clay bottom; I ploughed it Feb. 17, as it could not be done before, from its wet-state, though the field slopes to the south. I sowed it February 12, with white wheat; it was well manured for turnips in 1841, in drills, trench-ploughed, and well manured with horse and cow dung. The wheat came up tolerably in March, but in April it became very yellow, sickly, and evidently failing fast. A deal of plants died, so that I thought of ploughing it up for barley in May, when I accidentally heard, through my friend Mr Danson, of Liverpool, of guano. I tried a bag of one and a half cwt., costing £1.1s., mixed it well with an equal quantity of riddled old worn-out soil, and threw it broadcast on the field on the 6th of May, but did not harrow it in."

John Pritchard

Kirkdale, near Liverpool, December 21, 1842.[8]

[Pritchard then stated that after some rain, his guano treated crops did exceptionally well.]

Experiments of a supposedly more scientific nature, which had been presented in a report submitted by the French Ministry of Agriculture and Commerce, were also quoted. This document was based on trials made with guano at their experimental farm near the town and port of Bayonne. First they tried the manure on grass, spreading it rather lavishly at the rate of 1,600 lbs. to one acre, from which they were able to state that the vegetation produced was prodigious. Three crops of hay and after-grass till September 14 followed, which, they pointed out, was on land that had never previously produced more than two cuts in the year. Their scientist in charge concluded: "The quality of the hay produced by the guano was more tender, the smell more aromatic and agreeable, and the animals eat it with avidity."

Other items on the subject in the *Mercury* included the following:

> From Mr. John Taylor, Surgeon, Liverpool, to Mr W. Dawson. —Sir, Having noticed the progress of guano, from its numerous analytical examinations through all its phases of practical application to agriculture, it has afforded me considerable satisfaction to perceive how well its theoretical character has been sustained by the results of experience. In the comparative trials which it has undergone with farm-yard manure, ammoniacal salts, nitrate of soda &c., it has proved a concentrated animal mixture of richest fertilising properties, capable of producing larger crops, at less cost, than any other, taking into account its slow solubility in the soil, which gives it permanence beyond its rivals. The discovery of the best means of applying it, so as to render the greatest amount of service, has obviated any objections against its use, and manifested its superiority when appropriately combined with sulphate salts, or decayed vegetable and carbonaceous matters, with due reference to the description of produce expected. The latest analysis of the genuine guano, by Dr. Ure, shows an entire absence of sand and other impurities which had been discovered in larger proportion in other specimens, and describes it as a compact mass of the salts of ammonia in combination with soluble phosphates, than which nothing can be conceived more nutritious for the support of vegetation. The genuine guano therefore, when mixed with an appropriate compost, excels farm-yard manure by the less amount of labour expended in its use: it excels the various refuse compounds of ammoniacal salts by possessing the phosphorical salts in addition to abundance of ammonia; and the possession of these salts likewise gives it a preference over nitrate of soda, which, like the ammoniacal salts, merely stimulates the growth of plants at the expense of the phosphates contained in the salts. I am Sir, your most obedient servant,
>
> 17 Nile Street, Jan. 31, 1843.
>
> John Taylor[9]

The public, and in particular the farming community, were now becoming increasingly interested in this dynamic South American dung, which prompted the obvious question, does one have to go all the way around Cape Horn just in order to obtain the droppings of seabirds? Clearly unaware of the particular climatic factors that preserved the "ammoniacal salts" and other valuable compounds found in Peruvian guano, in December 1843, the editor of the *John O'Groats Journal* pointed out that guano was still scarcely known in Caithness, other than what the local farmers had read in the papers and excepting some minor trials made by a few wealthy proprietors and large local farmers. Consequently, he felt obliged to pass on the contents of a note the paper had just received in the hope that it would prompt some enterprising local landlords or tenants to experiment with this new and valuable manure.

> I wonder if I may not take up the subject of guano, and explain to your readers, more especially to your landed proprietors, that there is a great abundance of it [guano] to be found in Caithness, Sutherland, Orkney, and Zetland, among the islands, stacks, and cliffs of the rocks. There must be immense deposits of birds' dung on these coasts, which could be collected at a trifling expense. I last year made trial of it from an island near Inchcolm, took a boat in the morning, and with some small spades, mason's trowels, and some bags, clambered to the top, about 30 feet high, to the resort of the seafowl, from which, in an hour's time, three of us nearly filled the boat with excellent stuff resembling dirty lime. The season was past to try it on vegetables, and not being a farmer, I used it in top-dressing a flower garden, where it had astonishing effect. The feeding fibres of the plants came to the surface, and laid hold of the small pieces as greedily as a hawk would his prey; it was interesting to observe the feeders of the dahlias coming to the surface, a hundred at a time, as small as the threads, attached to a small piece, not bigger than a walnut. I had a delightful show of them, but will not have the pith of the guano until next summer. I am certain Sir George Dunbar could take a vast quantity of it from the rocks of his estate, of Hemprigg, Noss, &c.[10]

It is not, however, on record that Sir George took this well-meaning advice to attack his (rain-drenched!) rocks with spades and trowels in order to undercut the trade in foreign bird dung. However, interest in and advice on how to best use foreign guano continued to appear in the local and national press, of which the following is typical. After preparing the accompanying directions for using guano, for the information of Sir Charles Lemon's tenantry, it occurred to an anonymous expert that it might be a good idea to pass on his directions to the public at large, via the columns of the *Liverpool Mercury*.

> 1: It should never be used in contact with seeds, as it kills them immediately they begin to vegetate. 2: It should be mixed as equally as possible, with about four times its bulk of finely pulverised earth, burnt clay, turf, or peat ashes, after they have become cold. If sand is used, about twice its bulk will be sufficient. 3: The quantity per acre may vary from two to four cwt., according to the nature and quality of the land. Recent experiments have shown that a quantity that proved highly beneficial in poor soil, became deleterious upon land previously rich and well manured. 4: The best time for applying it is shortly after vegetation has commenced, and immediately before rain, or during damp warm weather. 5: The best mode of application is to divide the quantity per acre into two or three equal portions, and sow them broadcast at intervals of about ten days, or a fortnight. 6: For small allotments it might be more convenient to use it in a liquid state—in which case, mix four lbs. of guano with twelve gallons of water, and let it stand for twenty-four hours before being used. The same guano will do for mixing again, with the same quantity of water, after the first is drawn off.[11]

Sales of Peruvian guano continued to take place regularly throughout the 1840s. This was particularly so at Liverpool, where supplies of Peruvian guano soon began to be supplemented by the sale of recently discovered guano deposits at Ichaboe, Possession, and other isolated and rainless islands off the coast of southwest Africa. This was, of course, much to the consternation of the Peruvian government and their main guano contractors, Messrs. Myers and Gibbs. Whatever the source, adulteration of guano by some unscrupulous dealers continued to be a problem. In July 1844 the *Agricultural Gazette* raised the issue once more, pointing out that they had already asserted that guano was often an abominable mixture of all sorts of "brown ingredients" that were absolutely worthless. It would seem that one of their readers had recently purchased a large consignment, paying the substantial price of £12 a ton for what he thought was first-grade Peruvian manure. Alas, though, the smooth-talking guano salesman had seen this gullible farmer coming, and off-loaded absolute rubbish on him. On analysis it was subsequently found to contain just one-half percent of ammonia, not a trace of urea, and just minute quantities of alkaline sulfates and phosphates of lime; in short, it was estimated that the real guano present in the sample amounted to 3 percent. Even this, however, included feathers that appeared to have come from local sparrows and pheasants rather than Peruvian or African seabirds! Yet another quantity of guano, sold at Manchester, was found to contain 75 percent brick dust; another from Derbyshire contained 10 percent sawdust and 6 percent clay; and another Derbyshire sample had been "doctored" with 12 percent ground bark. With these facts staring farmers in the face, it was incomprehensible to the writer why farmers would "not throw themselves into the hands of the Chymists," who alone could help them.[12]

Four months later the *Times* brought readers attention to a more sophisticated scam, supposedly being operated by Liverpool skippers and shipowners. Increasingly, people were becoming aware that guano was being adulterated by dealers after it was unloaded from the ships. To get around this, farmers were making a point of buying it directly from the vessels in order to obtain what they thought would be the genuine article. Alas, the crooks were one jump ahead of them. The *Times* then went on to say that four ships had recently sailed from Liverpool for the African guano stations, ballasted with gypsum or plaster of Paris. On arrival at the islands, this "ballast" was not dumped but carefully mixed with the guano as it came on board. This ploy, the *Times* continued, allowed the unscrupulous Liverpool parties to deliver—straight from the hold—a rather nice-looking, although light-colored, guano. Finally, readers were advised that the favorite material for the adulteration of guano was umber, which is a type of brown earth containing iron and manganese oxides, used as pigment by artists. This was brought, in large quantities, from Anglesey, North Wales. The rate of admixture was about 15 cwt. umber to about 5 cwt. guano, from which a really excellent-looking article arrived at Liverpool to be sold as best African guano.[13]

But was this allegation true, for without delay this slur on the integrity of Liverpool merchants and skippers was hotly disputed by a dealer in African guano. This was Mr. Lloyd Phillips, who stated in the *Liverpool Mail,* at the end of November 1844, that the forgoing allegations, first made in the *Standard* and *Albion,* were untrue. Unfortunately, he added, these allegations were then repeated widely by other papers but were destitute of all truth, the writer, he added, being ashamed to reveal his name, for he knew that what he was writing was false. Phillips stormed, "I may well remark that every cargo of African [guano] on arrival here, is analysed by a chemist, and the analysis exhibited to the buyers before purchasing, who are governed, not by the colour, but by the quantity of available fertilising matter it contains, which quantity any respectable selling dealer or broker will guarantee. It is preposterous to suppose that adulterating substances would be sent out to Africa, where the genuine article itself can be had for gathering, and which on arrival here, would be chemically analysed and immediately detected." But he did concede that a great deal of adulteration had been going on, which none could deny. Nevertheless, this was bound to happen, with such a great demand for the product. He concluded, "The best and only security agriculturists can have against adulteration is to purchase either directly from the ship's side, from the bonded warehouses, or from parties whose standing in the trade is a guarantee against fraud."[14]

Despite minor problems with adulteration, throughout the second part of the nineteenth century demand for guano in Britain continued to grow steadily, and it was the general changes in English industry, agriculture, and society that was to give a continual impulse to guano extraction and importation. Since the early forties, British agriculture had prospered—notwithstanding the continual failure of the potato crop throughout this decade, particularly in Scotland and the west of Ireland—and even the repeal of the Corn Laws had not done the damage to the farm pricing structure some had feared. Improved inland transport and the concentration of population in large industrial towns and cities were great boons to the British farmer, providing him with a steady market and the means of reaching it.

Many more farmers were now trying to make use of the best methods known to agricultural science to increase production and meet demand. In these endeavors they were assisted by the Royal Agricultural Society, which was founded in 1840, just when Peru and the contractors were making efforts to promote guano in the United Kingdom. Of particular importance is the fact that agricultural science certainly did not stand still during this crucial period. The great importance of drainage was realized, and deep, covered trenches and clay pipes were used in place of the primitive method of throwing the land into high ridges and hoping for the best.[15]

The experiments of the German chemist, Justus Liebig, whose chief work was published in 1840, also opened up new, exciting possibilities of intensive cultivation. When only twenty-one years old, he was appointed professor of chemistry at Giessen, and in 1845 he was made a baron. Perhaps the leading chemist of his day, Liebig discovered various chemical substances, notably chloral and chloroform, and, above all others, he showed how the soil could be made more productive by the use of various fertilizers. To improve the land, the use of chemical and natural fertilizers became widespread and here, once more, Peru was in a position to meet demands for both products by supplying nitrate as well, a powerful chemical rival to guano. These nitrate deposits had, in fact, been discovered in the desert of Tarapacá, then the southernmost province of Peru, on the border between Peru and Chile, which, in fact, was soon to lead to war between the two nations.

Related to this was the fact that while British farmers were enjoying a period of prosperity during the forties, the shipping industry was in decline, and the urbanized masses, increasingly out of demand on the capital intensive and more mechanized country estates were enduring great hardship, this being particularly so in Liverpool. Here grinding poverty was the order of the day, with many families trying to survive on just a single meal of potatoes a day. Dr. Duncan, the first medical officer of health for the port, reported that in one area, 12,000 inhabitants crowded together on a surface of 105,000 square yards.[16]

Consequently, ships required to bring guano and nitrate back from Peru could, under these extreme social pressures, be manned cheaply, making the transportation of bulky commodities over great distances a viable economic proposition. Typically, during the "Hungry Forties," a Liverpool shipowner would pay his commanders just £10 a month; a first mate £5.10.0; second mate £4.0.0; third mate £3.0.0; carpenter up to £6.0.0; and ordinary seamen £2.0.0; with up to four apprentices working for just £5.0.0 a year.[17] Alas, by 1856 these rates had only risen slightly, with the crew of say the *Rimac,* then engaged in the Liverpool-Peru trade, receiving just marginally more; the first mate £6.0.0 and ordinary seamen £2.15.0.[18] A typical voyage to Callao would take ten months, but there would be a profit on a mixed cargo taken to Chile or Peru. Trading on the west coast itself and the carriage of precious metals, hides, and other items back to the United Kingdom with a bulk cargo of guano or nitrates meant that these small ships, many of only 200-ton burthen, could still make a good profit for the shipowner.

While the Chincha Islands poured millions into the Peruvian treasury, Tarapacá province also contributed the proceeds of its nitrate of soda trade to swell the riches of this strange, but favored land. This material was first exported to Britain in 1831, but this trade was quickly developed. Then, as mentioned, in the forties and fifties, vast fleets of sailing ships were to be found moored off ports such as Pisagua, patiently waiting for boatmen to bring a few bags of nitrate at a time over the pounding surf to their waiting vessels.[19]

Sir C. Markham calculated that the nitrate of soda grounds in this district covered fifty square leagues, with total deposits amounting to 63,000,000 tons. In 1860 the export of nitrate of soda from just the port of Iquique amounted to 68,512 tons.[20] The companies that were to become engaged in extracting nitrate, of which about five million quintals were exported annually, were soon competing with each other so ruthlessly that the low prices established by this cut-throat trade threatened to ruin both the guano and nitrate trades. Eventually President Manuel Pardo was obliged to take action in order to raise the selling price of both products. He did this by putting into force a government monopoly of nitrate. As a result of the war with Chile that followed, the nitrate fields of Tarapacá passed into the possession of that country.[21] Meanwhile, the guano trade, which had been exclusively consigned to Messrs. Gibbs and Myers between 1842 and 1849, and to Gibbs exclusively from 1849 to 1861, continued to expand into a major industry, as the following detailed statistics taken from British Parliamentary Papers indicate.

British imports of guano from Peru, 1841 to 1869[22]

Year	Tons	Year	Tons	Year	Tons
1841	02,062	1851	199,732	1861	161,566
1842	14,123	1852	86,293	1862	69,390
1843	01,589	1853	106,312	1863	196,704
1844	16,475	1854	221,747	1864	113,086
1845	14,101	1855	255,535	1865	210,784
1846	22,410	1856	177,016	1866	109,142
1847	57,762	1857	264,230	1867	164,112
1848	61,055	1858	302,207	1868	155,766
1849	73,567	1859	49,064	1869	199,122
1850	95,083	1860	122,459		

It was from 1841 that the product of the sales of guano began to feature as the principal factor in the Peruvian government revenues, although in the first seven years only about 289,000 tons were exported, the direct sale of which produced about $2,700,000. It was in view of these relatively poor results that the government resolved to consign the sale of guano directly to the account of the government. It was for this purpose that the aforementioned arrangements were made in January 1847, with the House of Antony Gibbs & Sons of London for the first consignments, and the following year other consignments were negotiated with local Lima-based firms. A new loan was then contracted in London for £3,734,400, with which to cancel the substantial loans negotiated in 1822 and 1825, to cover the cost of the wars of liberation against Spain. In the same year, for the first time, all the home debt was liquidated and consolidated in bonds gaining 3 percent interest, the amount of which was to exceed $5,000,000. Foreign debts were to hang like a millstone around the neck of the Peruvian government for the remainder of the century. To illustrate this, in 1850 the state of the public debt of Peru was as follows:

Debt	Amount
Home debt consolidated at 3% interest	$5,662,900
Foreign Dept (Anglo-Peruvian)	$18,682.000
Debt to Chile	$4,000.000
Floating debt	$2,500.000
Total	$30,844,900

Meanwhile the Custom House revenues were increasing, and soon reached the sum of $2,500.000 annually, while the direct revenues derived from guano stabilized at about $2,000,000 each year. However, between the years 1851 to 1854, the total amount of guano exported was 1,624,252 tons, which gave the government $16,838,600. The Custom House revenues during the same period amounted to $11,016,612. Thus we see that according to these figures the yearly income of Peru exceeded $7,000.000. Sadly though, extravagance by the government at that time only added to the problems of the nation. The inauguration of each new administration usually meant a complete change of employees, a list of debts for urgent payment, and the borrowing of more and more funds. The financial situation was further exacerbated by the liberation of the slaves, when compensation was paid out of the public purse to the slave-owners. Thus, by 1855 the home debt had risen to $24,429,700.

Having proved to be an excellent manure, the demand for guano increased until yearly sales reached 302,207 tons in 1858, and any financial difficulty was continually met by mortgaging the future sales of guano instead of making efforts to put the finances of the country on a sounder footing. As Peru continued to count on such receipts she made no effort to organize a financial system based on taxes. On the contrary, the easy money of the guano era led to the dangerous habit of contracting loans ruinous for the state, which became increasingly corrupt.[23] Meanwhile, during the years 1841 to 1845 the number of ships and seamen engaged in the Peruvian and African guano trade continued to increase dramatically, per these returns produced by the Custom House, London, in 1846.[24]

An account of the number and tonnage of vessels and number of seamen engaged in the guano trade

Vessels	British Vessels			Foreign Vessels		
Entered inward	Ships	Tons	Men	Ships	Tons	Men
1841	7	1,733	87	—	—	—
1842	41	12,000	560	3	1,091	59
1843	13	4,056	202	—	—	—
1844	286	81,902	4,313	1	207	18
1845	679	219,764	11,434	4	1,170	52

Back in the United Kingdom, the country that so much guano was bound for, the engineers were also making their contribution to the ever-changing agricultural scene. From 1850 onward machinery, often driven by steam power, began to be applied to every branch of agricultural labor. It was the golden age for landlord and farmer, although not for the ones that their joint prosperity rested on—the impoverished agricultural laborers, whose wages in 1861 averaged nine shillings and four pence per week.[25] Farm rents did rise, but to compensate for this, prices rose as well, and capital was plentiful, holdings were consolidated, farm building improved, and great advances were made in the breeding of cattle and sheep. But all good things come to an end, and, as might be expected, this prosperity did not last.

British agriculture was to suffer badly in the general depression of the seventies, and the lot of farmers made harder by a series of bad harvests from 1875 to 1877, followed by the worst season of the century in 1879. In earlier years farmers had often said that they made their best profits out of bad seasons because prices were high, as very little corn was imported to make up the deficiency. This remained partially true, even under free trade, because a bad harvest in England often meant a bad harvest over most of Europe, and no supplies were available. However, as the shipping industry developed, during the second part of the nineteenth century, bumper harvests of produce, in particular cheap American corn, could be moved over the Atlantic, with the result that prices remained low.[26] Furthermore, American farmers had also been mechanizing and importing thousands of tons of best Peruvian guano to maximize production.

Interestingly, the question of getting a good, cheap supply of guano from the Chincha Islands to the United States became a major issue between Peru and the United States in 1850. The Americans were then eager to build a canal between the Atlantic and the Pacific, mainly in order to shorten the long sea route to California around Cape Horn, but the high cost of shipping guano around the Cape also contributed greatly to their interest in this ambitious proposal. On the demands of farmers' organizations in Virginia, Delaware, and Maryland, several congressional investigations were held and the idea put forward that the United States should purchase a bird island to ensure a cheap supply of guano. While these proposals were not endorsed by Congress, resolutions were passed, calling upon the government to seek lower guano prices.[27]

In 1856 the question of Panama then dominated diplomatic relations between Britain and the United States. Palmerston was of the opinion that only three nations could constitute a threat to British power, namely, Russia, France, and the United States. It was at this point that a new and serious cause of conflict between Britain and the United States arose, namely the canal that the Americans were then eager to build between the Atlantic and the Pacific. The experts had advised that the shortest way across the Isthmus of Panama presented great engineering difficulties, so the United States turned their attention to Nicaragua. This, together with various other important issues, led to friction between the two powers.[28] In the event, however, the Nicaragua route was eventually abandoned in favor of Panama, the famous canal not being informally opened to traffic until August 15, 1914. Nevertheless, the forgoing interrelated issues serve to illustrate the influence that guano, and the small, insignificant Chincha Islands, were having on world politics in the second part of the nineteenth century.

Short-lived competition from the African guano islands of Ichaboe and Possession in the 1840s not only undermined attempts to raise the price of Peruvian guano, but also had the effect of letting many small, independent merchants enter this lucrative trade. However, after the third guano contract expired in 1847, the Castilla administration negotiated new one-year monopoly contracts with Antony Gibbs & Company of London for the exclusive rights to market guano in Britain and other parts of the world, and the Montane Company, of Paris, for a monopoly of the fertilizer sales in France.[29] Such arrangements, which became the norm, proved extremely unpopular with independent merchants, notably at Liverpool. A body calling itself the Commercial Association of Liverpool entered the fray in 1852. Claiming to have the support of "various associated commercial and agricultural bodies throughout the country," they sought to put pressure on the government to persuade the Peruvians "to open up the trade" to all and sundry. In a statement published in the *Times* in the winter of 1853, they pointed out that during the previous year memorials on the subject were poured upon the government from various agricultural bodies. These representations, they felt, might have proved more successful had they obtained the backing of notable mercantile and shipping interests. One of their main concerns was that the Peruvians were in possession of virtually unlimited supplies of guano, but the shipping was very badly organized. A huge fleet of ships, chiefly American and British, were constantly, in succession, waiting their turn at the islands. A vessel of 1,000 tons could be loaded through the shoots in a couple of days, but she generally had to wait for two to three months before she obtained her cargo. The trade, in fact, was clogged with obstructions from the first chartering of the ship to the final delivery of the cargo. While every separate transaction was clearly a source of income to the fortunate firms who had secured the monopoly contracts with the Peruvian government, due to the accumulated charges, the Peruvian administration had reaped little more than £4 per ton. In fact, from the previous year sales, and although the freight charges were only about £2.10.0 per ton, the remaining £2.10.0 had been "absorbed in the charges of management."

While they did not expect the Peruvian government to drop the price of their guano, which by and large offered good value for the money, they found it difficult to understand what prevented them from opening the trade to all nations at a fixed price. What they were suggesting was that the Peruvians should establish the average price they had realized per ton, under the monopoly, fix that price, and levy it at the islands from all applicants alike, free of cost and risk to themselves, all of which would result in an increased supply of this very marketable commodity. The writer continued, "Should an advance of money be necessary, it can surely be safely made on the same security as has proved satisfactory to the present contractors; and the interests of the Peruvian bondholders would certainly be improved by a transaction which might in a year or two double the revenue of that country."[30]

Further complaints about the Gibbs' monopoly reached the press in January 1857. The writer, who signed himself "A Lover of Free Trade," made the point that in 1855, 305,061 tons had passed through the hands of the firm, which enjoyed the monopoly of the Peruvian trade. He continued bitterly, "Last season I purchased 30 tons for the use of myself and my tenants at £11 per ton. I am now asked to give £13 for the same quantity; should I require only 29 tons I should have to pay £14.5.0 per ton—30 tons being considered a wholesale purchase. No cause is alleged for the increased cost of the article. The circular is silent as to harder terms on the part of the Peruvian Government, or exaction's from the shipowners. The trade reports of 1856, in your columns of January 3rd describe freights to be more easy. We cannot hide from ourselves that we have too much tonnage afloat for the purpose of legitimate trade."[31] The concerned landowner continued his subjective and ill-informed attack on the House of Gibbs by conceding that stocks of guano were low for the time of year, but added that this did not justify a company that was in a monopoly position jacking up the price. He concluded by suggesting that users should, perhaps, stop placing orders, as the accumulation of several thousand tons of guano at the various importing ports might impress on Messrs. Gibbs the need to trade fairly.

Alas, few buyers seem to have been influenced by the "Lover of Free Trade," for business remained as buoyant as ever during 1857, the press subsequently reporting that the quantity of guano exported from the Chincha Islands reached 490,657 tons in 1857, giving employment in that year to 620 ships. Financial returns presented to the Peruvian Congress by the finance minister also painted a similar picture, clearly showing how guano sales, far from dropping due to "consumer resistance" had increased and effectively become the dominant factor in the economic affairs of the Peruvian state. In 1860 the income derived by the state from net proceeds of guano amounted to $16,053,908, and in 1861 to $16,921,757; or at an exchange rate of 42d. per dollar to £2,809,433.18s. and £2,961,306.11s.7d, respectively.[32]

Messrs. Gibbs & Company remained active in the guano trade until the summer of 1861 when they let it be known in Lima that they did not wish to submit any further bids for the trade. Then in October they wrote that the finance minister had "again received our refusal to undertake the business." The phraseology, according to Mathew, "suggesting that they had received overtures." They subsequently changed their minds and put in a serious bid, but the new contract was awarded to a group of Peruvian businessmen led by Felipe Barreda. The contract was to run for eight years. On this deal their commission was to be 3 percent and 5 percent Advances were required by the government, and the share provisions showed that considerable outside help was required by these local entrepreneurs to finance this international operation, for which they were obliged to draw heavily on the London money market.[33]

Arrangements were then completed regarding the appointment of the agents to handle the business in Britain, the well-connected firm of Thomson Bonar & Company being appointed. Charles Edward Poulett Thomson (1799–1841), who at one time headed this enterprise, was the son of a merchant who, after receiving a private education, worked in a branch of his father's firm at St. Petersburg and then became an MP. After serving as vice president of the Board of Trade, in 1839 he was appointed governor-general of Canada, serving under the title of Lord Sydenham, but was killed in a riding accident in 1841.[34] At the time when this contract was awarded, William Gladstone, brother of Lieutenant Colonel Gladstone, was second partner in the firm, having joined the house in 1839, when Lord Sydenham went to Canada. The agents in Liverpool were Messrs. Gladstone and Serjeantson.[35]

However, in 1860, just before these new arrangements were put into operation, the national expenditure of Peru exceeded $20,000,000, more or less double what it was during the first years of independence. Notwithstanding this heavy annual outlay, the amount of direct contributions, including the sale of stamped paper, did not exceed $500,000, and the revenue of the Custom House was not more than $3,500,000. At the same time, guano sales of about 300,000 tons left the government with about $12,000,000, with which it covered just three-fifths of the general budget. The country was clearly not balancing the books, and consequently staggered from one financial crisis to another until it was obliged to consolidate in one sole debt the old foreign debts of Peru—the Anglo-Peruvian, the Deferred Stock, the so-called Urribarren debt, and that of the Arica and Tacna Railway. It was decided to contract a loan in London.

This massive loan—about which more detailed attention will be paid later—was issued in London in 1862, the year after the new Barreda guano contract was signed, the value of this amounting to £5,500,000 at 4.5 percent. Besides the general guarantee of all the government revenues, in this case the product of the sales of guano in the United Kingdom and Belgium was given as a special guarantee. When the conversion of the old loans had been effected, there remained at the disposal of the government the sum of £2,400,000, of which about one million sterling was remitted to Lima in the form of gold bars. Unfortunately, however, the servicing of this debt, with the expenses of the state, continued to reach 24 million soles per annum, and with receipts only amounting to 16 million, a deficit of 8 million each year became a regular feature in the Peruvian budget. Such was the condition of the republic's finances, so critically dependent on the continuing sale of guano.

Then, matters were made considerably worse by the unexpected occupation of the Chincha Islands by the Spanish fleet in 1864. This unexpected act of hostility on the part of Spain obliged Peru to arm herself in order to repel this aggression. With this object in view the Peruvians were obliged to return to the finance houses of London once more to raise a new even larger loan, this time for £10,000,000, at 5 percent backed, once more, by the product of the sales of guano. This loan, like the former of 1862, commenced with the conversion of the old debts of Peru. But as only £7,000,000 of this loan was placed, and allowing for various expenses, there only remained for Peru £1,300,000. With part of this sum, payment was made for the warship *Huascarr* and the *Independencia,* built by Laird of Birkenhead.

Notwithstanding Peru's continuing financial problems, the presidency of Colonel Balta, from 1868 to 1872, was marked with plans to convert the proceeds of guano into railways, in order to unite the principal agricultural and mining centers of Peru and thus bring about the progress of the country and the development of its resources before the guano deposits that the nation was so dependent on ran out.[36] When Balta came to power, the servicing of the foreign debts required an annual payment of £1,000,000 a year, and loans were contracted in 1870 and 1872, which raised this sum to £2,600,000. In August 1869, a contract was made with Messrs. Dreyfus & Company, a wealthy French business house, in order to pay off a debt to it of £3,900,000 by the sale of 2,000,000 tons of guano, delivery of which was to commence in 1872.[37]

It was against this ongoing political and economic background, outlined here, that ships from many nations rounded Cape Horn and made their way across the Pacific from Australia or down the coast from California to the guano islands of Peru. It was also the aforementioned economic factors that were allowed to dictate the working conditions for thousands of unfortunate men who were transported to these islands to work the valuable deposits, their short life on the islands being one of unremitting toil and misery.

6
Cape Horn and the Chincha Islands

AS NOTED, THE CAPITAL AND COMMERCIAL EXPERTISE REQUIRED TO establish the guano industry had, at least initially, come from abroad, that is, until the government had taken steps to place it in the hands of local merchants. The same government made no efforts, though, to reserve the unpleasant task of working at the guano diggings for Peruvians. At first they were obliged to use forced local labor, but later they brought in foreign workers for this unpleasant task, for, not surprisingly, there was no rush of willing local hands to work at the Chincha guano diggings. To appreciate just how unpleasant this work was, one has to understand that the centuries-old deposits had become hard and compacted, and in many places had to be blasted with gunpowder to release it. Then the stones and sand mixed with it had to be separated before it could be conveyed by ships' launches to the waiting vessels, anchored in scores off the islands, or alternatively, loaded directly down huge canvas shoots into the holds of the oceangoing sailing ships.

The actual working environment itself could not have been worse, for the islands are just three rocks, their brown surface cracked by a hot tropical sun whose savage beams are rarely intercepted by a cloud—rocks upon which no rain has fallen for centuries. Here men toiled at work as dangerous as mining, watched over by brutal overseers whose task was to ensure that each man fulfilled his daily quota of digging, moving, or loading the foul-smelling material. About this work Duffield wrote, in 1877, "No hell has ever been conceived by the Hebrew, the Irish, the Italian, or even the Scotch mind for appeasing the anger and satisfying the vengeance of their awful gods, that can be equaled to the fierceness of its heat, the horror of its stink, and the damnation of those compelled to labor there, to a deposit of Peruvian guano when being shoveled into ships"[1]—a far cry, indeed, from the genteel world of Peruvian politicians in Lima, Antony Gibbs in London, Dreyfuss & Company in Paris, and scores of shipowners engaged in this profitable trade, all of whom were, of course, dependent for their more pleasant lifestyle on the sweated labor of these unfortunate men who were slaves in all but name.

Under the 1842 contract, the guano export contractors were responsible for recruiting the required labor. However, where did enterprises, such as Quiroz Allier, Gibbs-Crawley, and Puimirol Poumaroux find the men to work the deposits? The Indians, genetically adapted to breathing the rarefied, cool air of the High Andes, could not be persuaded to leave the Cordilleras to toil on the coastal islands. The urban proletariat, of Spanish and mixed descent, was mainly tied to their craft guilds, and in any event, these proud descendants of the conquistadors undoubtedly considered such work beneath their dignity. Therefore, the only other group that could be considered was the Negro slaves, then working the undermanned vineyards and cotton and sugar plantations, but these could not be spared. The contractors therefore turned to the government, and with their active cooperation brought army deserters and convicts to the islands. These were supplemented with a few Negro slaves and some hired laborers.[2]

As might be expected, the aforementioned guano export merchants invariably managed to keep their distance from the unattractive bird islands, persuading themselves that other, more pressing matters required their attention in Lima or Callao. Organizing the work of digging and loading was therefore mainly left in the hands of subcontractors, such as Cipriano Roman, a Chilean who was prominent among these characters in the early 1840s. The government had provided the contractors with a limited supply of mainly penal labor, on which basis guano extraction continued throughout the 1840s, but as demand increased, the need for more workers soon became apparent. In January 1849 when the government of Ramon Castilla abandoned the arrangement of placing all trade in the hands of one main contractor, namely Antony Gibbs & Sons, they took the opportunity to draw up separate contracts for loading. Tenders were invited and then won by Domingo Elias, owner of many large haciendas on the coast near the Chincha Islands. Elias was also active as a prominent businessman and politician. The arrangement was to run for six years. Henry Witt, Gibbs' manager, then later a guano contractor in his own right, thought at the time that Elias would use his Negro slaves for the work, rather than free laborers, because the latter would demand wages for their work. From this contract, which incidentally was canceled in 1853, it was generally understood that he expected to make about $30,000 a year profit on the understanding that the government would pay him nine shillings per ton for his services, but as it happens, he had to settle for six shillings, then slightly more than this.[3]

However, contrary to expectations, Domingo Elias, acting in his capacity as the leader of Peru's plantation owners, did not use or even intend to use, his own slaves for this work. Just one month prior to signing this contract, he had managed to persuade the Peruvian Congress to pass an immigration law that granted a subsidy of thirty pesos a head to anyone importing more than fifty foreign "colonists" of either sex between the age of ten and forty. Elias and a colleague, Juan Rodriguez, were then, retrospectively, granted this subsidy for seventy-five Chinese coolies they had imported just before the bill's passage. They were then granted the exclusive rights over this task for the term of four years. It was mainly with these unfortunate Chinese men that Domingo Elias undertook to work the guano deposits and load the ships at the Chincha Islands. This was the beginning of Chinese coolie labor in Peru, which was to result in 90,000 Chinese coolies reaching the country between 1849 and 1875 with a further 10,000 perishing aboard the sailing ships that carried them across the Pacific.[4]

To understand the origins of this trade, mainly initiated by Elias, one must appreciate that he, in particular, had a very clear vested interest in not using his local labor for guano digging on the Chinchas. At the time the plain of Pisco was covered with immense vineyards that were mostly in his ownership. These included Buena Vista, Palta, Chacarilla, Santa Cruz, Hoyas, and Urrutia, which formerly belonged to Don Juan Aliaga, Count of Luringancho. From these lands he manufactured great quantities of wine and spirit called Pisco or Italia which he exported to all parts of the coast and into the interior of Peru. One of his great stores contained more than a hundred casks of wine of 280 to 300 gallons each, the Portuguese man in charge of this particular establishment making three types of upmarket wine and a delicious liqueur flavored with the cherimoya fruit. The common Pisco wine was stored in large warehouses on the beach and shipped off to various ports of Peru and Chile, all of which clearly required a skilled and experienced workforce with few to spare for other tasks, such as working on the Chinchas.[5]

During this period in Peruvian history, 90,000 Chinese workers were taken to Peru. Hundreds of these unfortunates were doomed to work on the Chincha Islands, with little or no hope of escape.

4. Chinese accommodation on the main Chincha Island. *The Illustrated London News*, July 9, 1864.

More than 5,000 were employed building railroads, and about 80,000 served on the coastal plantations. Virtually all had been duped into signing bogus "contracts" that guaranteed a return passage home, but there is no evidence to suggest that any saw their native land again.[6] By 1853 Elias's crew of guano workers on the Chincha Islands included about 600 Chinese coolies, 50 slaves, and about 200 Chileans or Peruvians, most of them convicts or army deserters, although a mere handful were free workers.[7] By 1854, though, British consular correspondence makes it very clear that control of the workers on the Chincha Islands had been passed back to Messrs. Gibbs & Company.[8]

Meanwhile, throughout the 1840s, the sailing ships of the ever-increasing guano fleet continued to make their way around Cape Horn from Europe and the eastern seaboard of the United States, bound for Callao and the Chincha Islands. For the Chinese the crossing of the Pacific to the Chincha Islands was rightly described as a one-way passage to hell, but the life of the mariners engaged in the trade was far removed from the proverbial bed of roses. Underpaid, overworked, badly fed, and exposed to the terrible weather conditions encountered off the Cape, few lived to a ripe old age. Captain David Cowans, in his memoirs, described what life was like in this brutal trade. His first visit to these islands was in 1849, when he sailed for the west coast in the Liverpool ship *Collector*. The vessel left the Mersey in June 1850 with a cargo consisting of bricks and patent fuel to be landed at Coquimbo on the coast of Chile. They had a good passage down the Atlantic, but as they neared Cape Horn, it became colder, and the nights longer. His graphic account of rounding the barren, isolated tip of South America in the *Collector,* a typical sailing ship of the day, is notable:

> No sooner had we set a little sail to get round this boisterous Cape than it had to be taken in, as we vainly tried to buffet the gale and make a little westing, tossing and plunging about in the tremendous seas ever and anon rolling along. Wet with salt water, perishing with cold, still we must get up and take in sail, but we managed it very well, if sail was not carried too long. A glass of rum was often served out to us, which for a time put a glow within us, but after its effects had died away, we felt chilled and almost as cold as before.
>
> On one particularly cold night, a small sail called the main trisail had to be taken in; it was blowing a perfect hurricane at the time, and the ship had to be wore round on the opposite tack in order to avoid drifting on an island to leeward. But the cold was so intense, together with the strength of the wind that the united efforts of sixteen men could hardly get it quieted and taken in for a whole hour. At length we managed to wear round on the opposite tack, and escape the much-dreaded island. We now had to make a desperate effort to carry some more sail in order to get clear, and it was some hours before we got sufficient sail set to make sure of keeping off the rocks.
>
> At length fatigued and perishing with the excessive cold, we were allowed some rest, and our glass of raw strong rum put a little heat in us for the time. Day after day and week after week the same fearful gales kept us back, and the long, dreary cold nights were enough to damp the courage of many a crew, for no sooner had we made a good distance by a favourable point or two of the wind, than again it would come down from the same quarter, hard, cold and furious as ever, driving us back more than we had gained.
>
> Some of our crew now began to have scurvy, which appeared in their legs and mouths, by the long use of salt meat and constant exposure to this terrible weather; our decks where the men's hammocks were slung being so leaky that a constant stream of water came through their leaky seams, saturating bed-clothes and hammocks. Various were the means tried to keep the water clear of our beds; greasing a track under the deck for it to run clear, but this was of little avail. Often as the watch was called "all hands shorten sail," have we got out and found our den of a forecastle ankle deep with water, as our deep loaded ship lurched and rolled

to and fro, try to dress on top of our chests to keep clear of the water, but in danger of being sent flying to leeward, chests and all, at each successive roll.

Such are a few of the many discomforts experienced by sailors in rounding Cape Horn; but there is no escape from these miseries, as round the Horn the ship must go, if we can only keep her afloat. Fortunately our ship made but little water in her bottom or top sides, and stood all this rolling, pitching and straining remarkably well. The captain was a good sort of man, on his first voyage as such; he had, however, a very headstrong way of carrying sail, which gave us all the more trouble, as we were aware that he did not attend to the warnings of the barometer. This instrument, when well understood, will always warn the shipmaster of approaching gales in those latitudes, and save much extra labour to the crew by attending to its warnings in time.

As we drifted about in this miserable way, scarcely holding our own at times, one after the other of our crew gave in with various ailments, scurvy being the most prevalent, till nine were laid up out of our crew of twenty-four. These ones being mostly working seamen, the work came heavier on the rest of the crew. Eight long weeks we had now been buffeted about off this weary, desolate cape, and very little chance of a change. At length about the ninth week we managed to get fairly round, i.e., to double Cape Horn, and keeping well off this much dreaded coast, were standing to the northward, under all sail, the warmth of the climate increasing day by day, until fairly within the limits of the south-east trades."[9]

Cowan then went on to describe in detail how they sailed up the coast until they sighted the lofty peaks of the Andes, some over twenty thousand feet high, which were visible seventy, eighty, and even ninety miles away, from far out in the Pacific Ocean. After a terrible passage of four months from Liverpool they landed their cargo at Coquimba and took in ballast for Callao, the port of entry for vessels bound for the Chincha Islands. The harbor itself, he noted, was entirely landlocked, so that a large fleet of ships could easily be accommodated there, but he considered the town to be a miserable, poor-looking place with few impressive buildings, and with mean, tortuous, and rugged streets. Here they filled up their water casks and, after final clearance, beat along the coast against the southeast trades to the islands, a distance of about ninety miles, the passage back against the prevailing trades taking eight days. Here, due to the cumbersome bureaucratic procedures of the Peruvian administration, and after already passing the islands on the way north, they were obliged to sail through the shipping moored off the Chincha Islands until they reached Pisco, the local port dominated by the aforementioned land baron, Don Domingo Elias. Here they had to anchor once more, and reenter at the Custom House before being allowed to return to the island for their cargo. The whole procedure was carried out in reverse on the return passage, all of which understandably attracted many complaints from exhausted mariners and shipowners who were worried by this needless waste of valuable time.

Off the islands the water was usually very smooth and though somewhat deep, there was good holding ground, at least for ships of large tonnage. They then prepared to take in enough guano by their own boats to ballast the ship until their turn came to move the ship in close to the base of the cliffs so that guano could be taken on directly. The longboat and pinnace were manned and hauled into the boat shoot each morning. Once in position the signal was given and a rush of guano came down through the canvas hose into the open boat, the evil-smelling dust almost blinding and suffocating the sailors waiting below. It was, however, via the ships' boats that vessels would initially get enough guano on board to allow them to discharge their main ballast. Once this unpleasant task was completed, they could wait off the islands until it was their turn to load the bulk of their cargo at the aforementioned *manguera* or loading shoot.

A few years later, on January 1, 1853, the writer Clements R. Markham boarded a small launch on the Peruvian coast manned by Chinese men and set out on a less-arduous voyage to the Chincha Islands. Unlike Cowans, who made no mention of actually landing on the islands, the following morning Markham and his party reached the North Island and by means of a steep ladder reached the top of the cliff. He at once saw that the principal guano cutting was about sixty feet high and about a hundred yards from the edge of the cliff. Here he watched about two hundred convicts shoveling down the guano, while a small steam engine of about twelve horsepower was being used for digging it out and also loading the cars. A crane projected from this engine, from which was suspended a large iron trough much like a coal scuttle, with six teeth at the edges and weighing 8 cwt. By working one chain, this scuttle could be plunged into the guano, thereby filling it. By connecting another chain on this ingenious machine, the crane turned and the contents of the trough would be discharged into a car. About four loads were required to fill these cars, which were then drawn down a tram road to the edge of the cliff where they were emptied, and the guano was shoveled down a canvas shoot into the hold of the vessel that was loading below the cliff. At the same time, unfortunate workers, who Markham described as "Strong-Brained Negroes" were stationed in the hold to trim the stinking cargo as it descended on the ship. These men received thirteen dollars per 100 tons from the captain of the vessel, but were forced to wear iron masks, "as the guano dust was more penetrating than coal dust, or steel filings, and stronger than volatile salts."

At the time of this visit Markham recorded that there were twenty-five merchant vessels, chiefly British, lying off the island, but conceded that there were generally many more, with the number often exceeding a hundred. He also noted that the convicts working on the island existed in a filthy collection of cane huts, besides which there was a little "town" containing two iron houses occupied by Peruvian officials, English carpenters, and an Irish doctor. In passing, Markham also made the point that in January 1853, Domingo Elias was holding the sole contract for shipping guano (by which he meant cutting and loading), and that he received twelve rials per ton, which, he understood, sold in London for about £10 per ton. Returning to the subject of labor, Markham noted that the center island was then being worked almost entirely by Chinese who were imported in shiploads to Callao. He then went on to say that "they were very badly treated, and, in consequence, frequently commit suicide, owing to the fearful nature of the work and a feeling of home-sickness."[10]

It was also in 1853 that George Washington Peck, celebrated author, journalist, and music critic, made his way to Australia before going on to Callao and then the Chincha Islands. His written accounts of working conditions on the islands did much to bring the horrors of the guano trade to the attention of the Great Powers and the international public at large. The influential George Washington Peck was born at Rehoboth, Massachusetts the son of George Washington Peck and his second wife, Hannah Bliss. He attended Brown University, graduating in 1837, then taught for a time in Indiana and Cincinnati before returning east to study law under Richard Henry Dana. Dana was of course, the world-famous author of *Two Years before the Mast,* which had brought the horrors of life at sea in the American Merchant Marine to the attention of the world. It may have been literary as much as legal ambition that led Peck to seek this association with Dana, but he was admitted to the Massachusetts bar on May 19, 1843, where he lived and worked for the next four years. In 1845 he founded the short-lived *Boston Musical Review*. In 1847 he gave up all connections with the law and went to New York and joined the staff of the *Morning Courier and New York Enquirer*. From this point on he devoted himself to journalism and was the author of several well-known books. Consumption reduced his output in later years, but he made a trip to Australia and the Chincha Islands in 1853, later writing letters to the *New York Times*. In 1854 he published an account of this voyage in his Melbourne and the *Chincha Islands*."[11]

After a long voyage from Greenwich to Australia, then on to Peru in the ship *Albus*, Peck eventually arrived at Callao on September 13. Like David Cowan, George Peck was not impressed with this Peruvian port. He ascended some steps, then went around a corner, fully expecting to find a normal, clean, well-built street. Instead he found himself confronted by a dingy mud-walled lane crammed full of sailors, Peruvians, and mules. He passed a chandlers shop where there was a group of captains sitting on a selection of old chairs, then came to an ill-paved, dirty-looking lane of mud-walled buildings occupied by clothing shops, of a sort. Eventually he came to the "Marine Hotel," which he described as being the meanest of sailor taverns, but then, to his surprise, discovered it to be the principal commercial house of the port. Peck spent some time in this dismal town and the capital city of Lima, but made a point of sleeping on the ship. He eventually arrived at the Chincha Islands on October 2, where he found 114 ships waiting to be loaded with guano.

The following morning he went ashore when a man he had met at Callao took him to the Middle Island. He found that the landing was on a ledge that projected out in front of a great cave over which, a hundred feet above, projected winding gear for hoisting up water and provisions. The top of the cliffs were reached by a series of staircases; the lowest one, Peck noted, was rigged so that it could be hoisted or lowered according to the tide. Significantly, it could also be drawn up every evening or, apparently, whenever the governor of the island chose to enjoy his dignity alone. The real reason, no doubt, was to ensure that no one ever escaped from the island. A few yards from the top of the cliff, and directly over the cave, Peck found the "palace" belonging to the "governor," who called himself "Kossuth." He claimed to be the brother of the great Hungarian leader of that name, a claim that most educated people seriously doubted. The "palace" itself was just a flat-roofed shanty constructed of rough boards and the canes and coarse rush commonly used in down-market Peruvian dwellings. It contained two apartments with a sort of portico and two or three benches; a table and grass hammock in front, surrounded by a low paling, forming a small yard where a huge dog usually kept guard. One of the apartments seemed to be used as a storeroom, while the other served as the bedchamber for Kossuth and his aids. It contained three or four cot beds, an old table and writing desk, and was "decorated" with a few newspapers, colored lithographs, and old German plans of the battles of Frederick the Great. The floor was nothing more than well-trodden guano. Over Kossuth's couch there was a selection of cheap, single-barrel pistols. From the windows they could look down on the shipping, anchored off the islands, while, in the distance they could just make out the hazy Bay of Pisco and far beyond the snowcapped heights of the Andes.

Peck described Kossuth as a middle-sized individual, half soldier-like, youngish, with quick gray eyes and an overgrown red moustache. He appeared to be shrewd and although full of life was clearly very hard and full of his own importance. Despite these traits, Peck seemed to like him, finding him polite enough, although he had heard that the captains often complained about his caprices. Kossuth invited Peck to come ashore and offered to tell him all the secrets of the island. First, he informed his visitor that he was one of a party of Hungarians who had come from New York on the representations of an individual by the name of Ujhazy who had obtained for them a grant of land. Alas, he explained, land was no use to them, for being soldiers they could not possibly be expected to work it themselves. Ujhazy who had been a landowner at home, and not a military man, had blundered in obtaining the land, as this group all wanted employment in the American army, or as engineers.

Finding how the situation was, Kossuth then stated that he made his way from New York to New Orleans, where he joined the infamous Lopez Expedition, from which he escaped and managed to reach Mexico. Significantly, he did not explain to Peck how he managed to get free, but here it will be recalled that the Venezuelan-born General Lopez had led a piratical adventure to Cuba, manned mostly by Americans, but was caught and garroted by the Spanish authorities. (This piratical invasion had the tacit support of the slave-owners of the Deep South who were concerned that Spain might release the slaves on the island and thus create unrest among Negroes in the United States.) At the close of 1851 the Spanish authorities on Cuba announced that they were going to release the captured American supporters of Lopez, and it may well have been that Kossuth did not actually "escape" at all, but was merely among those captured, then freed.[12] According to Peck, Kossuth then made his way to San Francisco where he joined Flores and so came to South America. He then obtained his post on this Chincha island, being in turn responsible to Deputy Commander Serrate, based on the North Island. From this post he made it clear he intended to make some money, in fact enough to buy some land, but not with the intention of working it himself, the idea being that others would do the work while he played the less arduous role of a wealthy landowner. All his actions on the islands were clearly motivated by a desire to fulfill this sharply focused ambition.

Kossuth then explained to Peck, whose intelligence he clearly underestimated, how he pitied the poor Chinese workers, but declared, what could he do? He could only make them work and so on. Good food and wine was then placed on the table for the distinguished journalist, while Kossuth rambled on about the difficulties of his position. It would seem that all the captains were constantly presenting him with presents of food—far more than he could possibly use. According to him they all expected cargoes at once, and as he could not accommodate them, they tried to influence him with flattery and gifts, to the point that he was wearied to death in his efforts to please them. All this he managed to recite with a straight face, but as Peck was aware of the exact sum that some captains had paid him, by way of a bribe to get loaded quickly, it was only with difficulty that he managed to stop laughing. Serrate was actually the chief person with whom the captains had to deal, holding a position superior to Kossuth, although the limits of the actual authority of each was difficult to ascertain. In practice, it would seem that a great deal of colluding went on between these two villains about the division of their spoils, mainly obtained from bribes offered by certain masters to obtain preference in loading and by grossly exploiting their unfortunate workers.

The guano, Peck stated, and confirming the procedure outlined by Cowan, was dug from the hills by Chinese coolies and wheeled to depots or open enclosures called mangueras on the cliffs at places where launches or vessels could be moored below. He estimated that there were about three hundred Chinese coolies then at work on the Middle Island, and seven or eight hundred on the North. These men, he stated quite incorrectly, were brought to Peru exclusively in English ships. Kossuth then advised Peck that under contracts made with them at home, the Chinese were to labor for five years, at one "York" shilling a day plus their rice, and after they had served their time out, they were free to return to their native land. A common ruse, he was advised, was to make them believe they were going to the gold mines. However, whatever they were contracted for, he felt they were being duped by the English, who brought them out, and the Peruvian government, for once in Peru they became, in effect, absolute slaves. About their life on the Chincha Islands, Peck wrote:

> They are condemned to be diggers of guano; their labour is much more severe and injurious than railway digging; they have no liberty days, no protecting laws, no power to obtain even the pittance said to be paid them, no proper seasons of rest. Most of them go nearly naked; none have more than enough clothing just to cover themselves; they live and feed like dogs; they are constantly within reach of the thongs of hideous black drivers—the link between men and devils; there are no women among them, nothing to mitigate their hopeless toil. Before and around them is the shining bay, and beyond it green groves and mountains; near at hand hundreds of ships coming up and going, filled with men like themselves, only free! They too have been free; they were not born in slavery; they are not domestic slaves or plantation slaves: but slaves without any title, or rights, or conceded customs—mere over-worked beasts of burden.
>
> Almost every week some of them commit suicide by throwing themselves from the cliff. They are said to do this in the belief that their spirits will awaken in their native land. Kossuth told Peck that more than sixty had killed themselves this way in the two years he had been there. One was driven over the cliff or jumped off, and was dashed to pieces, to escape the lash of a black driver, who chased him to the verge in sight of a captain of an American ship, the week before Peck left. The cliff where he leaped is two hundred feet high, and almost perpendicular. Kossuth, Peck stated, affects to pity these coolies; but he is said to overtask them. Each one, strong and weak alike under his overseers, is required to dig and wheel to the mangueras, five tons of guano per day. They are kept at labour Sundays as well as other days; under Serrate, however, on the North Island, Peck understood, Sundays were allowed them or, at least, they are said to be paid a little extra if they choose to dig guano on that day.[13]

The forgoing indicates what conditions were like on the Chincha Islands in 1854, but reports published later in the spring of 1856 by the *Nautical Magazine* would indicate that things had not improved by that date. Their correspondent, recently returned from Callao, confirmed that those who were employed on the islands to transport the guano to the loading places were Chinese, while Negroes and people of "mixed races" were employed stowing the cargoes. The Chinese, he was informed, were under specious promises, inveigled to the islands for a term of three years, but seldom lived to complete their term of slavery, "for the nauseous dust and overpowering effluvia of ammonia in which they work are of themselves rapidly destructive of life." This writer's view was that these men usually embarked in China but often at Melbourne, where they found nothing to do, and it was "well known that shippers receive so much per head for every Chinese they land at the Chinchas." Once on the islands there was no chance of escape, for they were detained by an armed force, housed in the most miserable manner, fed only after performing a specified amount of labor, and subjected to terrible treatment.

While the correspondent was on one of the islands, a desperate Chinese worker threw himself off the rocks and was dashed to pieces rather than submit to the tortures that awaited him. His "crime" was to have accidentally broken some equipment he was using, and, the writer continued, he formed a very good notion of the severity of punishment the Chinese were subjected to. This was brought by the horrible howling constantly heard on the islands. The following is just a selection of some of the atrocities inflicted on the enslaved workers by the orders of the commandants.

> hanging in ropes and chains round the waist, and in other ways, from sunrise to sunset, without food during that period, one, two, or more days, in proportion to the magnitude of the offence; and lashing to half-tide buoys, subject to exposure to the water, in addition to heat and cold. These punishments we saw inflicted in several instances, and it was reported that one man, whom we saw suspended daily for fully a week, had already suffered a fortnight previously to our arrival. We also saw a refined instrument of torture, combining the fabled labour of the Danaides, with the penalty of death staring the culprit in the face if he failed, from exhaustion or otherwise, in performing the task allotted him. This was a lighter with a large hole in the bottom; in which the offender was fastened, with a bucket to save his life by incessant baling.
>
> We were credibly informed that one of the punishments inflicted on the Chinese on the islands is that of placing them on a small point of rock, to which they are chained. The rock being so small that sleep or change of position must result in them falling off, to hang in their manacles, severely bruised perhaps, until the period of relief.
>
> But will it be believed that an English Captain whilst we were there surrendered a negro, whom we well knew, to the mercies of Peruvian Lynch

law after being flogged, and he was hung in a bow-line on the Commandant's hulk for three days successively, and this for merely swearing at "his honour"? I have seen on this hulk as many as eight or ten at a time; some swinging to the davits, and others, one above another, on masts temporarily rigged up. It is not long since that British and other seamen were subject to the same treatment, and a case is recorded of one who disappeared from the buoy, and it was then time for interference.

Does it not seem strange that civilised nations, banded together to suppress slavery, cannot, by remonstrance or force, with a trifling power like Peru, put an end to such inhuman practices at these islands? for they do not exist at Callao. And if the voluntary slavery entered into by the deluded Chinese cannot be prevented, surely something may be done by those who profit by their labours to alleviate their suffering.[14]

In view of the forgoing one can only be intrigued, if not amazed, by an account in 1852 of the Chincha Islands guano diggings that appeared in *Household Words,* the weekly journal produced by Charles Dickens, arguably the greatest of English novelists. The article, written by an anonymous sailor, describes at length his voyage to Peru from Australia, and conditions on the Chinchas. As they approached Callao, it would seem, they glided slowly along the coast, gazing in wonder at the huge mass of rugged brown mountains, rising in steps from the green sea, until they came to an anchor at Callao. Like many others he then made the point that although his ship was only bound for the Chinchas, they had been obliged to sail ninety miles past the islands in order to get formal clearance to obtain a cargo of guano. This, he pointed out, was a great annoyance to all masters of ships visiting Peru and a source of additional expense to English shipowners and charterers. Every guano ship was compelled to enter at Callao, then had to beat back against headwinds to Pisco, and then the Chinchas. However, when they eventually reached the islands, the writer and his party clambered ashore, reached the summit of one of the islands, and soon arrived at the "capital." This, he found, stood on a small space cleared of guano and consisted of twenty or thirty miserable shanties. Each one, he observed, was formed by four slender posts driven into the ground, topped by a flat roof of grass matting, one side of each shanty being open, the only furniture being a few rough benches and a collection of dirty cooking pans.

Clothes, they found, seemed to be almost discarded: an old poncho and a ragged pair of calico trousers forming the dress of the "aristocracy"—but many were virtually naked. One hut they came to that was slightly better than the others was occupied by two

English sailors who had taken a fancy to the islands and called themselves pilots, taking it upon themselves to moor and supervise the loading of ships. On the North Island they found a similar, but larger collection of dwellings, and the residence of the commandant, presumably Serrate, who the writer described as a military looking old gentleman—one of the high aristocracy, for he lived in a house that had a window in it! He then stated that there were about two hundred men employed on the North Island and about eighty on the south, the number varying with the demand for guano. In contrast to all other reports, he then stated that nearly all the workers were "Indians" and, quite amazingly, appeared to be happy enough in their dusty territory although everything about them, including their food, was impregnated with guano. No mention whatsoever was made of Chinese workers or brutality! Contradicting other reports already quoted, he continued, "They earn plenty of money, live tolerably well according to their taste, work in the night and smoke or sleep all day. To get rid of their wages they take an occasional trip to Pisco, where they spend their money much in the same fashion as sailors, substituting pisco and chicha (maze beer) for rum and ale, and the guitar and fandango for the fiddle and the hornpipe." One wonders how close this writer actually got to these workers. One can, in fact, just imagine the plausible "Kossuth" sitting back in his chair, offering the writer a drink and feeding him such a line about "good" conditions on the islands. Sadly, though, genuine reports continued to reach the international press regarding the real state of affairs on these islands of the damned.[15]

At the close of 1854 the *New Orleans Picayune* ran a story entitled "The Horrors of the Guano Trade," which was later quoted by The *Times*. The item stated that they had received confirmation of the horrors reported to be in the course of perpetration on the Chincha Islands. The workers, it was claimed, were hired for $48 per annum. Then, in complete contradiction to the questionable article in *Household Words,* the paper run by Charles Dickens, of all people, the *Picayune* gave the real facts. Far from smoking and sleeping throughout the day and working at night, the men commenced work in the morning as soon as they could see to move. Each day every man had five tons of guano to dig and wheel over a distance of one-eighth of a mile. It was all, or at least nearly all, so hard that it had to be broken loose by a pick. Those who did not complete their heavy quota by 5:00 PM were subjected to flogging with rawhide whips, sometimes five feet long, receiving one dozen stripes, each one of which lacerated their back, after which, dripping with blood, they were driven back to finish their outstanding work. Their reporter continued:

> I have known as many as 30 flogged in one day. They have no Sunday allowed, with the exception of one in a year, the same work going on on Sunday as during the rest of the week. The consequence of this ill treatment is suicide in various forms, such as leaping from the rocks 100 feet high, cutting their throats, and burying themselves alive. This last has actually been the case, to my knowledge. One morning three were found who had so buried themselves: two were dead and one alive. The last recovered to prolong his miserable existence for a short time.

"It is time," the writer concluded, "that the voice of civilisation throughout the world was heard in denunciation of such horrors as these."[16] The message was at last getting through to the "civilized world," for soon English mariners were to speak out against the horrors of the guano trade. Then, only six days after the above item appeared in the *Times,* a concerned shipowner with vessels in the trade sent the following note to the editor of this prestigious paper:

> Sir, A few months ago, the captain of a ship of mine that loaded at the Chincha Islands told me about the frightful treatment of the poor Chinese at the Chincha Islands, similar to that recorded in the American paper you lately quoted from, but I thought that such cruelty must be an entire exaggeration. Surely Anthony Gibbs and Sons can tell the truth, and it is for them to deny that the traffic is carried on at the cost of almost daily suicide. For mercy's sake, arrest such wholesale slaughter, if it be true; for I am sure that even the enriching properties of guano would be abandoned rather than it should be sent home at such a sacrifice of human life. A Shipowner.[17]

A few days later yet another reader of the *Times,* signing himself "A New Zealand Settler," submitted a contribution on this issue to the editor. He began by stating that in 1851 he had passed several months in Peru at Callao and in the neighborhood of the Chincha Islands. He then assured readers that he was able to confirm the recent statements that had appeared in the paper, regarding the aforementioned cruelties to which the laborers in the trade were subjected, adding that the accounts were not in any way exaggerated. He then made a disturbing allegation about the practice of English captains at the islands, namely, that if a dispute arose between the master and a member of the crew, it had long been the practice of some captains to hand over the sailor concerned to the governor of the islands for punishment. Invariably, the writer claimed, this punishment was to chain the sailor upon one of the many buoys that marked the soundings of the ocean near these islands, for one, two, or more days. "I knew myself," the writer concluded, "of more than one case in which the men so chained were found, when a boat was sent to release them, to have disappeared: the placid waters of the Pacific flowed softly over the friendless mariner."[18]

Another well-known incident in the Chincha scandal, related to American master mariners, demonstrates that commanders of ships at the Chincha Islands could themselves be treated brutally by the Peruvian authorities, who clearly called the tune that all others involved in the trade danced to. No doubt the ever-increasing demands of Peruvian society, so reliant on guano production, acted here and indeed in all matters relating to the islands as the motivating priority, rather than the civilized treatment of guano workers. Master mariners from powerful foreign nations clearly played their part in the following Chincha Islands drama.

Reports about the incident in question first reached London in October 1853, the press reporting that a serious disturbance had occurred at the Chincha Islands between a large number of masters of American vessels and the commandant of the island. It appeared that two seamen belonging to the American ship *Defiance* were arrested by the police and placed aboard the guardship for shooting a pelican. The birds were, of course, protected, and while no objection can be raised against the arrest of the men for this offense, one can only be amazed at the sequence of events that followed. The captain of the *Defiance,* upon learning about the incident, made his way to the guardship and asked the lieutenant in command what fine had been imposed on his men and was informed it was one dollar. This amount he tendered, then requested the release of his men. However, the proud, obstinate commander refused to release them, and thus set the stage for a major international confrontation.

All the American captains at the islands then held a meeting, remonstrating against such arbitrary proceedings. They then appointed a deputation of twenty-five of their number to visit the commandant and advise him of their concern. Upon their arrival on board the guardship the commandant treated them with contempt, brought his troops on deck with loaded muskets and fixed bayonets, and ordered the deputation to get back into their own boats. Without arguing they attempted to obey this instruction, but while in the act of getting into the boats, the troops rushed upon them with their bayonets, and several of them were seriously injured. The captain of the *Defiance* was at first thought to be mortally wounded, but fortunately this was not the case. Soon after this first notable incident, when the *Defiance* was going to sea, the proud master showed his own personal defiance by giving a rousing salute with his heavy gun to the American merchant fleet as he sped past under a heavy press of canvas. He was fined for this and paid the fine to the official, who boarded her, telling him, however, he might collect for another salute in a few moments!

Not surprisingly, the Peruvian commandant was enraged at the discharge of the second gun, went on board the aptly named *Defiance* once more, with three armed men, and after a prolonged struggle, seized the captain, bound him, and threw him into one of the boats, severely injuring him. A Peruvian officer and crew then took the *Defiance* to Callao, the defiant, but badly injured captain being retained in confinement. This situation, which began with the somewhat trivial offense of shooting two pelicans, was now becoming serious. War, or at least naval intervention, was clearly looming on the horizon! Mr. Clay, United States minister at Lima, forthwith chartered the British Pacific Steam Navigation Company's mail steamer *Bolivia,* and with her steam engines operating at their maximum capacity, sped toward the Chinchas to investigate this rapidly escalating affair.[19] The patriotic George Washington Peck now takes up the story.

In a long article published in the *New York Daily Times* in January 1854, Peck reiterated the observations made in his book about the inhuman treatment of Chinese workers on the Chincha Islands. Alas, though, he also managed to angle his report, more to embarrass the English government over British mariners' supposedly exclusive involvement in the coolie trade rather than directly condemning the Peruvian government for allowing such conditions to exist in their country. His attack was largely confined to a condemnation of the brutal Chincha commandant, Serrate, and his deputy Kossuth. Apart from these humanitarian considerations, more than half his article was devoted to the above incident and the political implications of the issue.

Here, Peck firmly condemned the Peruvian government for the action taken against American master mariners, a particularly fine body of men, he felt, who had each been entrusted with the sole charge of a large amount of property and the sole government of a crew of men sailing under the flag of the United States. People, he felt, "should be aware of the character of such men, selected by American merchants for such commands, for in addition to the experience and skill necessary for the safe management of large and valuable ships, they must have the firmness, and coolness, and knowledge of men to secure discipline on board; they must be familiar with the usages of trade all over the world, with the laws regulating their own in relation to freight, wages, crew, passengers, etc., under all the contingencies of long and hazardous voyages." There was clearly no way, Peck felt, that America could allow such a fine body of men to be subjected to such treatment. Therefore, he argued, the American government should take the matter in hand, without delay, and compel such redress "as shall teach these Peruvians the necessity of caution. I hope they will be made to pay for it roundly." Now clearly more mindful of the insult to the American flag than the suffering of the Chinese on the Chincha Islands, he called for an American warship to be sent to Peru:

> There ought to be an American vessel of war sent here at once. Had there been one at the time, the outrage to our shipmasters could not have occurred. An English frigate visited here sometime after, under Admiral Moresby, who immediately, at the request of our captains, remonstrated strongly with the Commandant upon his conduct; and had it been inflicted upon Englishmen, serious retribution would have followed at once. It is humiliating that our merchantmen should be compelled to look for protection to the ships of England, and made to feel how true it is that English seamen are better protected than ours. It ought to be mentioned in this connection that the commandant, it has been ascertained, had applied to the captains of two French ships then here, the *Ville de Lima* and *Pomone,* anticipating a rupture with the Americans; they had promised him their aid; and when the American shipmasters were driven at point of bayonet, and at peril of their lives, down the gangway of the hulk, the crew of the *Pomone* gave three cheers.

Despite these insults and complications, Peck concluded his thoughts on this issue by arguing that both English and Americans, and indeed all other nations freighting at the Chinchas, had much to gain by jointly urging the Peruvian government to take steps to have a more satisfactory management of the business. "Whether they will effect anything or not remains to be seen; it is said the nation is now on the eve of revolution. I believe the Peruvians require to be overawed a little for their own good, and that our ships can only obtain their freights here without unnecessary inconvenience when the authorities are fully aware that the rights of our seamen must be respected when they actually see a force able to afford protection"[20]

Despite some saber-rattling, war did not break out between the United States and Peru over this issue, nor did the pending revolution alluded to by Peck occur, although there was certainly much unrest in Peru at this time, mainly due to widespread corruption, but President Castilla kept order. From the early 1840s, the government had proclaimed the nitrate and guano deposits a state monopoly, and funds did begin to flow into the empty coffers of the state treasury. The country, it was felt, required "strong rule" at this time and got it from Ramon Castilla of Tarapacá, who dominated Peruvian politics from 1845–62, actually holding office for two terms, during this period, 1845–51 and 1855–62.

Autocratic and dictatorial, Castillo was praised by many for his administrative ability, which manifested itself in the judicious distribution of guano contracts and cash, by which he kept the ruling elite on his side. He also won the support of the Indians and Negroes by abolishing slavery and the forced tribute exacted from Indians. Alas, Castilla was not noted for his efforts to ameliorate the suffering of the Chinese workers on the Chincha Islands and must therefore be considered the man primarily, but not exclusively, responsible for this particular crime against humanity. Despite this rather obvious fact, in his long article about the Chincha Islands, Peck, as already noted, chose to hold the English as being primarily responsible for the ill-treatment of Chinese on these islands. The commendable stand then was taken by Britain against the slave trade, and the internal politics of the United States, then divided by the question of slavery, was undoubtedly the root cause of Peck's line on this issue. Specifically, on the question of Chinese labor on the Chincha Islands, he stated in his long article under the bold subheading "Brutality of the English Traders," that "it is certain they are shipped here in English vessels, and transferred or assigned (or whatever the word for such a transaction should be) to the Peruvian Government. I have known Englishmen who spoke of having been engaged in the traffic. The Government place them on these islands, avowedly under their original contract, to labour for five years; but who is to know how far this contract, if such it can be called, is adhered to? The truth is, the poor Chinamen are sold into absolute slavery—sold by Englishmen into slavery—the worst and most cruel perhaps in the world." Unfortunately, Englishmen were engaged in the trade, but far from exclusively so, as Peck seeks to imply. Nevertheless, he continued, without exaggeration, "Here are about eight hundred of the unfortunate creatures at work on these islands at a time: as fast as death thins them out the number is increased by new importation's."[21] However, this issue does reflect badly on *all* concerned. About Peck and his article on the Chincha Islands, a glance at British and American politics of the period will throw some light on this slanting of the issue.

In 1807, Great Britain, under the influence of the Abolitionist Movement, led by William Wilberforce, prohibited all her subjects from engaging in the slave trade. Then by the middle years of the nineteenth century, all the great powers of Europe had been induced by Britain to unite in expressing their abhorrence of this traffic.[22] Then, by the celebrated act of the imperial legislature, passed in 1833, compulsory labor was summarily abolished throughout the British Empire. At sea Britain was also foremost in mounting anti-slavery patrols, seeking to stop all ships engaged in the trade. In particular, this brought Protestant Britain into conflict with the Catholic powers of Spain and Portugal. The Catholic nations, whose conquistadors had brutally decimated South American society in the sixteenth century, in the nineteenth century gained the dubious distinction of being the main traders in African slaves across the Atlantic, despite anti-slavery treaties being imposed upon them by Britain.

Britain's abolitionist policies also brought her into conflict with the United States: first, by the Royal Navy claiming the right to stop and search ships, including American merchant vessels that were thought to be carrying slaves; and second, British opposition to slavery generally was not welcomed by the plantation owners of the Deep South who were still totally dependent on slave labor and anxious to preserve this situation. Among other things, they lost no opportunity to claim that American slavery was "better" than other forms of slavery. A claim, one might add, that is even to this day made by all apologists for slave-owning nations. At the same time, the slaves concerned steadfastly refused to argue about the merits of demerits of their particular form of slavery, but focused their attention on their fight for liberation. Peck, by implication, followed this well-worn ideological track in his article. But America was at this time moving toward civil war over the issue of slavery, and in this political atmosphere, reporting was very often slanted or distorted to embarrass Britain, which was then holding the moral high ground on the question of ending slavery, but at the same time participating in the transportation of indentured labor, primarily from China and India to the West Indies, as introduced by William Gladstone.

However, descending from the moral high ground of antislavery to the commercial valley of profit making, by 1853 an increasingly large number of Peruvians, Europeans, and Americans were making a great deal of money from guano. While there undoubtedly was growing international concern over labor conditions on the Chincha Islands, there was, by this time, even more concern about the continuing availability of this amazing fertilizer. Would the supplies hold out? How much guano was left on the Chincha Islands, and could other sources of supply be identified? Alternatives supplies from the West African Islands of Possession and Ichaboe had already been depleted, but others were being found and exploited. However, despite this factor, at Liverpool demand for guano was so great that in December 1853 the Liverpool branch of the Peruvian Guano Agency was refusing to take any more orders. Britain needed to know what the real situation was, and Admiral Moresby, in conjunction with W. H. M'Intosh, naval instructor, were charged with providing the answers. In August 1853 their reports were made public:

> There were at the Chincha Islands, on our departure, 100 vessels, capable of exporting nearly 100,000 tons of guano. The Americans far exceed in amount of tonnage. I enclose a list, showing that between the 15th of July and 24th of September 1853 there had been loaded, were loading, or waiting their turn to load, 65 American ships, carrying a gross amount of 61,982 tons. Other American ships were daily arriving, and they now take the superior quality. On the centre island there may be about 800,000 tons of guano of the first quality, and 700,000 tons of the second. This island is worked entirely by Chinamen; they dig and wheel daily about 1,290 tons, of which about 1,100 appear in the shipping dockets. The southern and smallest island has not yet been worked; from its windward position the guano is inferior, and has no great depth.
>
> A commission, consisting of the Peruvian Minister of the Interior, with a numerous staff, as per enclosed list, are occupied in surveying the island. A clerk belonging to the House of Gibbs and Co. was the only person that availed himself of the permission given to accompany the commission; in fact, the notice was short for others to avail themselves of the offer. From the plans and elevations of Mr M'Intosh, from my personal examination and information, gathered from those on the islands conversant with the workings, I am of the opinion that, at the present average rate of exportation, the islands would be exhausted of the guano

that would pay freight, or be saleable in the English Market, in eight or nine years.

I have the honour to be, Sir, your most obedient Servant,
Fairfax Moresby.
Rear-Admiral and Commander-in-chief.

Enclosure in Admiralty letter from Rear-Admiral Moresby.

Her Majesty's Ship *Portland,* at Sea, August 29, 1853

Sir, I have the honour to submit, for your information, the result of the calculations respecting the amount of guano now remaining on the Chincha Islands. The examination—for I cannot call it survey—taken by your order, was necessarily rough and imperfect, both by reason of shortness of time, and the want of proper instruments, as well as a desire not to excite observation. To avoid the possibility of underrating the quantity, I have estimated at the rate of 40 cubic feet per ton, and have allowed a considerable excess on the measurement given by the plans and sections. In laying this result before you I have the honour to state that, though no claim to great accuracy is made, I have no hesitation in pledging myself that the quantity here specified is greater than that absolutely remaining on the islands.

W. H. M'Intosh, Naval Instructor

Rear-Admiral Fairfax Moresby, C.B., Commander in Chief, &c.

Quantity remaining on north island	5,500,000 Tons
Ditto on centre island	1,500,000
Ditto on south island	1,600,000
Total	8,600,000 Tons

The mechanical engineer in charge of excavation on the northern island told me that since he came, in October 1852 a space of 450 feet had been cleared into the deepest cutting, which amounts to 300,000 tons. I have not been able to ascertain the exact present shipments on this island, but, judging from the number of check clerks, labourers, plant, &c., it may probably be estimated at one-fourth more than the centre island. M. Kossuth, the superintendent of the centre island, having allowed me access to his books, I have satisfactorily ascertained that his statement of shipping 1,000 tons per day is correct. The details of the work are—150 Chinamen, at five tons per day in barrows, and four shipshoots, at 135 tons each day. M. Kossuth further informed me that, when he commenced, in December 1852 the rail extended 150 feet from the

5. The principal mole on the main Chincha Island. *The Illustrated London News,* February 21, 1863.

> brow of the cliff; and that he has now obtained a distance of 850 feet, in a direct line into the deepest part of the cutting. This statement, on calculation, further proves the foregoing part, as the amount of guano from such an excavation would amount to 240,000 tons, which, in seven months is at the rate of 1,200 tons per day.[23]

Three weeks later all these statistics were disputed by James Caird, the British agricultural expert. First, he pointed out that although written honestly, the hurried publication of this report had, in the first instance, been made by a paper friendly to the guano monopoly (meaning, of course, Antony Gibbs) and had thrown the market into a state of confusion, and he was therefore suspicious about the frantic rush to make it public. "Fortunately," he continued, "we are not without additional information." Caird then pointed out that a French engineer who had recently been employed by his government to survey the islands had given a figure of 12,000,000 tons of guano left on the Chinchas, and the Peruvian government had declared the result of their last survey at 26,000,000 tons. He felt the Peruvian estimate could be thrown out of consideration, but this meant that the mean of the French and English estimate was 10,300,000 tons still remaining on the three islands.

Caird, however, correctly pointed out that these were not the only guano deposits on the coasts of Peru; there were also known deposits on headlands and other islands, including Pavillon de Pica and the Lobos group, which would lift the total known Peruvian deposits to 18,800,000 tons. Nor, Caird emphasized, was Peru the only country that guano was being obtained from. In fact, during 1852, while two-thirds had come from Peru, one-third had come from other places. Taking all factors into account, including the use of cheaper alternatives to guano, Caird concluded by calculating that there were, at existing and projected rates of consumption, Peruvian reserves, in 1853, that would last for about 90 to 100 years.[24] As it transpired, the Moresby-M'Intosh figures proved to be an underestimate, and the Caird figures a gross overestimate.

Speculation continued about the amount of guano available, but what we do know for a fact is that an ever-increasing number of ships were moving guano from the Chincha Islands during the years 1850, 1851, and 1853. In 1850, 169 British ships, and 45 "foreign" vessels moved 118,352 tons, and in 1851, 268 British, and 36 "foreign" ships moved 189,024 tons. Here it is interesting to note that of the total of 189,024 tons exported from the Chinchas in 1851, 150,653 tons were sent to Britain, none to France, and just 38,371 tons went to the United States. As noted, by 1853 this pattern had changed dramatically, for between July 15 and September 1853, 65 American ships did load at the islands, taking away no less than 61,982 tons of guano. The largest of these vessels was the *Tornado,* at 1,800 tons burthen, down to the 275-ton *Cabaja,* commanded by Captain Perkins, bound for St. Thomas. These ships sailed for various ports, but the main ones were Hampton Roads and New York.[25] In just over a decade the Spanish would be invading the Chinchas to lay claim to the far from depleted deposits left on the Peruvian guano islands. At this point, though, it should be noted that the short-lived West African guano industry, based on Ichaboe and Possession islands, did much in the 1840s to undermine the Peruvian industry. It also threw into disarray the pricing calculations of the existing guano contractors, in particular Messrs. Antony Gibbs of London, and Myers of Liverpool.

7
Chinese Bondage in Peru

THE EMANCIPATION OF SLAVES, THE EXTENSION OF CULTIVATION, AND the development of the guano industry in the middle years of the nineteenth century all gave rise to a very urgent demand for labor on the Peruvian coastal estates and the Chincha Islands. The racially prejudiced Peruvian elite actually preferred European immigrants, but the republic failed to compete successfully with the United States, Canada, Australia, and Argentina for European migrant farmers. The reasons for this were fairly obvious, namely, the reluctance of Peru's wealthy hacendados to make land, or indeed to have land that could be made available to ambitious European agricultural emigrants at competitive prices and also the high cost of a passage to Peru. However, neither the cost of the passage nor general political instability prevented British and other European urban migrants settling in Lima and other Peruvian cities.[1]

It was when the plantation owners failed to attract European labor to their estates—no doubt because these emigrants must have realized that these planters were only looking for cheap labor and not fellow settlers—that the hacendados were obliged to turn to Asia. As already noted, Domingo Elias, grape and cotton grower and one of Peru's wealthiest politicians, together with a partner, imported seventy-five Chinese at Callao in 1849. This marked the beginning of Chinese coolie labor in Peru, the immigration at first being encouraged by the Peruvian Congress, $30 being paid to the importer for each man arriving in the country.

On the issue of Negro slavery, unfortunately, but as might be expected, the abolition of black slavery in Peru was not linked to any redistribution of the land, the ruling white elite remaining firmly in control of this all-important commodity. The hacendados saw all these developments as "labor problems" for which a prompt solution had to be found. Indian and African labor had been exploited, and was still being exploited, despite the "emancipation" of the latter, but the time had now come for the Chinese to be added to this list of landless, superexploited workers. The emancipation of the black slaves, which was effected in Peru by progressive stages, was made complete in 1855 when the proprietors received a compensation of $300 from the government for each slave released.[2]

The "government" being largely composed of landed proprietors, it is perhaps not surprising that no thought of offering any form of "compensation" to the freed slaves seems to have come under active consideration. In this respect, though, it has to be said, Peru was merely following the example set by Britain, who had "compensated" her slave-owners at the time of emancipation. In this case, the offer of "compensation" was a considered tactic of the abolitionists in their ongoing struggle against the parliamentary defenders of the plantation interests. Ironically, the funds to meet the Peruvian "compensation" payments were to be met by the sale of guano, produced by Chinese laborers working in conditions akin to—if not worse than—slavery!

However, the mid-nineteenth-century Peruvian elite were not without their admirers and supporters, among whom was the celebrated historian, Clements R. Markham, the man who had written critically and objectively about the early history of Peru and the deplorable record of the conquistadors. In a highly defensive article about Peru and her record on the treatment of Negroes and Chinese, which appeared in the *Geographical Magazine* in 1874, Markham argued that the modern Peruvians had set a noble example, as regards the treatment of the laboring classes. He also felt that the landed proprietors of Peru were, as a class, most kindly and considerate employers of labor, all of which deliberately missed the point, for the issue was not employer-employee relations, but freedom or slavery, and the disputed right of any man—kindly or otherwise—to hold property in man. He continued by advising readers that he had traveled for hundreds of miles along the coast and over the Andes, and had stayed at the cotton, vine, and sugar estates in the different valleys. On these estates he states that he found that the Negroes were a happy and contented race, "endeared to their masters by the traditions and experience of kind and considerate treatment." They could also attend church and numerous fiestas, and all were well fed and housed within the spacious *galpones*. He felt that the Peruvian hacendados were, in reality, an excellent class of country gentlemen, habitually considerate in the treatment of their dependants. He did though concede that the Chinese laborers had "introduced a disturbing element" into this idyllic scene, and that the want of women among them was deplorable and aggravating the position. Clearly holding the Chinese responsible for their own misfortunes, he concluded his thoughts on these social issues by enthusiastically praising the noble hacendados: "Such men as the Count of Monte Blanco, the Count of Torres de Oran, Don Mariano de Osma, Don Pedro Paz Soldan, Don Manuel Quintana, and a host of others of similar stamp, are not to be spoken of in the same breath with ordinary planters and speculators, whether English or American. Peruvian hacendados, such as those I have mentioned, have received their estates from their forefathers, and are not planting adventurers merely seeking to make money rapidly."

Slavery had survived in Peru for more than thirty years after independence precisely because the ruling elite considered that this institution was of vital importance to the nation's economic recovery and prosperity. Needless to say, it was equally crucial to the individual wealth and social position of all planters, noble or otherwise.[3] And while one can allow for the fact that some slaveholders undoubtedly did treat their "dependants" better than others, which is in itself commendable, all things are relative, and this was only by comparison with other exploited, landless, oppressed workers and slaves whose conditions were invariably abysmal. Indeed, far from being universally satisfied with their lot, over the years thousands had tried to escape from their respective owners' estates. Slaves had actually been fleeing from their owners since the first days of African slavery in Peru and well into the nineteenth century, the incentive to flee being all too clear. The vast majority did not live well, and poor rations and bad housing were the general order of the day on many, if not most, of the estates. Illness and mistreatment among the slaves and deficiencies in health care, clothing, and excessive labor demands were all part of the abuse and exploitation that both urban and rural slaves had to face daily.[4]

Slave resistance was common, one example of a rising being in 1838, when slaves on the San Pedro estate forced the majordomo and employees to flee. They sacked and robbed the estate store of corn, then killed the livestock to eat and sell. Yet despite clear and continuing indications of slave discontent, for a long period the slaveholders showed but limited concern, that is, until the Chicama Valley rebellion of January 1851, which marked the culmination of slave resistance during this period. It warned the "country gentlemen" that slaves were reaching the end of their tether, and a desire for freedom had reached the point where they were ready to fight and die for it. By the 29th of the month, this uprising had attracted about 150 slaves, and came into public view as the result of an armed confrontation on the Cajanleque estate. This northern revolt served as an example that others soon followed. Less than two months later about fifty slaves from the great Casa Blanca and La Quebrada estates in the Canete Valley arose, proclaiming "Liberty or Death." This isolated revolt was soon brought under control, but just two years later, a lone individual tried to rouse the Casa Blanca slaves again, but the local hacendados quickly armed their men, hunted him down, and executed him.

It was only through the slaveholders' continued use of terror and brutality that Markham's "happy and contented" race of black slaves were kept under control. This in itself indicated that the slaveholders viewed the slaves as a very real threat, and there can be no doubt that such fears existed ever since the arrival of the first African slaves in Peru at the beginning of the colonial era. Slaves were continually running away, attacking their owners and rebelling. While this type of resistance could not end Peruvian slavery, such actions caused much concern among the individual hacendados and revealed the dangers of maintaining this brutal, oppressive system. Soon prominent members of Peru's ruling elite began to add their weight to the call for abolition. One voice raised was that of Alfonso González Pinillos, a prominent planter and slaveholder from Trujillo. In January 1852 he freed his 136 slaves, mainly because of the recent slave rebellions, but also because of his growing awareness of the slaves' distress. His voice was now added to the growing number in Peru arguing for the emancipation of slaves.[6] In addition to the internal forces that were weakening Peruvian slavery, during the first three decades following independence, considerable pressure was being exerted by foreign nations. Foremost among these was Great Britain, whose crusade to eradicate the international slave trade, and eventually to abolish slavery in all its guises, included Peru within its purview.[7] Accordingly, a further brief glance at the development of this great, humanitarian movement would be in order at this point.

For two hundred years the unholy practice of slave trading had corrupted British society, choking the arteries of the social and even of the religious life of the nation. However, during the years 1787 to 1833, first under the leadership of Wilberforce, then Buxton, Britain had moved from being a principal participant in the trade to the main international opponent of slavery. As noted, the abolitionists first worked to get a bill through Parliament banning the slave trade, which they finally achieved in 1807. Unfortunately, the slave trade had in the meantime increased, and the checking of its international development then became one of the main aims of the Duke of Wellington.[8] In Parliament the fight for the abolition of the slave trade lasted eighteen years; for the emancipation of the slaves in the British colonies, another twenty-six years.[9]

By 1840 about 25 percent of the Royal Navy was employed in efforts to suppress the slave trade, the Africa squadron being foremost in this struggle. The British government then responded to popular demands to increase the strength of this squadron, for by 1842 this fleet, previously composed of sailing ships, was strengthened by the arrival of five steamers. During the 1840s Britain also used her imperial strength to persuade other nations to cooperate, by signing appropriate treaties, who then sent out their own antislavery patrols.[10] The naval historian Christopher Lloyd estimated that in the middle thirties 135,000 Negro slaves were being taken across the Atlantic each year, mainly to Cuba and Brazil.[11] By the 1840s Buxton estimated that this had increased, and that no less than 150,000 human beings were then being conveyed each year from Africa, across the Atlantic, and sold as slaves in the Americas.[12] A large number of these slaves were being conveyed across the Atlantic in Spanish and Portuguese vessels, running the gauntlet of the British patrols.

It is of particular significance, in this chapter on Peru—and her exploitation of Chinese workers—that Portugal was then putting herself in opposition to Britain by conniving at the illegal movement of all these slaves across the Atlantic. It should also be noted that much of this traffic in slaves was being undertaken in ships belonging to her private merchants. It was, in fact, from the Portuguese colony of Macau, on the Canton River, China, that the majority of Chinese were to embark on their one-way passage to this Latin American republic. The nearby British colony at Hong Kong was also, but to a lesser extent, involved in this trade but, as will be noted, this met with a good measure of official opposition, due to the antislavery position of Palmerston and the imperial government.

The Treaty of Friendship, Commerce, and Navigation between Great Britain and Peru was signed on April 10, 1850. Through this document Palmerston put pressure on Peru to abandon all links with the slave trade by proposing that the Slave Trade Article, which was included in the 1837 British–Peru Treaty, was included in the new one. The Peruvians wanted "Slave Trade" to read "African Slave Trade," but Palmerston, to his credit, refused, commenting, "Slave Trade is Slave Trade whether the slaves bought and sold be Africans or Americans; and such Traffic ought equally in either case to be put an end to."[13] The Peruvian Congress, which had to confirm it, actually procrastinated, which meant that the document was not formally ratified and exchanged at London until October 15, 1852. The relevant clause was Article XV, which stated: "The Republic of Peru engages to co-operate with Her Britannic Majesty for the total abolition of the Slave Trade, and to prohibit all persons inhabiting the territories of the Republic, or subject to its jurisdiction, in the most effectual manner, and by penal laws, from taking any share in such trade."[14]

One can be in no doubt that the growing dependency of Peru on the London money market also had much to do with the final ratification of this treaty and many subsequent developments. In October 1849, a new loan had been arranged, at the instigation of the Peruvians, between the republic and William Gibbs & Company in Lima, involving substantial drafts on London. This appears to have been independent of any formal guano contract, although it was clearly the intention to repay it through guano sales. "We are to advance $400,000 without interest," reported Samuel Went, their manager in Lima, "by paying 18% in paper, from which, and from the Exchange we shall get some 9 or 10%." Two days later he wrote that Pedro de Candamo, a Chilean merchant, had also become party to the transaction, taking a one-eighth share, Gibbs's part of the loan, therefore, amounting to $295,000.[15] As Gibbs & Company were soon to be directly involved in the employment of Chinese workers on the Chinchas, they inevitably became central to the whole issue of Chinese bondage in Peru and therefore subject to pressures from London via the local British consul based at Lima.

While Britain led international efforts to end the slave trade, she was, as mentioned, also responsible for establishing the "coolie trade." From 1837 to the early years of the twentieth century, the British shipowners in this trade were to be responsible for transporting countless thousands of indentured Indian and Chinese workers to various British colonies, notably the islands of the West Indies and British Guiana (now Guyana). Critics saw this as a thinly disguised attempt to replace African slaves with Indian and Chinese laborers, working under conditions akin to slavery. Supporters of this emigration argued that it was a legitimate emigration, operating under stringent regulations and controls, and therefore bore no resemblance whatsoever to the slave trade. Whatever the case may be regarding British participation in this trade, it undoubtedly set the pattern for making use of cheap Asian labor as a replacement for freed slaves, which was soon emulated by other nations, including Peru.

One of the first acts of the Reform Parliament of 1832 was the Act of Emancipation, which granted liberty to the slaves of the West Indies at the cost to the English people of £20,000,000. This sum was the amount required by the slaveholders of the West Indies to "compensate" them for their loss of "property." While the abolitionist forces in Parliament were strong at this time, and growing stronger, the plantation owners, opposed to emancipation, also had much support. The planters were, in effect, bought off by this large payment. Never was money better spent, and yet it was a gross injustice. It was like paying a man for property to which he had no intrinsic moral right, and for which, according to the highest law of equity, he could establish no claim.[16] In fact, many planters received in "compensation" payments that amounted to more than the value of their estates. However, despite reservations about the "justice" of these payments, it remains to the credit of the British people generally, who met these payments, that they had, collectively, broken the chains that bound black Africans in perpetual slavery.

Soon after the British government had bribed its own planters and the slavers of foreign nations to free their slaves, it became apparent that the plantation economies of many colonies would collapse. That is, if alternative sources of cheap labor could not be found, who could stand the severe tropical conditions on the coffee, sugar, and cocoa plantations. In just one colony, Demerara (British Guiana), 100,000 slaves were freed; the actual number on which compensation was claimed was 82,824.[17] Soon after emancipation many of the plantations lay in ruins, for the freed slaves, quite understandably, refused to cultivate the fields and work the mills anymore. It was under these circumstances, and the resulting urgent quest for labor, that the eyes of the West Indies planters focused on the "Jewel in the Crown" of the British Empire—India—and also China, with their huge populations and "surplus" labor.

As far back as 1834, the year after slavery had been abolished throughout the British dominions, forty Indian coolies were exported to Mauritius.[18] In 1837, the first "Coolie Emigration Act" was passed which, among many other things, laid down very stringent regulations concerning the safe transportation of emigrant labor from the Far East to the West Indies. Notwithstanding these stringent regulations, many shipowners entered this trade. However the "main players" in the coolie trade were, undoubtedly, John Allan & Company of London, James Nourse & Company, and Sandbache Tinne & Company of Liverpool.

The clipper ships employed in this trade, at least by these three named firms, were, indeed, a far cry from the vessels used by earlier generations of British shipowners and mariners, for they were among the finest ever built. Sleeker than the legendary tea-clippers of the period, some would also carry up to 50 percent more canvas than was normal for vessels of their size. Capable of circumnavigating the globe with ease, the Sandbache Tinne emigrant ship *Shiela* once outsailed the legendary tea-clipper *Cutty Sark*.[19] Getting to the colonies safely was one thing; working conditions when they arrived, and ever getting the "guarantied" return passages were quite another matter. It was, of course, these crucial factors that continued to cast a long shadow over the whole trade, making it a highly controversial issue for a period of more than sixty years. Apart from these major enterprises, which were subject to proper controls, many other ships were also employed in this trade, which escaped from, or were not subject to, United Kingdom legislation, and conditions on these vessels were invariably atrocious.

So far as the general emigration of Chinese workers from Hong Kong is concerned, this can, in the main, be traced to the opening of the gold fields in the Sacramento Valley in 1848. This discovery set in motion a rush of prospectors and general workers to the West Coast of North America. Many nationalities, including Chinese in great numbers, headed for the western states. Alas, there was no "pot of gold" in line for the vast majority of these Chinese men, many of whom soon found themselves dragooned into the ranks of railroad construction gangs, work that was virtually as bad as working the guano islands in Peru.[20] By the close of 1849, it should be noted, the population of California was about 100,000. (Interestingly, a state constitution was ratified on November 13, 1849, that prohibited slavery, the actual admission of California as a free state forming part of Clay's famous "Omnibus Bill" of September 9, 1850.)[21] The massive influx of "Gold Rush" adventurers into California in 1849 and the early 1850s placed many demands on the limited resources of the area, which obliged the Californians to turn to Hong Kong, where they bought such items as clothes and wooden houses, which were shipped in frames. Chinese artisans were sent to California to set up these houses. These were followed by an annually increasing stream of Chinese emigrants embarking at Hong Kong for San Francisco and a steadily developing trade in all sorts of articles. In 1851 forty-four vessels left Hong Kong for California, and this line of trade was to remain constant throughout the remainder of the nineteenth century.[22]

Almost synonymous with this development was the establishment of the Chinese contract labor system, by which means African slavery gave way to a thinly disguised form of Chinese slavery, in which many nations participated. During the period 1847–74, it has been estimated that between a quarter and a half million laborers were shipped from Amoy, Canton, Hong Kong, and Macao, especially from the last two ports, to Cuba, Peru, Chile, and the Sandwich Islands. In 1864, for example, 4,479 were shipped from Macau to Cuba and 6,243 to Peru; in 1865, 5,207 Cuba and 8,417 to Peru. Sailing under the French flag during the same years, 2,716 laborers were shipped by Cuban agents from Canton to Cuba. The need for cheap labor in the West and the overflowing population of China built up many lucrative business enterprises for astute but ruthless traders in the East and West. According to a contemporary account, the supply came chiefly from three sources: "Prisoners taken in the clan fights of the province of Kwangtung, and who are sold by their captors to Chinese or Portuguese man-buyers upon the interior waters; villagers or fishermen forcibly kidnapped along the coast; and thirdly, individuals who are tempted by prowling agents to gamble (in Macau) and who on losing, surrender their persons in payment according to the peculiar Chinese notions of liability in this respect." Others were simply duped into signing bogus "contracts," and many that were destined to work on the Chincha Islands of Peru were under the impression that they were being taken to the gold fields of California. Writing about this trade in 1933 professor Harley Farnsworth MacNair of St. John's University stated, "The suffering of these labourers caused by the methods used by European, American, and Chinese agents in getting them to leave China; the terrible conditions under which they were shipped abroad, as bad as those on the old African slave ships; and their exploitation on the plantations of the New World combine to form one of the darkest stains on the record of the relations of China and the West, a record, it may be added, for which the blame must be pretty equally divided between Chinese and Westerners."[23]

The "crimps," as the collecting agents were called, received up to $10 a man delivered to the "coolie depots" or barracoons in Macau. Here the Chinese laborers were duped into signing a "contract"—which, of course many, if not most, would be unable to read—that bound them for eight years' service. The least fortunate of all then found themselves heading for the Chincha Islands, Peru, with others, slightly more fortunate, ending up in places such as Cuba. On reaching this latter country, the surviving coolies would be put up for auction with their "contracts" and sold in a manner almost indistinguishable from that of an imported African slave, $400 to $1,000 being the going price for a Chinese coolie in the mid-nineteenth century. Theoretically, the coolie had the legal right to appeal to the Spanish courts for enforcement of his rights in case of bad treatment or lack of payment, but no instance is on record of such a proceeding.[24] So far as Cuba is concerned, of the 140,000 Chinese who are estimated to have sailed for this island as indentured labor under such schemes, it is estimated that 11.4 percent, that is 16,000, died on the passage.[25]

As with Cuba, every Chinese laborer bound for Peru was furnished with a copy of a contract, printed in Spanish and Chinese, by which he was bound for a period of eight years. In Peru, on average, $450 was paid by the hacendado, or employer engaged in other work, to the immigrant contractor for his service. One significant clause in these "contracts" stipulated that "the period of service of eight years being concluded, the Chinaman is free to dispose of his labor—no debt of any kind being sufficient to impede his liberation, as any such debt must be recovered by the laws of the country." However, as there was no guaranteed right of return to China at the end of his service, this "liberation" was little more than a delusion.[26] In any event, those who ended up on the Chincha Islands would have been dead from overwork and abuse long before their term of service was completed.

Throughout the 1850s the flow of Chinese emigrants from Hong Kong to California continued to increase. As many as 14,683 were shipped from Hong Kong in the year 1855, and 13,856 in 1858.[27] But accurate figures regarding the importation of coolies into Peru at this time are more difficult to establish, since Peruvian statistics of the period tended to be incomplete. However, Juan de Arona quoted a Peruvian writer to the effect that Chinese arrivals in the decade 1850–59 numbered 13,000.[28] Beyond this point, Thomas J. Hutchinson, British consul general in Peru in the early 1870s and

6. Flogging a Chinese "coolie" on board a ship. *Harpers Monthly Magazine,* June, 1864.

author of the notable work *Two Years in Peru,* gave in this book the following statistics, namely that between 1860 and 1870 a total of 43,301 Chinese sailed from Macao for Callao. Of these 38,648 arrived and 4,653 died on the passage. In 1871 the captain of the port, Senor Palacios, advised Hutchinson that between January and September 1871, 9,693 had sailed from Macao, 9,021 had arrived, and 672 had died on the passage.

During the period from January 1 to October 3, 1872, it is interesting to note that twenty-six ships arrived in Peru, bringing 10,977 Chinese emigrants, out of a total of 11,933 who had embarked, 956, or about 8 percent, had died on the passage. Of these ships none were British, 18 were Peruvian, 4 were French, 2 were Portuguese, and 2 were Dutch. But the average rate of mortality distorts the picture, for the horrors of this traffic are exposed by the facts relating to several of these ships. One of these vessels, the French barque *Antares,* commandeered by Captain Nantle, arrived in Callao at the end of June with a "cargo" of Chinese from Macao. Out of 263 put on board at the port of embarkation, only 181 reached Callao, having had the appalling mortality rate of 31 percent on the voyage. During the same period the 1,043-ton Peruvian ship *Lama Canevaro* arrived at Callao with 547 passengers on board; having left China with 739 emigrants, this gave a mortality rate of 26 percent for the passage. The Portuguese ship *Emigrante* lost 107 of her 499 passengers and the 1,562-ton Peruvian ship *America* that arrived on June 13 lost 105 of her 690 passengers.[29]

On July 3, 1852, a particularly sad case concerning a British ship and Chinese emigrants was brought to the attention of the public, which will serve to illustrate just how bad things could be in this trade. In June 1852 the British ship *Lady Montague* arrived back in London after a voyage of nearly four years' duration. The Board of Trade was then advised that 274 people, principally Chinese emigrants bound for California, had died while on board this ship. The 760-ton vessel had left Southampton in May 1848, laden with coals for Aden, and under the command of Captain Wells. About six weeks later Captain Wells died, and the chief mate, Mr. Samuel Robinson Smith, assumed command of the vessel. After discharging the coal at Aden, Smith proceeded to Bombay, then to Canton, Amoy, and Shanghai, and continued trading backward and forward between those ports, eventually chartering the ship at Cumsingmoon to take Chinese emigrants to California via Callao. Why Smith should have chosen to take Chinese emigrants to North America via South America is not abundantly clear, unless he was trying to hide the true destination of the vessel from his passengers. It is worth noting that the statistics regarding ships that had been engaged in the Chinese emigrant trade, presented by Samuel Went to Chargé d'affaires Sulivan on September 21, 1854, clearly lists the *Lady Montague* and notes that she "had lost many men from sickness," all of which probably confirms that she was engaged in the Peruvian, rather than the Californian, emigrant trade.

However, she eventually sailed again on February 11, 1850, having on board, including passengers and crew, no less than 500 people. Within a few days of her departure, the crew and passengers began to go down with sickness and fever. The water and provisions that had been provided for the emigrants became putrid, a fact that was duly recorded in the log. Soon scores of men had died, and the suffering of the sick was almost beyond description. Many also committed suicide by jumping overboard, and by the time the ship put into Hobart Town, no fewer than 193 had perished. At Hobart the governor responded promptly by sending all the assistance that was possible to alleviate the suffering on the ship. By April

30, the medical officer, who had gone to the relief of the emigrants, succeeded in restoring those who survived to a better state of health, and the ship resumed her long voyage to Callao. Within days, however, the sickness broke out again, and before she reached her destination, nearly 100 others had died. The only letter that Mr Vaux, the owner of the ship, had received from Samuel Robinson Smith regarding this tragic voyage, reads as follows:

To John Vaux, Esq. Southampton. Callao, July 13

Sir, I beg to advise of having arrived here on the 20th ult. I have had a most awful passage of it, dysentery and fever having broken out among the Chinese emigrants shortly after leaving China, which carried off 274 souls, including 26 of the ship's crew. Among the latter were poor Mr Brazier and the apprentice J. G. Paul. I had promoted Mr Brazier to second officer on leaving China, but, poor fellow, he had only one week of duty, ill all the passage, and died the night the ship got to Hobart Town. I was obliged to make for the nearest port to save the ship, the remainder of the crew, and passengers. I have also been attacked, and lay at death's door for a whole fortnight; but Divine Providence spared my life a little longer. The only person in the ship who has not been sick is the apprentice Huscroft. You may be sure I have had a dreadful time of it on the passage. For weeks and weeks I have had no more than four, five, and six men besides myself to navigate the ship. No officers neither, and in a high southerly latitude, with a cold stormy weather to contend with. Happily, through the blessing of Almighty God, I have arrived with the ship here safely. I was put in quarantine until the 9th at St. Lorenzo Island, allowed to go on shore on the island, and everything that was required was sent to us at Callao.

James R. Smith

The above was the sum total of all information that the Board of Trade had initially been able to obtain respecting this disastrous voyage. Only three out of a crew of thirty-six who went out with the *Lady Montague* eventually got back to the United Kingdom. Soon after receiving this note, however, the following letter from the owner of the ship was received by the board:

Sir, I beg to acknowledge the receipt of your letter, of the 9th inst., respecting the number of deaths on board my ship, the *Lady Montague* on her voyage from Cumsingmoon to Callao. I regret to say I was unable to furnish any information beyond that already obtained by you from the log-book, or to give the number of passengers who originally embarked. My order to the captain who originally sailed in the *Lady Montague* was to bring her directly to England. He unfortunately died, and the command was assumed by the chief mate, James Robinson Smith, who, in disobedience to my orders and entirely contrary to my wishes, chartered her for a time at a fixed rate per month, to be employed [to] carry emigrants to Callao. The number taken on board was not communicated to me, but it was stated that the charterer and a surgeon sailed in the ship. I so strongly disapproved of his conduct that I despatched another captain to China, with a power of attorney to supplant him, which, on the return of the *Lady Montague* to China was done, and Smith returned as passenger in another ship. He is now in London, but I have not seen him. There has been no dispute between us, though I expect there will be.

Should I be able to throw any light upon this lamentable occurrence, I shall be most willing to do so. I am, Sir, &c.,

To Mr T. H. Farrer John Vaux[30]

Soon after this trade had started, news about conditions in Peru, and other states Chinese emigrants were being taken to, clearly got back to China, and cases subsequently occurred of coolies deliberately attacking the crews or setting fire to their ships, obviously preferring death to slavery. A "memorial," compiled by a group of English master mariners addressed to the lords of the Privy Council of Trade, which was later published by the press, throws an interesting light on one of these incidents and also confirms previously mentioned disturbing reports about the Chincha Islands. First, the mariners made the point that Don Elias, as the main labor contractor, was the man responsible for the atrocities taking place on the islands. Then they drew their lordships' attention to the fact that, from time to time uprisings had taken place on board emigrant ships sailing from China to Callao. Reports also indicated that in one of these uprisings the brother of Don Elias was killed. Whether this story was true or not, it was being given by many as the reason for the cruelties taking place on the islands. If true, it was all the more reason why no more Chinese workers should be placed under the vindictive and brutal control of this man. Their account continued:

No sooner are they [the Chinese workers] landed from the ships than they see tall African Negroes placed over them as boatswains, armed with a lash of four plaits of cowhide, laid up in the form of what seamen call "round Sennet." Five feet in length, and an inch and a-half in diameter, tapering to a point, and such as we, who have never been in slave-countries without witnessing floggings, could not have thought could be applied to human beings without causing death, and can only compare to the Australian Stockwhip.

During the forenoons, except for regular offences [or such as the overseers please to term such] this instrument was not so much used, but at, about 4 o'clock in the afternoon, many of the weakest had not performed their task work, the boatswains [when the middle island, on which Chinese only were, was under the control of Kossuth] freely used it to start those behind to bring the day's supervision to a close. The slightest resistance was punished by a flogging little short of murder, as on many melancholy occasions we witnessed, being nearer than we desired. The first six to twelve cuts started the most agonising cries, that range through the fleet—cries that we heard day by day, but only then knew the full amount of suffering that called them forth. There was no tying up; the nearest Chinaman being compelled, by a cut of the lash, to lay hold of an arm or leg and stretch the miserable sufferer on his stomach on the guano. The mere weight alone of the lash made their bodies shake, blackening the flesh at every blow, besides cutting into it like a sabre, and when a convulsive movement took place, a subordinate placed his boot on the shoulders to keep the quivering body down; two dozen made them breathless, and when released after thirty-nine lashes, they seemed slowly to stagger over, reeled, and fell, and were carried off to the hospital—in most cases, if they recovered; committing suicide; for no human heart, unless elevated by Christian training, could, after undergoing so cruel an infliction, ever have more than two feelings, that is, death to those he suffered from, or death to himself. Accordingly, during our stay there many sprang over the cliffs, many buried themselves alive in the guano, and many hid themselves in the caves of the islands to starve to death, their dead bodies floating all around in numbers. In one instance, two, emboldened by pity shown them by a shipmaster, hid themselves on board his vessel, one of whom survives, and is now in this country. We hope this miserable fugitive may live to plead the cause of his countrymen, and that the almighty will retain him in the possession of his faculties, which so far as his appearance goes, we think impaired by the sufferings he has undergone.

The mariners then stated that all the American shipmasters at the Chinchas, from the southern as well as the northern states, declared that they had never seen slavery approaching that of the middle Chincha island. Only the good relations established between them and the American shipmasters stopped the latter, they felt, from taunting the English for engaging in slave traffic. It is also clear from this that the British felt that the Americans were primarily holding their nation responsible for events on the Chinchas, rather than Elias, Kossuth, and the Peruvian authorities. Sadly, this was substantially true because British ships at that point in time were most active in bringing these unfortunate emigrants across the Pacific. It would seem that one of the masters signing the memorial had, in fact, managed to act on a clause in the ship's charter that enabled him to obtain permission to work with sailors on the main island. For just 1s. per ton, on top of their ship's wages, they had dug and wheeled down the guano until ordered off by the Peruvians. It was felt that this was done because this official was concerned that they would try to protect the Chinese on the middle island. However, the captains continued, "sailors were not allowed to land, for if they had they would certainly have interfered." The point was then made that while the ships lay for months waiting to be loaded by these brutally treated workers, hundreds of sailors were idle in their ships, who, if allowed to land, could have loaded their ships in a matter of days. However, even if the trade was not made free, the trifling addition of 1s. 6d. per ton would not be felt when guano was fetching £10 a ton. Surely, such a trifling addition would make digging guano a favorite pursuit of free laborers who would not have to be driven by brutal thugs, they argued.

The shipmasters objected strongly to British ships being allowed to take emigrants from China to Peru. In their penultimate paragraph the signatories urged their lordships to take steps to ensure that all future deportations of Chinese to Peru, Cuba, and other slaveholding countries were stopped without delay. "By means which your official wisdom will suggest to you, means of which, if we had the knowledge, it would be presumptuous on our part to point out to your official experience." The final paragraph of this notable document read:

> We trust that your Lordships, after a hard day's labour, called for by the circumstances of war in which this country is placed, will not, when snatching a glance at your family circles, and the Christian blessings surrounding you, forget the claims the miserable Chinese have on your active sympathy; and that, amid the pressure of public business, while contributing to the discomfiture of a colossal and encroaching despotism, will you stretch out a merciful and helping hand to helpless and unresisting sufferers. That the God of mercies will direct your Lordships' most humble servants.
>
> (Signed) James Turnbull
> Frederick Acock
> John Henderson Smith
> John Coulter
> John Purdon
> John W. Symons
> Chas. Robertson
> William Caithness
> London, June 27, 1854 Edward Oager[31]

It is indeed gratifying to record that without a moment's delay or reservation, the "merciful and helping hand" *was* stretched out to those suffering on the Chincha Islands. In direct response, the British foreign secretary, Lord Clarendon, wrote to Chargé Sulivan at Lima, enclosing a copy of the sea captains' memorial and instructing him to take immediate action. Accordingly, on September 2, 1854, Sulivan wrote to the Peruvian minister, His Excellency Don José Luis Gomez Sanchez. Enclosed was a copy of the memorial advising him that Her Majesty's government had read this report and noted with disgust the details of the cruelties being practiced on the unfortunate Chinese laborers who were working under the authority of people responsible to the government of Peru. After diplomatically stating that he assumed the Peruvian government was ignorant of these revolting atrocities, he added that he hoped not a single day would be allowed to pass without the most stringent measures being taken to put an end to the atrocities, "the toleration of which would inflict indelible disgrace upon the Peruvian Government." On the sensitive issue of British ships being used to transport workers from China to Peru, Sulivan wrote:

> Her Majesty's Government learn with deep regret that by British Agency and under the British flag these Chinese labourers have been brought to the Chincha Islands and placed in a state of slavery more horrible than any yet recorded; but this fact imposes an additional duty on Her Majesty's Government. Under any circumstances they would interfere in the defence of outraged humanity; but they are now specially called upon to protect these victims of brutal cupidity, and from that duty they will not shrink, if unfortunately the Peruvian Government should hesitate to perform the duty which in the first instance devolves upon them.[32]

Sulivan continued by stating that he hoped the required orders would be issued, and that if this was done, a British officer would be permitted to accompany a Peruvian official to the islands, in order to verify the shipmasters' report. On reflection, though, it is clear that no atrocities would occur if and when such a delegation was actually on the islands making such "official" verification impossible. Apart from this fairly obvious consideration, Sulivan, speaking on behalf of the British government, continued by advising Minister Sanchez that instructions were also being sent to the Commander of Her Majesty's naval forces on the Pacific station, these unambiguous instructions calling on him to visit the Chincha Islands, "to ascertain the real state of things there, and at once to adopt such measures for the protection of the Chinese and the punishment of the overseers and others as humanity and justice demands."

Sulivan's final paragraph opened on a friendly but firm note, stating that he was also instructed to point out how much the interests of the Peruvian government would actually be promoted by putting an end to such "misdeeds." He then concluded with a final commercial observation, for consideration by His Excellency, this being the inconvenience of ships being obliged to touch at Callao before proceeding to the Chinchas, which he was particularly requested to raise with the foreign secretary by the ships' captains.

Two days later Sulivan wrote to Samuel Went, the junior resident partner of William Gibbs & Company, at Lima, raising the issue and enclosing a copy of the memorial. In this note he pointed out to Went that the loading contract, formerly held by Elias, was now held by Messrs. Gibbs and Company. Accordingly, he requested a full report on the matter, adding, "You have the control over these Chinese labourers and it is for the honour of your House that the truth should be stated."[33] On the same day Went gave Sulivan the required assurance that the matter would be looked into with as little delay as possible.[34] On the 11th of the month, Sulivan wrote back to Clarendon. This advised him that matters were in hand and assured him that he had requested a full report from the House of William Gibbs. He also advised the foreign secretary that this firm had succeeded to the contract, formerly held by Don Dominigo Elias, for the shipping and loading of guano on the Chinchas, and that consequently the Chinese laborers were now principally under the direction of that British commercial house, but, he continued, "Both the Peruvian Minister and Mr Went do not deny that at the time when there was no Governor of the Chincha Islands, and when the contract was held by Don Domingo Elias the Chinese labourers employed in the digging of Huano were severely treated and the chief overseer of Don Domingo Elias, Mr Kossuth, was an individual of a cruel disposition, but he has been long ago dismissed."

Sulivan then advised the minister that Went had assured him that his first step, on carrying on the government contract taken from Elias, had been to ameliorate the condition of the Chinese laborers. These men, he claimed, were now being well fed, well treated, and not overworked, they were receiving their pay regularly, and if they chose to work extra hours, they received additional pay. Most importantly, Went had assured him that the best men among the Chinese workers had now been appointed overseers to their own countrymen.[35] Just ten days later, Went submitted his detailed report to Sulivan.

In this long document he began by making the point that the masters who signed the memorial had, with one exception, all completed their loading between November 25, 1853, and January 23, 1854. He then stated that his house only took up the contract on January 22, 1854, therefore they had no control over loading and labor prior to this date. While they felt the memorial was exaggerated, they had to admit the charges were not altogether unfounded, but they felt bound to state—for the honor of Don Domingo Elias—that any ill treatment of the Chinese could not have taken place with his knowledge, due to the fact that from the month of August 1853, because of his "overt disaffection" to the government of Peru, he was not able to visit the Chinchas. Due to these circumstances, things were left under the direct control of the respective overseers, and Kossuth, on the Middle Island, had abused his position, taken the law into his own hands, and badly treated the Chinese workers. He then confirmed that measures had promptly been put in hand to ensure that these men were properly treated. Steps, in fact, had been taken to allow some ships to load with their own labor, and he had obtained permission for vessels to leave direct from the islands but, rather surprisingly, only a small proportion had availed them of this facility.

On the crucial question of which ships were actually bringing the Chinese emigrants from their homeland to Peru, Went stated that he understood they had been transported across the Pacific by both English and Peruvian vessels. Unfortunately, though, he was not able to state in what proportion. However, as things stood, in September 1854, as far as he could ascertain, the vessels then employed in the trade were confined entirely to those under the Peruvian flag, but concluded by giving details of ships that had been employed to carry Chinese to Peru. The following is a memorandum of vessels that were employed to carry Chinese to Peru:

BRITISH FLAG

Lady Montague	Lost many men from sickness, No. landed not ascertained
Marina	Landed about 400 men
Coromandel	Landed about 400 men
Nepal	Landed about 500 men
Susannah	Landed about 325 men (Afterwards sold to a Peruvian)

Amazon	Embarked 250 men and landed safely 248
Victory	Did not arrive, the Chinese having mutinied and landed on the China Coast.

FRENCH FLAG

Albert	Chinese mutinied and relanded
Manuelita	Condemned at Manilla and Chinese landed there
Chile	Lost

AMERICAN FLAG

Ohio	Landed about 300 men
Tague	Number landed not ascertained

PERUVIAN FLAG

Empressa	Three voyages landing about 1000 men in the three trips.
Isabel Quintana	(Formerly the *Sussanah*) Two voyages landing about 325 men each time.[36]

On December 12, 1854, His Excellency, José Luis Gomez Sanchez at last replied to Chargé Sulivan's letter of September 2. First he advised him that as the mediation of the British legation in this matter could only be considered as a simple notice in favor of humanity, he would respond. He did, however, point out that his government was of the opinion that the allegations made by the shipmasters were completely wrong, and as they had linked this to observations on other commercial matters, their real motives had to be questioned. His government had, in fact, conducted its own inquiry into the matter, through General Charles Lagomarcino, the governor of the islands, from which it was absolutely clear there were no grounds whatsoever for the statements "respecting the supposed sufferings of the Chinese." The government had, however, given express orders that the Chinese should be treated with humanity, and they had, forthwith, doubled their wages. Sanchez closed by assuring Went that for the honor of their own administration, they were "interested in removing every imputation which could represent it as capable of permitting the execution of acts of cruelty upon any class of men, whatever may be their race or condition."[37]

There can be no doubt that the removal of Elias led to a great improvement in conditions on the Chincha Islands. Nevertheless, in 1853, when he was in control, it is estimated that his crew of guano diggers included about 600 Chinese coolies, 50 slaves, and about 200 Chileans or Peruvians, a large proportion of them being deserters from the army or convicts, although a small minority were free workers.[38] The terrible truth about Elias and Kossuth was, however, confirmed in a letter from Sulivan to Clarendon in July 1855. In this he noted that statements made by a Captain Kennedy, of the ship *India*, only went to prove that in the year 1853, when Domingo Elias had his contract and Kossuth was on the island, the Chinese were indeed badly treated. He was, however, pleased to be able to report that he had recently spoken to many shipmasters coming from the Chinchas, and the state of the Chinese laborers was then satisfactory.[39] A further letter from Sulivan to Clarendon, written two years later, would tend to verify a pattern of continuing improvement:

> My Lord,
> As Admiral Bruce had decided to send H.M.S. *Vixen* to the Chincha Islands, I availed myself of that opportunity to visit those huano deposits, and to ascertain the actual condition of the Chinese labourers, and I am happy to be able to report to your Lordship that whatever may have been formerly the ill treatment of the Chinese labourer, no such complaint can be made now. There are at present about four hundred Chinese under contract and about one hundred and fifty free labourers. The Chinese who are under contract are paid eight dollars a month, are well fed, lodged, and clothed. The free Chinese, that is to say, those whose contracts are ended, are paid according to their work, at the rate of two and a half reals a load of about eighteen hundred pounds of which they can with ease dig four a day and many of them dig six. Most of the Chinese have saved money and some of them are wealthy, they appear to be perfectly satisfied, and the Peruvian Government connive at the erection of a temple in which they can celebrate their religious rites.
>
> (Lima 11th August 1857).[40]

All this went some way to calming British concern about the treatment of the Chinese on the Chincha Islands, and as the number of independent reports itemizing brutalities fell away sharply after the removal of Elias and Kossuth, one must assume that this provided evidence of a genuine improvement. Indeed, as Mathew has pointed out, it actually made little economic sense to allow brutes like Kossuth to have men incapacitated through sadistic actions, for they were thus rendered incapable of working. As for remuneration, while one can be sure it was never as generous as Chargé Sulivan had suggested to Lord Clarendon in August 1857, there is evidence that it did improve to an extent. "Free labourers were paid a higher wage than coolies, and were probably required to meet their own subsistence costs." These men earned six reals a day in 1853 for moving four tons of guano to the loading bays on top of the cliffs, and the men who did the dangerous and dirty job of loading into the shoots received double that amount. However, they earned it, for there was a constant danger of falling into these huge, open shoots: "It was accordingly, reserved for free labourers: a dead contract worker represented lost money."[41]

In all more than 100,000 Chinese laborers were taken to Peru between 1849 and 1873, in the main to work on the coastal cotton and sugar plantations, on railroad construction, and for guano digging on the Chincha Islands. Those who failed to abide by the disciplinary code of the hacendados were, on occasion, chained and shackled, to prevent escape, but this, we are confidently assured, was an extreme form of punishment only meted out to the most "chronic rebels."[42] Mortality was high among these workers due in part from overcrowding on the ships and ill-treatment in Peru. Although, and in common with many European mariners taken to distant parts of the globe, many also succumbed to foreign ills to which neither Europeans or Chinese had any natural resistance. The worst recorded case of this nature was in 1870 and 1871 when the celebrated American railroad contractor, Henry Meiggs, was building the famous Oroya Railroad. Meiggs, in the main, employed Chilean and Chinese men on this and other projects. However, in the first two years of this particular project, 10,000 of these men are estimated to have died while this work was in progress, most of whom were victims of a fever that was said to be peculiar to the Rimac Valley.[43] It was actually soon after this catastrophe that the emigration from China to Peru was stopped. In fact, a temporary prohibition was placed on the coolie trade to the Chincha Islands on September 1, 1854, when the trade was being rated as an "aggravated form of slavery." However, this was withdrawn again on February 3, 1855, after the aforementioned measures had been taken for the better treatment of Chinese workers on the islands. All this, incidentally, conveniently coincided with an improvement in the Gibb's guano contracts, for in 1854 their monopoly trading area was extended by an additional contract that gave them the exclusive selling rights for Australia and the British West Indies.[44] One can assume, therefore, that they in particular, as the main export agents, had a vested interest in seeing labor relations put on a better footing.

At about the same time new regulations concerning the diet and provisions of Chinese passengers in emigrant ships were made (March 7, 1855). While Hong Kong continued to be the main port of embarkation from which all south China emigrants, able to pay their passage, embarked for various foreign countries at this time, Macau was soon the main port of embarkation for the coolie trade to Peru because regulations there were less stringent. The existence in March 1857 of closed coolie barracoons in Hong Kong came as a shock to the authorities and was soon put down by the order of the governor, Sir John Bowring.[45]

In 1867 opposition to the coolie trade at Hong Kong was led by Sir John Smale, the chief justice of the colony, and James Whitall who, in June of that year, wrote a memorial on the subject to the governor, Sir Richard Graves MacDonald. They felt constrained to loudly condemn the trade; it was so inherently bad and so dependent on crime for its very existence that they felt it should be stopped without delay. It was, they were convinced, little more than a modern form of slavery. Their thoughts on the trade were neatly encapsulated in just one paragraph of their long letter:

> We do not require to relate in detail to your Excellency the grounds which lead us to thus strongly depreciate what is commonly known as the "Coolie Emigration" and to pray that any promotion of it, within colonial waters, at least, may be made illegal. You are well aware that all assertion and evidence, so called, to the contrary notwithstanding, few Chinese peasants enter into contracts for service or labour abroad, possessed of any clear, intelligent sense of what they are doing. Too often the miserable wretches are doomed by this dreadful traffic to a lifetime of exile and slavery. (For although the trade has now existed for years, few, if any, of its victims have returned to China) are torn by violence from their friends and homes, or have been obtained by means of deception and misrepresentation; it being notorious to all persons acquainted with Chinese character, and manner of thought, that none of these people would consent to quit their native land, did they thoroughly understand the nature of the lives, which even in the most favourable localities, say the British and Dutch West Indian Colonies and the Hawaiian Islands, lie before them.

The governor promptly sent the memorial to the Duke of Buckingham and Chandos. A reply, directly to Smale and Whittall from the colonial secretary's office in London, made the point, among many others, that they were asking the governor of Hong Kong to

7. The Oroya Railroad, crossing the Verrugas Bridge. *Harpers New Monthly Magazine* (European Ed.) December 1890.

repeal an act of the imperial Parliament, which he obviously had no power to do. Although they had made the point that abuses were then taking place, primarily at Macao, this in itself was not grounds for stopping emigration of all contract labor from the colony. Also, it was felt many Chinese emigrants were fully aware of the nature of the work that they were contracting to undertake. Interestingly, paragraph 13 and 14 of this detailed reply read:

> 13. It would also appear to have escaped your attention, that to close this port to all Chinese emigration would be running counter not merely to Imperial legislation, but apparently to the action and wishes of the Chinese Government, which, in the Convention made at Peking last year with the British and French Ministers has shown its willingness to promote emigration on sufficient guarantees being given for the moral and physical well-being of the emigrants.
>
> 14. In a dispatch of Prince Kung dated 15th March, last year, whilst declaring that the emigration from Macao is wholly unauthorised by the Chinese Government, his Highness renders a just tribute to former benevolent efforts of the British Government to promote the welfare of the labourer, and expressly notifies Chinese sanction of coolie emigration, even to countries with which China has no treaty relations, if Great Britain could pay proper attention to the coolies sent there.[47]

Unfortunately there is invariably a large gap between agreements entered into by governments and those responsible for implementing them. Making regulations, and actually making sure they are enforced, are two different matters. Nevertheless, during the winter of 1865–66, the British and French ministers in Peking had conferred with Prince Kung, head of the Chinese Ministry of Foreign Affairs who, it was clear, was as opposed to the malpractices of the coolie traffic as were the foreign envoys themselves. Elaborate and specific regulations for the protection of the emigrants, whether free or contract, were then put down. In the case of the latter type the specifications of the contract were prescribed, including, among other things, the hours of work, the number of working days a year, the length of the contract, provision for illness, and the return of the laborer to China. Prince Kung also made three declarations, the most significant of which was the second, which, by a law of the Chinese Empire, was to punish by death those who, by fraud or force, kidnapped Chinese subjects for the purpose of sending them abroad against their will.[48]

Sadly, though, there is a great deal of evidence to suggest that a large percentage of Chinese emigrant workers continued to be taken abroad against their will, or at best were duped into signing bogus contracts. This inevitably led to mutinies on the ships, when the men suddenly realized what was happening to them, and often soon after sailing. The merest hint of such an outbreak would result in captains keeping passengers belowdecks to prevent the crews being killed. Unfortunately, the 9,000-mile passage across the Pacific from Macao to Callao often took four or five months. Thus, with hatches battened down and ports closed due to bad weather, or concern that the emigrants would attack the crew, life on the unventilated emigrant decks in the humid tropical heat soon become intolerable. It was under these conditions that they rapidly fell prey to fever, dysentery, and other diseases. Even when the ships were first class and the food was adequate, these Chinese emigrants had to endure a grueling voyage. Unlike European emigrants, though, they invariably faced a grim existence when they arrived at their destination, particularly if it was Peru.

According to Markham, between 1850 and 1853, 2,516 coolies landed in Peru, and from 1860 to 1872, the number increased to 80,458. Agents and brokers, for enlisting coolies, Markham conceded, set up business in Macao, and there was much kidnapping, overcrowding, and ill-treatment. Nevertheless, he was convinced that "these evils have been grossly exaggerated." According to Markham the ships taking coolies from Macao to Callao could be divided into two classes: those belonging to the emigration companies established at Lima and those that were chartered. The first class consisted of large well-found ships, with 6' 6" between decks and sufficient space for each emigrant. These ships, he was confident, were well ventilated, and there was provision for medical attendance. He continued:

> The *Isabel, America, Camilo, Cavourr, Fray Rentos* and *Rossalla* are good of their class; and Messrs Samuda have recently built a steamer on purpose for this traffic, in which hygiene and ventilation have been especially studied. The rations for the Coolies are sufficient, and include rice, frijoles, preserved vegetables, and fish, tea, and tobacco. The vessels of the second class, which are generally French, and are hired for the voyage, are not so good, and it is on board these that the abuses and cases of neglect, which have been so much talked of, and so seldom proved, have occurred, or are alleged to have occurred.[49]

The uprisings on the emigrant ships were explained by some as being due not to poor provisions, but more to the fact that such a large percentage of these Chinese workers had been deceived or kidnapped to get them on board.[50] The coolies were, in many cases, so determined to avoid going to Peru—or for that matter other destinations—where they felt they faced a grim future, that they set fire to or scuttled their respective ships. To illustrate this, such an event happened on one of the largest sailing ships owned in New York, this being the *Norway,* which, in 1859, took on board at Macao 1,000 coolies for Havannah.[51] Unfortunately, this practice continued, for during the year 1870, the author, Thomas J. Hutchinson, then serving as British consul-general in Peru, recorded that during that year a few dreadful cases of burning of ships had occurred, when bringing Chinese coolies to Callao.[52] In an editorial that appeared in the Peruvian newspaper *El Comercio* on July 25, 1871, it was stated that ships with more than 3,000 coolies on board had been scuttled, burned, or in other manners destroyed. In other cases the ships were taken over by the Chinese, and often with great loss of life. This allegation was made while making reference to a particular case, that of the ship *Nouvelle Penelope.* In the same article mention was also made of the case of the Chinese emigrant ship *Maria Luz.*[53]

The case of the *Maria Luz* is particularly interesting. She was a Peruvian vessel of 600 tons, commanded by Captain Herrera. She sailed from Macao with 225 emigrants on board and put into the Japanese port of Yokohama from stress of weather in July 1872. It appears that during the night of July 13, one of the emigrants swam across to the man-of-war *Iron Duke* and asked the captain for help because the emigrants were being badly treated. This was promptly brought to the attention of the Japanese authorities, the result being that Captain Herrera was tried and sentenced to receive 100 lashes. A pardon was subsequently granted, but all the emigrants were taken out of the ship, and the owners were subjected to heavy losses. This was all brought to the attention of the Peruvian government, and the president, Don Manuel Pardo, resolved to dispatch an envoy to Japan to demand reparations for the "outrage," and at the same time to establish treaty relations with Japan and China.

After reaching an agreement with the Japanese about the *Maria Luz* affair, which was based on putting the case to independent arbitration, a treaty of commerce and friendship was drawn up between the two nations, which was signed on August 21, 1873. The Peruvian envoy, Senor Garcia y Garcia, then proceeded to China, reaching Tientsin on October 31, 1873, where he opened negotiations with Prince Kung. Because of reports (which Markham, characteristically, considered either false or exaggerated) about the condition of their compatriots in Peru, namely, that they were being insulted, overworked, and ill-used, and the emigrant ships taking them out were overcrowded and ill-found, the Chinese were in a hostile mood. The first Chinese dispatch concluded with a demand that all the Chinese emigrants should be returned to China forthwith. However, after it was pointed out that this was impractical, and that many regulations had been introduced for the protection of the emigrants, a treaty was eventually signed between the two nations, this being on June 26, 1874. As part of the deal it was also agreed that a Chinese commission could visit Peru in order to inspect and report on the conditions and prospects of the Chinese emigrants.[54]

Prior to these developments in 1871 Senor Palacios, captain of the port of Callao, provided Hutchinson with the following immigration statistics, to which some reference has already been made. The data throws much light on the total scale of this emigration. It will be noted, however, that for obvious reasons, the Peruvian official based at Callao, who was responsible for recording the arrival and departure of vessels, would not be in a position to include details of emigrant ships that had left Macao bound for Callao but failed to arrive! The inclusion of all the many China-Peru emigrant ships lost due to mutinies (and shipwreck) would clearly paint a very different statistical picture. Nevertheless, the information provided from this source is disturbing enough:

Immigration of Chinese to Callao

Year	Arrived	Sailed from Macao	Deaths on Passage
1860	1,413	2,007	594
1861	1,440	1,860	420
1862	1,003	1716	713
1863	1,628	2,301	673
1864	6,410	7,010	600
1865	4,540	4,794	254
1866	5,929	6,543	614
1867	2,184	2,400	216
1868	4,266	4,387	121
1869	2,291	2,366	075
1870	7,544	7,917	373
Totals	38,648	43,301	4,653

Immigration of Chinese into Callao from January 1, to October 3, 1872

Arrived at Callao	Nationality of Ship	Name of Ship	Tons	Embarked in China	Died on voyage
January 20	French	*Mille Jonnes*	735	432	39
January 21	Peruvian	*Hong Kong*	458	314	8
January 24	Peruvian	*Providencia*	574	416	5
February 12	Peruvian	*Peru*	570	400	10
February 12	Peruvian	*Callao*	1,049	629	19
March 24	Peruvian	*Lola*	890	592	04
April 12	Peruvian	*Fray Bentos*	410	375	6
April 24	Portuguese	*Cecilia*	533	380	8
April 25	Peruvian	*Clotilde*	1,314	760	9
May 16	Dutch	*Johan den Villen*	494	260	13
May 17	Peruvian	*Lama Canevaro*	1,043	739	192
June 11	Portuguese	*Emigrante*	965	499	107
June 12	Peruvian	*Rosalin*	816	457	64
June 13	Peruvian	*America*	1,562	690	105
June 30	French	*Antares*	401	263	82
August 31	Peruvian	*Camilo Cavour*	854	650	57
Sept. 10	Peruvian	*Sara*	638	346	23
Sept. 12	Peruvian	*Hong Kong*	458	314	37
Sept. 16	French	*Canadienne*	853	507	19
Sept. 19	Peruvian	*J. Righam*	337	193	7
Sept. 22	Peruvian	*Callao*	1,049	695	10
Sept. 22	Peruvian	*Providencia*	574	422	10
Sept. 27	Peruvian	*Peru*	570	406	34
Sept. 28	Dutch	*Inrust*	836	453	45
Sept. 29	French	*Radama*	487	305	4
October 3	Peruvian	*Macao*	603	436	39[55]

As part of the China–Peru Treaty of 1874 it was agreed that if cases should be found of ill-treatment of Chinese immigrants, whose contracts had not expired, these could be put to local tribunals for consideration and even carried to higher courts of justice for further investigation. Cases with immigrants whose contracts had expired were dealt with under a separate clause; namely, where there had been a stipulation that the employer should send them back to China, the Peruvian government agreed to compel the employers to comply with their contract. In similar cases, where there had been no return stipulation, the Peruvian government promised to "cause them to be repatriated gratuitously in the ships which leave Peru for

China." With the ratification of this treaty, to which this special agreement was appended on August 7, 1875, the worst abuses of the unregulated Chinese contract labor came to an end.[56] Unfortunately, what percentage of all these Chinese emigrant workers ever got back to China, under these improved provisions, still remains decidedly unclear.

8

The Lobos Islands Adventure

SINCE 1841 THE UNITED STATES, GREAT BRITAIN, AND EUROPE HAD been heavy importers of Peruvian guano. In Britain the fertilizer was selling at £9.5s. and delivered to an American farm, it was costing $50 a ton.[1] In the early 1850s farmers and shipping interests on both continents thought this was too much and were becoming vociferous in their condemnation of the whole import system, which they felt made such high prices possible. Though all agreed these prices were exorbitant, there was apparently little that could be done about it, for since the African reserves had been rapidly depleted, in 1845, Peru was, once again, the only source of supply. What also rankled with the British farmer was the fact that the protectionist "Corn Laws" had just been repealed—in the interests of free trade—but against their perceived interests; yet now they were being subjected to exploitation by an anti-free-trade manure monopoly. They objected strongly to this political inconsistency. Prices of agricultural produce had been falling, and farmers were looking to the government for support.

Not surprisingly, Gibbs & Company and the Peruvian government were becoming increasingly unpopular with farmers and shippers alike, the latter still being in the grip of recession and anxious to obtain profitable employment for their ships. Both interest groups resented being so dependent on this tight monopoly. By 1852 they were in a mood to back any development that could break the Peruvian-Gibbs stranglehold on the guano market. However, short of persuading the government to declare war on Peru and taking over the Chincha Islands by force, there seemed little that could be done. There was, of course, no political support for such an ill-considered adventure, so there seemed only one other way forward, and that was the discovery and exploitation of other bird islands that fell outside, or at least appeared to fall outside, the legal jurisdiction of Peru. It was in this political context that two international spotlights fell on the Lobos Islands in 1852, the one in Britain being manipulated by an English country squire, Thomas Wentworth Buller, and the other by a somewhat obscure American mariner, Captain Jewett, the latter clearly taking his lead from the decidedly less obscure Wentworth Buller.

Thomas Wentworth Buller was the quintessential English country gentleman. A former naval officer and a governor of the Royal Agricultural Society, he was also wealthy, for he was the Lord of the Manor of Whimple, Strete, Raleigh, and Cobdon in Devon. A dedicated opponent of the free-trade policies advocated by such radicals as Messrs. Ricardo, Cobden, and Bright, whose collective views had led to the repeal of the protectionist Corn Laws, Buller had, many years earlier, written a challenge to Ricardo's advocacy of free trade in grain. His provocative role in this particular saga was to question the ownership of the Lobos Islands. The Lobos de Tierra group was actually just twelve miles from the coast of Peru, and Lobos de Afuera roughly forty miles distant. Like Captain Livingstone of Liverpool, Buller had read Benjamin Morrell's book, *A Narrative of Four Voyages*, which had led to the exploitation of the African guano islands, and from which Buller noted that the same intrepid mariner had visited the Lobos Islands in September 1832. Here he had seen vast guano deposits, sufficient to load a thousand ships. Excited by his "discovery" on April 18, 1852, Buller wrote to Palmerston, citing Morrell and mischievously suggesting that Peru could hardly have any legitimate claim over such a group of uninhabited desert islands, far out in the Pacific.[2] This was the second approach that Buller had made to the government about this issue. On this occasion, however, he also made his views public by writing to the editor of the *Times,* who promptly published his long letter. It began by stating: "There have been various accounts lately in the public papers relative to the discovery of guano upon some islands in the Pacific," and he continued, "Allow me, through the medium of your columns to put the public in possession of the facts relative to this discovery."[3] He then solemnly advised readers that Lobos de Afuera was 50 miles and Lobos de Tierra 20 miles from the coast of Peru, when in reality, most reports indicate that the former is 40 miles and the latter just 12 miles out in the Pacific. Notwithstanding this less than objective prolegomena, he continued by citing the relevant item from Morrell's book: "The Indians sometime visit these islands in large parties on fishing excursions or frolics; and frequently stay three or four weeks. I have always found them to be very civil and accommodating, having frequently received kind offices at their hands, such as presents of fruit, vegetables, &c., from the main. They always bring their fresh water with them in their catamarans, as there is none to be found in the islands, which are covered with sand, rocks, and the dung of aquatic birds; the latter sufficient to load thousands of ships, having been accumulating for untold ages. It is called 'guannar' by the Spaniards, and is probably the richest manure in the world."

Buller then advised the public that as he appreciated the value of such a discovery to the shipowners and agriculturists of Britain, he had at once applied to the government to take possession of the islands, and then, under the protection of the British flag, make the export of the guano free to all nations. With this objective in view, he assured readers that he had, by inquiry at the Foreign Office, ascertained that these islands had not been enumerated among the dependencies of Peru at the time that she had declared her independence and defined the extent of her territories. They were, Buller proclaimed, just desert islands, and no state had ever exercised dominion over them. In such circumstances, Buller proclaimed, international law decreed that "all mankind have an equal right to things which have not yet fallen into the possession of anyone; and those things belong to the person who first takes possession of them." It is clear that to the mind of Mr. T. Wentworth Buller, the continual visits of Peruvian Indians to these islands in no way constituted any recognizable form of "possession." On the other hand, the planting of a flag on these islands by the natives of a more technically advanced island—albeit, from the opposite side of the globe—would constitute a fair, legal territorial claim.

Nevertheless, after taking into account what he considered to be the best legal opinions of the day, Buller advised readers that in 1851 he had asked the government to plant the required flag on the Lobos Islands, but "got nothing but trouble at the Foreign Office." Buller then stated that "when the present extent of our empire in different parts of the world is considered, perhaps the disinclination to make even the smallest addition can scarcely be condemned. Suffice to say that I did not succeed." Finding it impossible to prevail on the imperial government to take possession of the islands, Buller, with characteristic British determination and grit, "determined to try what private enterprise might effect." By making inquiry in London, Buller then established contact with a shipowner who had for many years commanded a trading vessel in the Pacific, this being

Captain Lawson, the mariner who had visited the Lobos Islands, and while he had no knowledge about the nature or extent of the guano deposits, he spoke confidently about the excellence of the harbor, the rainless climate, and the large numbers of seafowl that inhabited the islands, thus, to an appreciable extent, confirming Morrell's story.

More importantly, however, Lawson had a vessel on the point of sailing for San Francisco, which, he promised Buller, he would order to touch at the Lobos Islands on her outward passage. Accordingly, on December 14, 1851, Captain Dixon, of the ship *Bombay*, wrote the following note to Lawson while he was at San Francisco: "Went to Lobos. The very thing I have said to you years before this. I think I could load a thousand ships as well as one, good anchorage. I think at one place I could load with a spout into the ship." At the same time he forwarded a sample of the guano taken from the island.

With this additional evidence Wentworth Buller had appealed to the government for support once more, and claims that he received an assurance that a ship of war would visit the islands. On a change in the Ministry, Buller then managed to obtain an interview with Lord Malmesbury, from which he hoped to obtain naval backing for his adventurous proposal, but at the time of writing, April 1852, he had to concede, "the matter was still under his Lordships consideration." In the meantime, it appears, several ships had already sailed for the Lobos Islands, due to the influence of, or acting under instructions from, the enterprising Captain Lawson, on which point Buller noted "that the Peruvian Minister is acquainted with the fact." With a merchant fleet already on the high seas bound for the Lobos Islands, Buller continued by acknowledging that the matter could no longer be kept a secret. Consequently, he felt obliged to put the whole issue before the public, in full confidence that the agriculturists and shipowners of Britain would not allow such a "glorious opportunity" to be lost, adding, to rally the fainthearted: "I fearlessly assert, that according to the law of nations the Peruvian Government can have no claim to these islands. On the other hand, the monopoly of guano now maintained by the Peruvian Government is injurious to the whole-civilized world, but especially injurious to the British farmer and British shipowner. I fearlessly assert, that according to the law of nations the Peruvian Government can have no claim on these islands." Then raising the banner of free trade aloft, which he and his fellow agriculturists had just been grudgingly forced to sail under, he added, "They must see that all idea of protection is abandoned. They must feel, that whoever may be Minister, they are equally doomed to suffer all the disadvantages of free trade. It will be their own fault if they do not obtain some of its advantages."

While Buller was writing to the *Times* over this issue, Robert Rankin, chairman of the powerful Liverpool Shipowners Association, had also been taking the question of the Lobos Islands up directly with the lords commissioners of the Admiralty. In a letter to them dated April 13, he asked if any instructions had been given to the Royal Navy regarding the protection of British ships loading at the "recently discovered" guano islands in the Pacific. Could our ships so loading rely on the protection of the government from "interference" by Peru or, for that matter, any other power claiming a territorial right to these islands? Then, to stress the urgency of the situation, he added, "I am informed that several members of this Association are engaged in sending out ships to load guano at the above island; and it is of the utmost importance that they should know their position and security as regards such trade."[4] The letter was replied to the following day by the secretary to the Admiralty, W. A .B. Hamilton, who advised Rankin that the admiral in the Pacific had orders to protect legal British commerce. However, no specific directions had been given with regard to vessels loading with guano, all of which hardly amounted to the open-ended support Robert Rankin was seeking.[5] On April 20 an even more anxious shipowner wrote to the foreign secretary, the Earl of Malmesbury, seeking support. This was, in fact, the rather impetuous Allan Edward, who had already sent his ships out to the Lobos Islands immediately after receiving information about the islands from Captain Lawson and before ascertaining the true status of the islands:

Dundee, April 20, 1852

My Lord,

In Consequence of information and encouragement which I received from Captain E. Lawson, I lately fitted out and dispatched some vessels for the island of Lobos Afuera, off the coast of Peru, to load guano for this country. A few days ago I was surprised to hear that the Peruvian Government through their Chargé d'Affairs in London, had laid claim to the island, and threatened to prevent any vessels taking guano therefrom.

Under these circumstances I take the liberty of appealing to your Lordship, and of inquiring if any vessels, in case of their being interfered with by the Peruvian Government, will receive the protection of the Government of this country; and whether any British ships of war have been, or will be dispatched for the safety of British vessels resorting to the aforesaid island?

May I beg the favor of an early answer to this communication, as the nature of the answer will greatly regulate me in the proceedings to be adopted for the security of my vessels.

I have, &c.
(Signed) Allan Edwards[6]

Needless to say, officials at the Peruvian legation in London had wasted no time in refuting the proposition put forward by Mr. T. Wentworth Buller, namely that the islands of Lobos de Tierra and Lobos de Fuera were desert islands and had never been claimed by any nation. In a strongly worded letter to the *Times,* published within days of Buller's provocative article, Emilio De Althaus, first attaché to the legation and vice-consul, made the position of his government crystal clear. This was, of course, to serve as a warning to all adventurers who might be tempted to proceed to these guano islands. He assured the public that the islands had not been "discovered" by Captain Morrell but had been known ever since the discovery of the west coast of South America by the Spaniards, and consequently were, and always had been, an integral part of Peru.

Here Althaus was careful not to mention that the Spaniards had, in turn, taken the islands, together with the entire land of Peru, from the indigenous Americans, as this would have rather undermined the moral and historical claim of ownership he was presenting. He did, however, make the point that the fishermen of Lambayoque had, from time immemorial, been accustomed to inhabit the islands. However, he added, for some years past the Peruvian government had prohibited their doing so, in consequence of their destroying thousands of birds and bringing away boatloads of eggs, which was disturbing the birds and thus preventing the accumulation of further deposits of valuable guano. This was the reason why the occasional visitor found the islands empty and deserted, and not because the islands were undiscovered or unclaimed. Althaus concluded by stating that these islands were part and parcel of the Republic of Peru. Consequently, any attempt to load at the islands, without a proper license, would lead to the immediate seizure of any such merchant vessel by Peruvian government ships appointed to cruise off and visit all the guano deposits.[7]

On April 21 Rankin decided to write another letter on the subject, this time to the prime minister, the Earl of Derby, in which he made the point that the Lobos Islands would be of great value to the nation. They would, in fact, afford a great deal of employment for the shipping industry; an industry, he added, that was still in the throes of a major depression. This was a simplistic argument that conveniently avoided making any mention of the interests of the City of London and the Peruvian bondholders who, having lent Peru large sums of money based on repayments being made from guano sold at a high price, had every reason to oppose such a price-cutting development. Rankin then continued by pursuing a more moderate line with Derby over the question of the sovereignty of the islands: "The Shipowners' Association feel confident that your Lordship will direct every step to be taken, consistent with the Law of Nations, to obtain the benefit of the discovery of those islands for this country, in common with other nations or, if they belong, as has been suggested, to Peru, then your Lordship will take into your immediate consideration the expediency of endeavoring to negotiate a treaty, under which this country may be enabled to avail itself, on the most favorable terms, of the guano on the islands."[8]

The day after this letter was written, the Earl of Malmesbury received another, but considerably longer, letter on the subject, this one being from Captain Andrew Snape Hamond, RN, who opened by apologizing for intruding upon his lordship's valuable time. He then went on to explain that his only reason for doing so was that he was very concerned about the line being pursued by Wentworth Buller. His fear was that if it was acted on, it could embroil them in a very unjustifiable act of aggression against a friendly power. In his mind there was no doubt whatsoever that the islands did belong to Peru, and, in fact, had never heard that a doubt was entertained on the subject until he read Wentworth Buller's letter in the *Times*.

Hamond then advised Malmesbury that the Lobos Inner and the Lobos Outer Islands formed two distinct groups off the coast of Peru, situated at the respective distances of ten and thirty five miles off shore, instead of the 20 miles and 50 miles, as stated by Wentworth Buller. Hamond then added that for many years the islands had been frequented by local Peruvians for the purpose of sealing, fishing, and removing the guano. These two island groups were among many similar groups off the coast of Peru. They clearly belonged to that nation, many of them, in fact, being as far off the coast as the Outer Lobos, facts that Mr. Wentworth Buller, an old stationer out there, should surely be aware of. Surely, Hamond argued, it would hardly be an act of justice on the part of such a powerful nation as our own to give any countenance to a proceeding that might lead to the most lamentable results? Hamond then went on to exemplify his arguments by recounting an event that had happened when he was left as senior officer on the coasts of Peru and Chile during the year of 1843.

It would seem that while Captain Hamond was lying at Valparaiso, he was given to understand that a Captain Fielding of the merchant ship *Vitula* had made his plan of action known to his fellow mariners at Valparaiso, namely, that he intended to take his vessel down to the Chincha Islands and load without clearance from the Peruvian authorities. In a conversation he happened to have with this most daring and reckless character, Hamond strongly advised Fielding against such action, but unfortunately this headstrong mariner ignored what was clearly sound advice.

After Fielding had done his utmost to induce other merchant captains, then in port, to follow his example, but without success, he armed his crew and set sail for the coast of Peru, eventually mooring off the Chincha Islands. Needless to say, word soon got through to the authorities at Pisco, the town opposite the islands, who wasted no time in taking steps to stop the actions of this adventurer. Arming three or four launches with guns and men, the Peruvians set off in the middle of the night and reached the islands before daybreak, without Fielding and his men being aware of their arrival. The armed party then made their way to the summit of the island and waited for Fielding's crew to commence loading the ship. Soon after they had arrived and started work, the Peruvians surrounded them, made prisoners of the whole crew, and then called upon the captain to surrender his ship. True to character, Fielding refused, and a desperate fight ensued in which he was badly wounded and made prisoner, together with the remainder of his crew, and the *Vitula* was taken possession of by the Peruvian officers. The case was subsequently tried before a tribunal at Lima, and the ship was condemned as a lawful prize. However, Captain Fielding and his crew, after undergoing a short imprisonment, were set free.[9]

Another even more relevant case concerning foreign vessels that called at Peruvian offshore islands without authority was also brought to the attention of British ministers in 1852 following the publication of the Wentworth Buller letter, this being the case of the 110–ton, Liverpool-owned brigantine, *Hibernia,* on which the owner's son, Mr. Henry Dempsey, was serving as supercargo. Originally fitted out with diving apparatus for getting pearls, which she unsuccessfully searched for near Panama, her master then died, and the mate, John Kennedy, assumed command. The ship then made her way down the west coast and, in November 1844, she was at Callao. On the 14th of the month, the *Hibernia* cleared out of this port, ostensibly on a fishing expedition, based on the port of Lambayeque. However, instead of proceeding there, she went directly to the Lobos Islands without having obtained permission to do so, where the ship arrived on November 19. She remained there until January 10, 1845. It was only then that Dempsey decided that they should make their way over to Lambayeque in order to obtain information and also to procure formal permission to go over to the Lobos Islands, having supposedly only just learned that it was necessary to do so. They had, it would seem, not actually been fishing as declared, but searching for the wreck of a Chilean vessel, the *Manuel*, which had recently been lost with specie on board on the Lobos de Afuera rocks.

However, once at Lambayeque, the required license was issued by the sub-prefect of the district, although it was well known that the vessel had already spent some time at the islands prior to applying for formal permission to go there. Dempsey and Kennedy then established contact with the owners of money that was lost in the wreck. The captain of the port then took on board a Peruvian customs officer and once more headed for the scene of the wreck, but once again failed to recover the lost specie. The *Hibernia* then made her way back to Lambayeque. Here the vessel was seized on the grounds of the master having altered the date of the clearance from Callao. This showed that he first arrived at Lambayeque and then went to the islands, which the Peruvians had forbidden because all guano on the coast was declared public property. The ship was then seized, and Dempsey, the captain, and some of the crew had to make their way to Callao, where the former had a protracted legal struggle to get his father's ship released. The point here is that fully seven years before Wentworth Buller had written his provocative and misleading letter, the *Hibernia* adventure provided irrefutable evidence that the islands were then under the jurisdiction of Peru, and British mariners were fully aware of that fact.[10] However, the public debate, initiated by the publication of Buller's letter, continued throughout the year of 1852.

Typical of the letters appearing in the press on the subject was one published in May, signed by an "Old Farmer" from Godstone, which is a village just to the south of London. Having read Buller's letter, this gentleman stated it gave great relief to his feelings for, if true, he understood there was a good chance he would soon be able to buy guano at just £5 a ton. Unfortunately, his hopes were soon dashed by a stockbroker who advised him that vested interests would take care to see that no cheap guano reached the market, for if the price received by the Peruvian government dropped, the Peruvian bondholders would get no dividends.[11]

On which point Mathew makes the very valid observation that "As for the Derby government of 1852, it was about the last that could be described as representative of some new, middle class order. The Cabinet comprised a duke, a marquees, four earls two barons, a baronet and four commoners, and many of them owned vast tracts of land. The average property in the Cabinet extending to about 35,000 acres."[12]

Nevertheless, the old farmer was not a lone voice crying in the agricultural wilderness of the home counties. The interrelated questions of a cheap supply of guano, Peru, the Chincha and Lobos Islands, the Gibbs guano contracts, and the Peruvian bondholders were now matters of national, and indeed international, concern. In Britain, the highest in the land were focusing their attention on the issues. In June a deputation of noblemen and gentlemen, representing a broad body of interests, met with the prime minister. Among organizations represented were the Royal Agricultural Society of England, the Highland Agricultural Society of Scotland, and many local associations concerned with the cultivation of the soil—and shipping enterprises. Their mission was to impress upon the government the great importance of using every possible means to obtain a cheap and abundant supply of guano. Among those present were the Duke of Richmond, the Duke of Buccleuch, Lord Berners, Sir James Graham, MP, Baron Goldsmid, Captain Stanley Carr, Professor Way, and Mr. Fellowes, MP.

The first to speak was none other than the ubiquitous Thomas Wentworth Buller who, while playing down his earlier, totally bullish line on the sovereignty of the Lobos Islands, still wondered if Britain could obtain guano from the "newly discovered" guano deposits on these islands at a cheaper rate. He looked to the government to at least take this opportunity to negotiate better terms and do away with the unacceptable guano monopoly situation. The Duke of Richmond presented a memorial from Banff signed by 870 "agriculturists." In this he stated that if they could get guano at £6 a ton, the present consumption would be doubled, both in England

and in Scotland, and for his own part he would use, with advantage, four times the quantity that he did at present.

The next to speak was a Mr. Hildyard, a lawyer acting on behalf of the shipping interests who took up the dubious line first raised by Buller. He argued (once more) that the Peruvian government had no legal title to the Lobos Islands. "The highest authorities," he assured all present, "could be quoted to support this view." Hildyard did not actually waste valuable time by quoting from the "high authorities" alluded to, but chose to press home his case by dwelling for some time on the fact that the Lobos Islands were uninhabited, and that their products were not the result of human industry! The obvious, but inconvenient fact that many small, uninhabited islands also lie off the coast of Britain, and this was not being used as a criteria by Peru to question British sovereignty over them, was tactfully ignored by Hildyard. He concluded his address by making an extremely radical observation, namely, that "materials" that were not the product of human labor should be freely available to mankind generally, a radical view that clearly had implications for the landed gentry present at this meeting, and therefore perhaps best left out of the argument.

The Earl of Derby, who spoke next, promptly poured cold water on Messrs. Buller and Hildyard by pointing out to the audience that the legal right of the Peruvian government over the "newly discovered" Lobos Islands had been finally settled by the opinions of former law officers of the Crown. They had, Derby continued, confirmed that as far back as 1834, the question was raised with respect to seal fishing and was referred to the late Sir Herbert Jonnor, who gave his strongest opinion that these islands did indeed belong to Peru. This nation had, in fact, for an unlimited period of time exercised sovereignty and jurisdiction over them. Consequently, the Peruviang Government had full right to prevent any seal fishing close to the islands. Derby then assured his distinguished audience that this legal opinion naturally applied to the guano issue as well. Therefore, he was afraid that he must deal with the question on the assumption that the Peruvian government had absolute sovereignty over these islands. He could, therefore, only treat the issue as one of monopoly.

On the question of price, Lord Derby continued by pointing out that Messrs. Gibbs' position was that of agents who received commissions and accounted for sales. They therefore had a vested interest in increasing sales, but there was another question involved, namely, that this firm had obtained loans for the Peruvian government on more favorable terms than they could otherwise have secured. For security, Antony Gibbs held the guano sent over, and consequently, without Messrs. Gibbs' consent, or that of the lenders, it was not, Derby argued, in the power of the Peruvians to reduce the price even if they were willing to do so. To the shipowners present he then added that the search for other guano islands would be "a very good employment for our cruisers." If any, in fact, could be obtained from another country, it might be used as a lever to put pressure on Peru and others to moderate their demands.[13] In fact, by 1852 a great global "Treasure Hunt" for guano was indeed already well under way. Merchants and mariners, eager to make a fortune, needed no prompting by Lord Derby to look for guano. This search was to take mariners to some of the most remote and inhospitable islands on the face on the planet.

Since the 1840s the United States had also been a heavy importer of guano, particularly in the upper south, where prodigal farming methods had been ruining the soil. Like their British counterparts, American farmers were pleased with the performance of guano, the new "wonder fertilizer," but less than happy about the price they were being charged. Delivered to an American farm, it had at one point cost $50 a ton, but as Peru was the only source of supply, and the English house of Antony Gibbs had exclusive distribution rights in America, it seemed there was little that could be done about the situation. At this point, however, word got through that the Gibbs' contract (circa 1841–42) to supply the United States was about to expire. An American firm then offered the Peruvian government a better price of $20 a ton, as they were confident that they could retail guano for less than the going price of $50 and still give themselves a fair return on their investment. However, the offer was refused in favor of one from Messrs. F. Barreda & Brother, a Spanish-Peruvian concern. As many Peruvian officials had an interest in this enterprise, it was therefore pointless to argue that the American bid had been much higher.

As all this would keep the price of guano up, when outspoken American farming interests had an interest in keeping prices down, the American secretary of state, Daniel Webster, began to take a keen interest in the guano issue. This was, however, only after he had been approached by an American mariner, Captain Jewett, a rather dubious character already playing a provocative role in this affair. Jewett first wrote, and then delivered by hand, a letter to Webster, in which he suggested that guano could be taken from the Lobos Islands by Americans. In this respect Jewett was, almost certainly, taking his lead from Captain T. Wentworth Buller, RN, for he was suggesting to Webster that Peru had no legal jurisdiction over the islands. The fact that the United States secretary of state was very ill at this time, and destined to die on October 24, may go some way to explain why he responded promptly and robustly to this unknown mariner's communication, clearly without considering the full implications of his oversupportive response. Webster at once declared that Peru had no title to the Lobos Islands, either by discovery or occupancy, but that our old friend Captain Morrell was their "probable" discoverer in 1823. This was despite the fact that Morrell had made it abundantly clear in his book that he found the islands were occupied by Peruvian "natives" when he arrived! Unmoved by this consideration, Webster said this obviously gave Americans the right to take guano as they pleased, adding, significantly, that the United States Navy would back them up!

It then became clear that Jewett had a partner, a New York speculator named Benson, who had for some time been anxious to make money from the guano bonanza. Heartened by the support of Webster, Benson promptly advertised in the newspapers for ships, and on the strength of Webster's supportive remarks, promised them full naval protection. Needless to say, these activities prompted the Peruvian minister in America to assure Webster that the Lobos Islands had been an integral part of Peru for centuries. Webster, at first, stood his ground, so Peru made preparations to defend the islands. It was then that John Randolph Clay, American minister to Peru, argued against Webster's position by showing that the islands had indeed been Peruvian since the days of the Incas. The highly embarrassed secretary then decided to admit, but only privately, that he had fallen for a scheming sea captain's tall stories, but by this time the damage was done. Lima was preparing for war, and an American merchant fleet was on the high seas, outward-bound for Cape Horn and the Lobos Islands.[14]

At the close of October 1852, the *New York Herald* picked up on this fascinating saga by advising readers that they had just received a report from the Lobos Islands, dated August 12, dispatched by the master of the American ship *Manlius* of Boston. The vessel had been sent out by its owners for the specific purpose of loading guano at the Lobos Islands. The voyage had, of course, been undertaken

8. Daniel Webster, U.S. Secretary of State. ***Illustrated London News,*** **November 13, 1852.**

on the strength of Daniel Webster's opinion, given some months previously, that the Peruvians had no jurisdiction over the Lobos Islands, and that consequently the mariners of all nations had a right to avail themselves—without payment—of that "wonderful deposit." Interestingly, it was then made clear that the *Manlius* did not belong to the fleet sent out from America by Messrs. Jewett and

Benson, which vessels, the editor felt, must now have reached the islands. Their fleet, it would appear, consisted of no less than twenty ships and was organized "in this grand commercial speculation" under private arrangements made with Webster. The venture also had the support of the secretary of war, who had sent out orders to Commodore M'Auley, directing him to cruise near the Lobos Islands and afford protection to American subjects that were there and engaged in the guano trade. Unfortunately for the *Manlius,* she clearly arrived before these preliminary guidelines were ratified. The captain of the *Manlius* then reported that he was ordered off the islands by a Peruvian brig of war. He then refused to obey such orders, as he was fortified by copies of the letters of Secretaries Webster and Graham, and consequently expected Commodore M'Auley to carry out his instructions and extend the promised protection to his ship. Unfortunately for the owners of the *Manlius,* and Messrs. Jewett and Benson this "protection" was never to arrive. It was at this point that the arguments contained in the official letters and documents presented by the Peruvian minister at Washington to the American secretary of state had the effect of undermining Webster's previously held position, thus compelling him to do a full-scale retreat. Having virtually recanted his previously held position on the Lobos Islands he followed this up by issuing a fresh series of orders to Commodore M'Auley, countermanding his original instructions and forbidding him to countenance any violation of the rights or laws of Peru by American citizens.

Reports, subsequently received across the Isthmus of Panama, that reached New York in October then indicated that the Peruvian government had acted swiftly by stationing a formidable force at the islands. It was therefore highly unlikely that any of the vessels that had sailed from New York under the directions or influence of Jewett and Benson would have been permitted to load. In any event, the dispute was resolved without bloodshed, largely through the statesmanship of John Randolph Clay, whose emphatic stand, clearly going way beyond his minor diplomatic brief, had shot the ground from under his superior's feet, but at the same time prevented war over the issue. At the most critical point in this saga, Clay asked an American naval vessel then in Callao harbor to proceed to the islands to stop American ships' crews from making trouble. Messrs. Jewett and Benson lost a considerable amount of money over the deal, but the Peruvian government was so relieved over the outcome that they agreed to foot the bill for the fraud that had influenced the American State Department. The owners of the ships chartered for this bold but unrewarding commercial enterprise were also paid for their lost time.[15] Both the handling and outcome of this issue did not please many Americans, all of which is reflected by the way the *New York Herald* concluded a long article on the subject:

> It will be seen that, owing to the dubious, hesitating, and pusillanimous conduct of our Administration, the guano speculators in the city, who anticipated such splendid results from the trade to the Lobos Islands, are doomed to sad disappointment. The Government here has shown itself too facile in according its own preconceptions in favor of the claim put forward by the Peruvian Minister to the exclusive right inherent in Peru over the disputed islands. Senor De Osma's letter to Mr. Webster put forward what he conceives to be incontestable evidence of this right. The Lobos Islands, he says, have been known to navigators since the time Pizarro conquered the empire of the Incas, and have been occupied and made use of both under the ancient and present regimes; and further adds, that not only were they the subject of express prohibition for the last 20 years, but in 1844 or 1845 an official survey was made of all the guano deposits within the territorial dominions of Peru, in which were comprised the Lobos Islands, the ownership of which had never been called in question by any nation. As a still more emphatic declaration, Senor De Osma avers that the title of Peru to the Lobos Islands is as plain and evident as that of the United States to Governor's Island.[16]

The Lobos Islands saga had been a revealing one, mainly because it had shown that by 1852 farmers in Britain and America had become, to some extent, dependent on guano, and looked to their respective governments to ensure that large quantities were available and at a reasonable price. The restraint shown by Lord Derby and his government, which was mainly composed of aristocratic landowners with a vested interest in obtaining this commodity cheaply, is also revealing. Here, though, one may assume, like the outspoken "Old Farmer," that the power and influence of the city and the bondholders' interests played their part in shaping the government's attitude toward Peru. However, although the power of the city and industry was growing at this point in time, it still did not outweigh the power of the landed gentry, unless we allow for the fact that surplus capital generated by large landowners found its way into the city; and surplus capital produced by city merchants was, almost always, invested in a country estate. The two power groups and their interests, therefore, to an appreciable extent, were not antagonistic, but interrelated.

Apart from the forgoing considerations, Derby's administration was a weak one. Early in 1852, the Russell ministry had been defeated on a militia bill and resigned, having held office for four years. It was only then that the Earl of Derby had formed a conservative ministry. Soon after the second Burmese war broke out, which occupied the attention of the imperial government throughout the year, until the British forces won and the province of Pegu was made an integral part of the British Empire.

Preoccupation with this venture in the East, where Britain was the dominant imperial power, may well have deterred Derby from engaging in a dispute on the west coast of South America, where Britain's power and influence rested, primarily, on the financiers of the City of London. Direct military or naval intervention in this part of the world would also have aroused concern in Washington, for America was, even then, becoming very involved in the commercial development of the area. In any event, the new House of Commons assembled in November, but although the government had abandoned Protection, it failed to secure a majority. It was defeated on the budget proposals and resigned in December 1852. Aberdeen then formed a new ministry that, among other things, was pledged to a free trade policy, and it was, one can reasonably assume, these varied considerations and political developments that prevented the relatively minor Lobos Islands dispute of 1852 from escalating into a major international confrontation. In America the secretary of state, Daniel Webster, who had initially favored intervention over this issue died on October 24, 1852, the short-lived Lobos Islands dispute being buried with him.

9

The Brocklebank Line and the Cape Horn South Pacific Traders

SEVERAL NINETEENTH-CENTURY LIVERPOOL SHIPPING ENTERPRISES regularly sent vessels around Cape Horn to Callao, a large percentage of which were involved, to a greater or lesser extent, in the guano trade. Among these in 1847 were Messrs. Rankin & Gilmour, Cotesworth Wynne, Imrie & Tomlinson and W & J. Tyrer & Company.[1] Collectively, these ships were known as the "Cape Horn South Pacific Traders." However, the old established House of Thomas & John Brocklebank first started trading to the west coast in 1821, and it was their ship, the aptly named *Bonanza,* that was responsible for bringing the first commercial load of Peruvian guano back to England in 1841. This enterprise traded their small wooden ships to many parts of the world, but the South Pacific trade featured prominently in their operational strategy, and it therefore requires a special mention in this history of Peru and the Chincha Islands. Several of their mariners, notably Captains Ray, Anderson, and Ellery, also left interesting accounts of their experiences at sea, with the former making a special mention of his involvement with the Peruvians and William R. Grace on the Chincha Islands. These memoirs also give us a unique insight into the life of these nineteenth-century mariners in their diminutive wooden sailing ships.

The long and romantic story of the Brocklebank line of Whitehaven and Liverpool begins in the reign of Queen Anne, when the Reverend Daniel Brocklebank, father of the founder of the line was born in Cumberland in 1705. In 1734 young Daniel Brocklebank married Sarah Slack at Ireby, and it was one of their children, Daniel Jr., born in 1741, who founded the line. Placed as an apprentice carpenter to a shipbuilder at Whitehaven when he was fourteen years old, he remained in this port for the next fourteen years as a single man. Then, at the age of twenty-eight, he married a Miss Anne Cuppage. The young couple remained at Whitehaven for another year before seeking their fortune in the New World. This was in 1770 when Daniel and Anne set sail for America, the aim being to establish a shipbuilding yard at a place called Sheepscutt, New England, where, over the course of the next five years, Daniel built five ships, the last of which was the *Castor.* The timing of their move to America was intriguing, for as Daniel Brocklebank must have been aware, events in America were drifting inevitably toward war owing to the resentment on the part of the colonists against the taxes imposed on them by the British government. The famous Boston Tea Party occurred in 1773, and in 1775 hostilities broke out at Lexington. On May 8, 1775, Daniel Brocklebank, who remained loyal to Britain, decided to get out while the getting was good, so he assumed command of the near completed *Castor,* and set sail for Whitehaven, where he soon arrived safely with his young family.

Back in Cumberland Daniel Brocklebank then applied to King George III for his official license to become an accredited privateer and his "Letters of Marque" were granted in August 1779, which authorized him to "seize and destroy the ships, depots and goods belonging to the King of Spain." Armed with this useful document and with no less than twenty-six guns aboard the *Castor,* Brocklebank entered a new, more robust phase of his career. He appears to have done quite well out of this dangerous venture, for he was soon able to place an order for another ship with a local builder, prior to establishing his own building yard at Whitehaven. Daniel died in 1801, and it was his two bachelor sons, Thomas Brocklebank (1776–1845) and John Brocklebank (1779–1831) who gave their name to this fast-developing shipping and shipbuilding enterprise. Daniel's fourth child, Anne (1777–1830), married Captain Wilson Fisher, and it was their son Thomas (1814–1906) who, after being obliged to assume the name Brocklebank, continued the business, and in 1845 he became the first baronet.[2]

From 1815 to 1845 the number of vessels owned by the Brocklebank Line steadily increased, as did the departures from Liverpool. In 1831, ten years before the Peruvian guano trade was established, the firm was trading five ships to India. These included the famous 514-ton *Princess Charlotte.* Eight ships were being traded to Brazil and Argentina, the largest of which was the 320-ton *Balfour.* The *Affleck, Tampico, Dash, Buoyant,* and *Jamaica* were sailing to the West Indies, the *London* to New Orleans, and the following vessels to Chile and Peru:

Ship	Tonnage	Rig	Age
Bonanza	176	Schooner	1 year
Maypo	173	Barque	2 years
Esk	217	Barque	3 years
Oberon	150	Brig	4 years
Courier	142	Schooner	5 years
Globe	212	Brig	9 years
Swallow	141	Brig	9 years
Ariel	154	Brig	11 years[3]

The remarkable 176-ton schooner *Bonanza,* which initiated the Peruvian guano trade, was built by Thomas & John Brocklebank at Whitehaven in 1830; she was just 85 ft. 6 ins. in length, with a 21-ft. 8-inch. beam, and was 13 ft. 2 ins. deep.[4] She was mostly employed in the South American trade, her first voyage being in 1830 to Vera Cruz under the command of Captain Storrs. Her most notable voyage was the one in 1841 to Callao and the Chincha Islands,[5] but her longest voyages were undoubtedly made between April 14, 1846, and April 20, 1849, when she was commanded by Captain Mossop, with Francis Wise acting as his first mate. Then rigged as a brig, the first of these voyages were, briefly: Liverpool to Callao 102 days; at Callao 16 days; Callao to Hong Kong 100 days; Hong Kong to Shanghai 30 days; at Shanghai 59 days; and Shanghai to Liverpool 91 days. The total number of days spent on this epic voyage was 398, or just over fourteen months.[6]

Two other well-known Brocklebank ships engaged in the Cape Horn South Pacific trade were the *Rimac* and the *Kestrel* the former being a 214-ton brig built by Thomas & John Brocklebank at Whitehaven in 1834. A Cape Horn trader for many years, Francis Wise was her master from 1855–58, during which time William Ray served as one of his apprentices before becoming a master, then marine superintendent, of the company. This ship was in service for thirty years, being sold in 1864, then wrecked while under the command of her last owner/master, Captain W. Heron of Liverpool. This disaster took place on December 12, 1874, when Captain Heron was off the English coast near South Somercoates.[7]

The *Kestrel* was a 231-ton brig, built by the firm at Whitehaven in 1840. In service for twenty-three years, she was mainly employed on voyages to Callao, the Chincha Islands, and Iquique. Abraham Vaux Wise Jr., joined this ship as first mate to Captain Farrell in June

1840. The ship arrived at Callao on September 6, 1841, with a crew of twelve and carrying a cargo of general merchandise. She remained in port until October 20, when she set sail in ballast for the Chincha Islands, returning to Callao for clearance on December 14.[8] This was a typical sailing schedule for small vessels then employed in the west coast trade. Abraham was born on June 26, 1812, and became master of the *Kestrel* in November 1841. He died at sea while in command of this ship on January 17, 1855. In all, he rounded Cape Horn some thirty times. Abraham's most notable officer on this ship was James Anderson, later Captain Sir James Anderson, who left us a brief but interesting insight into his own early life and his experiences at sea on Cumberland-built Cape Horn South Pacific traders.

Born in Dumfries, Scotland, on June 4, 1824, James Anderson was the fifth son of the late Mr. John Anderson, bookseller and founder of a well-known library in the town. After leaving the Dumfries Academy, where he received an excellent education, at the age of fifteen he was apprenticed to the printing trade under a Mr. Craw of the *Dumfries Herald.* Finding the work extremely boring, Anderson and a fellow apprentice, John Hamilton, decided to run away to sea, and promptly made their way to Portsmouth. Their plans, however, were discovered. An enforced spell ashore was then put into force by their concerned parents. In fact, Hamilton stayed ashore for the rest of his life, returning to journalism and becoming the first editor of the *London Morning Star.* Young James Anderson, however, was so clearly set on a life at sea that his parents at last gave way. In 1840 he made his way to Whitehaven, on the south banks of the Solway Firth, and entered the service of Thomas & John Brocklebank, being bound apprentice in the *London,* one of the finest vessels owned at that time by the firm.[10]

The *London* was a 351-ton ship that carried ten guns for protection. Built at Whitehaven in 1820 by Thomas & John Brocklebank, she was to remain afloat for forty-three years, thirty-five of these years being in the service of Messrs. Brocklebank. At first she made voyages to the West Indies under the command of Captain Frazer. Later she was engaged in voyages to Honduras under the command of Captain Kerr. In 1820 Captain Robert Wise took her to Savannah. She was then commanded by Captains Brown, Johnson, and McLean, and traded mainly to the Southern states of America until 1834, when McLean took her to Calcutta, and she was to remain in that trade for the remainder of her Brocklebank service.[11] In 1840

9. Sir Thomas Brocklebank (1814–1906). W. Burnett Tracy. *Lancashire at the Opening of the Twentieth Century.* 1903.

Captain Joseph Benn was given command of the ship, and one of his young apprentices on this voyage was James Anderson of Dumfries, Scotland.

In later life Sir James always spoke with kindness and affection about Joe Benn of Whitehaven, whom he described as a genial old skipper. From him James Anderson learned the rudiments of navigation as they steered the old brig from the River Mersey to the Bay of Bengal. On the third voyage Captain Benn was so unwell as to be unfit for duty and, as he seemed to have had confidence in Anderson and another young apprentice, but not his officers, the two youths, rather than the older hands, were entrusted with the navigation of the ship. What the "older hands" actually thought about this arrangement is not on record, but one can well imagine their concern! However, after serving his time, James Anderson was then fortunate enough to get a berth as second mate aboard the *Horsburgh* under John Smith, a skipper who had the reputation of being an excellent sailor. This vessel was a 320-ton barque built by Brocklebank's in 1838, and employed by them in the South Pacific trade.[12] James Anderson joined the ship when Captain Smith was taking her to Callao, this being about 1845. Smith's estimate of his second mate is notable: "I never had an unpleasant word with him, never saw him in a passion, never heard him 'damn the eyes' of man or boy. An oath, I do believe, never passed his lips, there wasn't a bit of the bully in his composition, and yet, youth though he was, there was in his manner and voice which, when he gave orders, made every man jump to his work, feeling them to be orders of one who meant to be obeyed."

From the *Horsburgh* Anderson was appointed first mate to Captain Abraham Vaux Wise on the *Kestrel,* and his experience as a navigator and his courage in storms were put to the test time after time in the voyages he made round Cape Horn with Abraham. Apart from the rigors of a life at sea, one is still left wondering how these long ten-month voyages showed a profit to shipowners, with vessels that could only carry a few hundred tons of cargo, out and back, to the west coast of South America. This was, on reflection, only possible because the remuneration received by crews was exceptionally poor. Nevertheless, there are indications that mariners enjoyed working for the Brocklebank family, finding them good employers. There can, however, be no doubt that pay and conditions, notably for ordinary seamen and apprentices, were far from satisfactory. On the question of pay and conditions, it should also be noted that vessels such as the *Kestrel* would carry a crew of about thirteen, including the master, but five of these would be apprentices, such as James Anderson, who were paid just £20 for four years' service. Thus, James Anderson, who was bound for four years at the age of seventeen on July 10, 1840, received £4 for his first year, £5 for the second and third years, and £6 for his final year. By error he was actually paid

£20.7.3, but this overpayment was later corrected by deducting 7s. 3d. from his wages when he was serving as a seaman.[13] Apart from learning the skills of a mariner, these youngsters did the work of able seaman for about £4 per voyage. A typical crew list and wage bill for one of these voyages is given below.

Voyage of the *Kestrel* from Liverpool to Lima, July 16, 1842 to May 27, 1843

Name	Age		Total Wages
Abraham Wise	30	Master	£100
James Chester	24	First Mate	55
George Raymond	22	Second Mate	40
Anthony Mossop	23	Carpenter	45
Thomas Guthridge	42	Steward	27
Peter Kent	33	Cook	24
George Mitchell	23	Seaman	20
Arthur Smith	35	Seaman	20
Hugh Grange	19	Apprentice	4
Thomas Fairclough	19	Apprentice	4
James Bower	17	Apprentice	4
William Duncan	15	Apprentice	4
Thomas Truck	15	Apprentice	4
Total (estimated) wages for voyage			£351[14]

After serving with Abraham Vaux Wise on the *Kestrel,* James Anderson was appointed captain of the *Aliwal,* which sailed from London to Port Natal with emigrants, but no sooner had he weighed anchor than cholera broke out on board. Fortunately he managed to keep the scourge under control until he reached port. For two years Anderson traded between Mauritius, Singapore, China, and the Persian Gulf until he realized that his future lay in steam, not with sailing ships. In 1851 he entered the service of the Cunard Company. In practice this virtually meant beginning all over again on the lowest rung of the ladder, as third officer on board one of their liners,[15] but in the same year he took his "Extra Masters Certificate" at Liverpool, which ensured that his promotion was rapid. After serving as mate on three ships in 1855, he was appointed commander of the *Melita;* he then commanded in turn the *Cambria, Niagara, Africa, Etna, Canada, Europa, China, Australasian, Asia,* and *Arabia.*[16] Then, in 1865, Captain Anderson took command of

Brunel's greatest creation, the *Great Eastern*, with which the Atlantic cable was eventually laid, linking the "Old World" with the "New," for which service James Anderson was knighted. All of this, however, is another long, but interesting story, and far removed from his life as a Cape Horn South Pacific trader on board the *Kestrel.*

Meanwhile, the diminutive wooden sailing ships of the Brocklebank Line continued to force their way around Cape Horn bound for Chile and Peru. The Brocklebank involvement in this trade was notable, a point that is illustrated by the fact that during the years 1854 to 1857, no fewer than forty-nine sailings were made under their house flag from Liverpool for Valparaiso and Callao, and a large percentage of the latter obtained a return cargo of guano from the Chincha Islands. Here, though, one must acknowledge that although these voyages represented a large proportion of Brocklebank sailings, in total they would only have been responsible for moving a very small percentage of the guano exported from Peru during these years. Nevertheless, profits made in the Cape Horn trade were used to finance the development of their East India trade, for which the firm built some exceptional vessels. However, the details of Brocklebank South Pacific voyages for this three-year period are notable:

Ship	Master	Crew	Sailed	Bound for
Horsburgh	H. Mounsey	15	2/2/1854	Callao
Dryad	R. Barnes	14	26/2/1854	Callao
Bonanza	A. Penrice	10	19/3/1854	Callao
Callao	G. Fletcher	10	12/4/1854	Callao
Kestrel	A. V. Wise	13	28/6/1854	Callao
Globe	C. Mossop	13	20/7/1854	Valparaiso
Camana	P. Smith	10	30/8/1854	Callao
Mindanao	J. Ponsonby	22	9/9/1854	Valparaiso
Courier	F. Wise	9	22/9/1854	Lima
Rimac	Fearon*	13	13/10/1854	Callao
Valparaiso	J. Joughlin	15	9/11/1854	Valparaiso
Lanercost	J. Tully	10	30/12/1854	Lima
Dryad	J. Chambers	13	9/1/1855	Lima
Horsburgh	H. Mounsey	15	21/1/1855	Valparaiso
Sir Henry Pottinger	R. Barnes	16	8/2/1855	Lima
Bonanza	A. Penrice	10	4/3/1855	Callao
Petchelee	Overend	17	30/3/1855	Callao
Callao	G. Fletcher	11	4/4/1855	Callao
Lord Althorp	W. Ronald	13	4/4/1855	Lima

(*continued*)

Ship	Master	Crew	Sailed	Bound for
Globe	J. Jordan	13	18/5/1855	Callao
Kestrel	P. Bowman	13	2/6/1855	Callao
Patriot King	Osborne	17	22/6/1855	Lima
Camana	P. Smith	11	30/8/1855	Callao
Earl Grey	E. Curwen	?	14/9/1855	Valparaiso
Courier	J. Candlish	9	17/10/1855	Callao
Rimac	F. Wise*	12	16/11/1855	Lima
Dryad	J. Chambers	13	10/1/1856	Valparaiso
Lanercost	T. Tully	12	12/1/1856	Callao
Sir Henry Pottinger	R. Barnes	16	18/2/1856	Callao
Petchelee	J. Overend	17	27/4/1856	Callao
Lord Althorp	W. Ronald	13	12/5/1856	Valparaiso
Callao	N. Paul	10	13/5/1856	Lima
Kestrel	P. Bowman	13	7/7/1856	Lima
Patriot King	P. Smith	17	11/7/1856	Valparaiso
Valparaiso	E. Curwen	15	30/8/56	Lima
Mindanao	J. Ponsonby	20	13/9/1856	Valparaiso
Globe	A. Penrice	13	15/10/1856	Callao
Earl Grey	W. Bell		9/11/1856	Valparaiso
Rimac	F. Wise*	13	14/12/1856	Lima
Callao	W. Pole	11	27/2/1857	Lima
Dryad	J. Chambers	13	22/3/1857	Valparaiso
Lanercost	Tully	15	14/4/1857	Callao
Sir Henry Pottinger	R. Barnes	16	15/5/1857	Valparaiso
Kestrel	P. Bowman	13	21/5/1857	Callao
Patriot King	Lowden	17	28/7/1857	Valparaiso
Camana	J. Jordan	11	8/8/1857	Callao
Valparaiso	E. Curwen	15	20/9/1857	Lima
Rimac	F. Wise*	14	18/11/1857	Callao
Globe	A. Penrice	13	11/12/1857	Callao

* William Ray serving as an apprentice on these voyages of the *Rimac.*[17]

William Ray was born at Hensingham, a small village to the south of Whitehaven, Cumberland, on August 31, 1839. Educated at the famous St. Bee's School, when still very young William Ray decided that he was going to become a mariner. Accordingly, he went south to Liverpool, made his way to the offices of Thomas & John Brocklebank, and on October 11, 1854, he signed the appropriate documents and was bound apprentice for five years. He then reported to Captain Thomas Fearon, then master of the *Rimac,* and the following day he left the Mersey on this small vessel bound for Cape Horn and Callao. Fearon, who came from Whitehaven, had served as master of the *Bonanza* in 1852,[18] and was now making his second voyage on this ship. His first mate for this long voyage was Alfred Sargent of Falmouth, an experienced mariner who, at this point in his career, had been at sea for over nine years. The second mate, John Leech of Norfolk, then age twenty, had just completed his apprenticeship on the Brocklebank Indiaman *Hindoo,* a barque of 266 tons that had been traded to the Far East since she was built in 1831. David Brand, from Aberdeen, also twenty years of age, had just completed a voyage on the Liverpool ship *Triton;* the Brocklebank clerk noted against his name in the company records, "A stranger in our employ—shipped at the Sailor's Home." Also serving with Ray was a fellow apprentice, E. McKinna, from Creetown, the same clerk writing against this youngster's name "Drunk and Disorderly at the Sailor's Home."[19]

The *Rimac* then made her way down the Atlantic until the first albatrosses would have been seen, probably somewhere around the latitude of the River Plate, and Captain Fearon and the crew of the *Rimac* would all have been aware that bad weather was not far distant. The temperature would then have dropped rapidly, as the ship sailed south, and Fearon would have insisted on all his crew keeping a sharp lookout for drift ice, even before they reached latitude 50 south by the Falkland Islands. Some of the drift ice in these waters can be of an incredible size, as much as fifty miles long, and broken-off icebergs, carried by wind and current, could be met as far north as the latitude of Buenos Aires. Cape Horners, such as the *Rimac,* usually sailed west of the Falklands, keeping close to the land where, with luck, a more favorable wind would often be located.

When south of the Falklands mariners knew that the wind frequently hauled around to the southwest so that a ship could make headway taking it on her starboard beam. As soon as they reached Staten Island, however, experienced mariners knew that any attempt to make westing was invariably met with a strong headwind. Statistics also show that winds in this area hardly ever blow at less than forty-five miles per hour for twenty-two days out of thirty, and for five days out of seven they blow from the west. The mountainous seas in this area also have the temperature of melting ice, which meant that any sailor or apprentice that fell from the rigging into the water was inevitably doomed to a watery grave. In addition to this, the air temperature in winter often falls to thirty below. Nevertheless, men and boys would still have to man the rigging, if "Cape Stiff," as the mariners called it, was to be rounded. Quite amazingly, however, the Brocklebank sailing schedules clearly indicate that sailing around the Cape continued throughout the year, with no attempt whatsoever being made to adjust departures to seasons. Interestingly, the Brocklebank Company, in common with most shipping enterprises of the day, would give their masters "Sailing Instructions." The French firm of A. D. Bordes produced notable ones for their commanders in the South Pacific Cape Horn trade: "The weather round Cape Horn is nearly always bad, even in summer. The winds blow almost continually from the west, and although the gales do not last so long in summer as in winter, they are more frequent and stronger. On the other hand, the winds are more variable in winter, the cold is more bitter and the hours of daylight are much reduced—lasting at most from nine to three—and there is mist and snow to make things worse. In short, navigation is nowhere more difficult than in these waters."[20]

Cape Horn is actually situated some 180 miles southwest of Staten Island; 57 miles farther to the southwest is the isolated Diego Ramirez Island; and 45 miles northwest of that are the treacherous rocks of Ildefonso. Here sailing ships often spent four or five weeks beating about in the open seas, considering themselves to be extremely lucky if they made fifty miles in a day, but it was often only five or ten, and on numerous occasions unfortunate mariners would lose hard-won ground. In the days of the small three-masted wooden ships, such as the *Rimac,* a captain could more easily pass through the Straits of Le Maire, where the seas would be calmer. This, however, was not a viable option to the masters of the big four-masted barques or the American "Down Easters," as they were not as easy to maneuver, so they tended to go eastward of Staten Island and beat about in the open sea south of Cape Horn. Here the crews were constantly on call, as no opportunity could be lost to trim the sails and beat into the wind.

Here, as noted, a ship could often spend many weeks beating about in the open sea south of the Horn, which would leave crews sick and exhausted. Whenever there came the slightest improvement in the weather, the crew would be obliged to make more sail; consequently they never bothered to undress when they came off watch, merely taking off their seaboots, tumbling into their bunks, and falling asleep in the damp, cold atmosphere, all of which explains why few seamen above the age of thirty-nine are listed on the crew lists of these Cape Horn traders. Conditions were, in fact, horrific, for the great westerlies that met the ships off the Cape often produced waves 50 to 60 feet high, known by the Cape Horn crews as "Greybeards." The force of these monsters flung against the ship was calculated to be the equivalent of 20–30 tons for each square yard of impact. When the wind reached 45 miles an hour, the pressure it exerted against a four-masted barque, under reduced canvas, was estimated to be 100 tons a second. The fight to round this dreaded Cape actually began well before ships reached it. The reason for this was that most of the sailing vessels chose not to chance a passage through one of the straits but moved down from the latitude of 45 south in the Atlantic, this being way past the Horn, then up to 45 south in the Pacific—a distance of about 1,300 miles, and it was a relentless struggle all the way.[21]

Such were the conditions that faced young William Ray on his first voyage around Cape Horn in 1854. Interestingly, though, when he was writing about this event sixty-seven years later in 1921, he initially makes no mention of the harsh climatic conditions, but complains bitterly about the captain, who he considered to be a rather tightfisted tyrant! "On my first voyage I was drafted as an apprentice in a little wooden vessel called the *Rimac,* of 212 tons register, carrying a cargo of about 340 tons weight, and trading round Cape Horn. My first voyage in the *Rimac* was under the command of a master who was the most tyrannical and selfish individual you could possibly imagine, and although the instructions from the owners was that the people on board should always have a sufficiency of good food without waste, he, in his position of master of the ship, took no notice of this instruction, and seemed to take a delight in apportioning as little as possible, and the consequence was a most unhappy voyage."[22] It is, however, gratifying to note that Ray makes no mention of any really brutal treatment of the crew, by either Captain Fearon or his officers. Such behavior, however, was common practice in those days on American Cape Horners, as recorded by Basil Lubbock, with characteristic relish when quoting the utterances of American masters and mates in the Cape Horn trade:

> You know a man has to be rough going deep-water. When you get a tough or weak or know-nothing crowd for'ard, as sometimes happens, you have to handle them rough or you'd never get the ship's work done" was the general opinion from the mates' side of the deck. And American captains and mates even went so far as to study the various methods of "taming"

> a man, but, thoughtfully, without rendering him unfit for duty. "Never strike a man near the temple, especially with an iron belaying-pin or a hand spike; and when you have him down, kick him in the legs or above the short ribs. It's altogether unnecessary to disable a man, and unwise with a short crew." The opinion of a "shellback"—that is a seaman, on board one of these ships, about such behavior, being "I'd rather be in hell without claws than aboard a Yankee ship with the mates down on me."[23]

Despite problems with Captain Fearon, William Ray survived his first voyage round Cape Horn in the *Rimac,* and on November 15, 1855, set sail once more in this ship for Callao, via Leith, but under a different master, this being Captain Francis Wise of Cumberland, then aged thirty. Francis Wise had, since serving on the *Bonanza,* acted as first mate on the *Sir Henry Pottinger, Aden,* and *Arachne* on voyages to Calcutta and Hong Kong.[24] His previous voyage, though, had been as master of the Brocklebank Cape Horner *Courier,* a vessel of just 135 tons register. On this voyage his first mate had been Michael King of Whitehaven, age 22, the oldest member of the crew being an illiterate seaman, George Williams from Cheshire, age thirty-six, who had just completed a voyage on the ship *Catherine.*[25] On this voyage of the *Rimac* Alfred Sergeant remained on board as the first mate. The oldest seaman on board was James Day, age thirty-three, from New Jersey; the cook was John Phillips, an "old man" of thirty-six, who had been born in Bombay. Serving with William Ray as an apprentice was Mark Ridley, whose date of indenture was November 15, 1855, the day when the *Rimac* sailed down the Mersey bound for Leith, and then on to Callao.

William Ray seemed pleased to be serving with Francis Wise, whom he generously described as a fine shipmaster who was the most gentlemanly and courteous man that he ever came across in his career. According to Ray, Francis Wise "revolutionized" the state of things on board the *Rimac.* In common with all other Brocklebank masters, and the British merchant marine masters in general, Francis Wise found it quite possible to get his ship around Cape Horn, and to all other destinations for that matter, without beating and kicking his crew. In fact, according to Ray, Francis Wise seemed to get a great deal of pleasure from making everyone as comfortable as he knew how, or circumstances would allow. William Ray was to make three voyages around Cape Horn with Francis Wise, during which they all had to meet the same weather as on the first voyage in navigating that stormy part of the world, which brought exposure to the elements, when they were often cold, wet, and miserable. Despite all of this, Ray stated that these voyages were, nevertheless, very happy ones, in spite of the rigors of the climate.

William Ray then recalled an interesting episode on the Chincha Islands while on what he later thought might have been his third voyage, but which, for reasons that will become clear, was his second voyage. The first mate apparently sent William Ray and another apprentice named George to bring back Captain Wise, who had gone ashore on business, back to the ship for his midday meal. George made his way to the store on the main Chincha island, which was then kept by William R. Grace, an Irish emigrant who was destined to play a major role in the development of Peru. Later in his career Grace became mayor of New York and established a multinational company about which much more mention will be made. At this point in time, however, Ray recalled that there was a captain of the port at the Chincha Islands—a Peruvian official—and also a man-of-war in the harbor, a sort of guardship placed there for the maintenance of order. While George was at Grace's store, William Ray remained in the boat, and as he was waiting for George and Francis Wise to return, a boat belonging to the Peruvian man-of-war came alongside the *Rimac*'s boat. In the course of a minute or two the captain of the port and the captain of the man-of-war walked down the jetty and took up their positions in the stern of the boat. They were in full regimental dress and obviously returning to their man-of-war for their midday meal.

When the Peruvian boat shoved off from the jetty, the sailor in the bow of the boat had a boat hook, and instead of putting this in the jetty, this seaman had the cheek to stick his hook into the bottom of the *Rimac*'s boat. Ray, who was sitting in the stern of the boat waiting for Francis Wise to return, felt that this was too much, considered it to be an insult, and decided to retaliate. Notwithstanding the fact that men had recently been tortured or put to death on the Chincha Islands for the most trivial reasons—and Ray must have been aware of this—the proud, high-spirited young apprentice brought a tiller down on the boat hook handle and smashed it. A Peruvian boatman at once retaliated by smashing Ray over the shoulder with an oar, and Ray fought back by cracking one of the Peruvians over the head and pushing him into the water.

Before William Ray realized what was happening, the Peruvian coxswain gave orders to the rest of the boat's crew—about eight of them—to arrest Ray. Needless to say, the young lad was soon overpowered and dragged onto the jetty, where he continued to struggle but was eventually forced to march up the jetty between two "gendarmes" and taken to the jail. This was a simple structure, without a roof, but because of this unusual deficiency for a jail, it was furnished with two lines of stocks, and into one set of these medieval devices, Ray was promptly secured. Alongside William was a Frenchman, the boson of a ship then at the Islands who had tried to desert from her. This sailor spoke a little English, and William learned from him that prisoners were not actually fed by their captors, and if their shipmates did not bring any food, they would starve to death. Fortunately, the first mate of the *Rimac* turned up at 4:00 PM with a good supply of food, and Ray survived. It was, no doubt, even more fortunate for William Ray that Kossuth no longer reigned on the island, otherwise he might not have survived to tell the tale.

Next morning a deputation went to the captain of the port on Ray's behalf, the result being that he was taken out of the stocks and released. The captain of the port then kindly explained to the proud young apprentice that he had been put under arrest because of the insult he had offered to himself and the captain of the man-of-war, not because of the injury he had done to the seaman. Ray later conceded that his release was secured by the solicitations of a gentleman called Forbes, a Scotsman who was building a jetty for the government on the Middle Island, William R. Grace, owner of the store, and Captain Francis Wise. Later in his story of the Chincha Islands, William Ray stated that the acquaintance he then made with William Grace lasted for the rest of his life, and that afterward, when he was first mate on the *Rimac* and found himself in a very difficult position, William Grace was of very great assistance to him.

When William Ray wrote these memoirs in 1921 he was eighty-two years old and clearly working from memory rather than notes, which will, no doubt, explain certain interesting anomalies and omissions. According to the crew list for his second voyage, his fellow apprentice was Mark Ridley, and on his third voyage on the *Rimac,* which left the Mersey in December 1856, William Ray, then age seventeen, sailed as a seaman, not as an apprentice. For this voyage he was paid ten shillings for ten months' work. The two apprentices on board the *Rimac* for this voyage were Patrick McKenna and Joseph Lawson, "George" not being listed, all of which would indicate that William Ray was being punished for upsetting the Peruvians on his second voyage. Perhaps understandably, Ray makes no mention of his spell as an ordinary seaman, when he was, no doubt, hanging on to his career by the skin of his teeth! It is certain that Francis Wise would have felt obliged to report an incident that could have damaged company interests, if not British relations with Peru. One suspects, however, that Thomas Brocklebank would have been both concerned and, on the quiet, amused. Demotion for a year seemed an obvious response for such an incident. The crew list for this voyage is as listed below.

Voyage of the Rimac, Captain Francis Wise, Liverpool to Lima, December 8, 1856.

Crew member	Age	Last ship	Capacity	Wage
John Roat	24	*Imperador*	Mate	£6. 0. 0
J. Leech	24	*Rimac*	2nd Mate	£4.10.0
W. Simpson	22	*Sea Horse*	Carpenter	£5.05. 0
William Bravo	26	*Beirout*	Steward	£3.05.0
John Laidlow	40	*Patriot King*	Cook	£3. 0. 0
Philip Gome	30	*Sarah Jane*	Seaman	£2. 15.0
William Walton	32	*Hastings*	Seaman	£2. 15.0
Richard Kennedy	29	*Lizzy*	Seaman	£2. 15.0
William Ray	17	*Rimac*	Seaman	£0 10 .0
William Woods	21	*Baines*	Seaman	£2. 15.0

Apprentices on board	Date of Indenture
Patrick McKenna	3rd May 1854
Joseph Lawson	23rd December 1854[26]

William Ray sailed with Francis Wise on the *Rimac* until he completed his service as an apprentice in 1859. In January of that year Francis became the commander of the Brocklebank Indiaman *Harold,* a full-rigged ship that was traded exclusively to Calcutta. William Ray was offered the position of third mate on this ship with his old skipper. This offer, however, was declined, namely because Ray felt that serving in that capacity did not count for the next certificate. He therefore accepted an offer to return to his old ship, the *Rimac,* as second mate, under Captain Jenkins, and they returned to Peru once more, loading a further cargo of guano at the Chincha Islands, bringing it back to Queenstown where they waited for orders. Ray then took the opportunity to pass for chief officer and returned to the *Rimac* in that capacity. After eventually discharging their cargo, they took on a cargo of coal at Leith for the Gas Company at Lima and set sail for Peru once more.

However, this time the captain elected to take the *Rimac* around the north of Scotland, where they found that the conditions off Cape Wrath in winter were almost as bad as those experienced when rounding Cape Horn! By taking this route, it was seventy days before they crossed the equator, making it a very long passage to Callao. On arrival there, the captain—who had a serious alcohol problem—vanished, leaving Ray in charge of the ship for the next three weeks while the alcoholic skipper went on a drinking spree.[27] After being on board their ships for several months, and struggling to get around Cape Horn, one can well understand why so many master mariners did turn to drink and spent too much time in low drinking dens. Callao, in common with all nineteenth-century seaports, responded to these "market forces" by providing numerous dives to cater for this particular human weakness. The port of Callao, whose delights were then attracting the master of the *Rimac,* and which in itself is so central to this story of Peru and the Chincha Islands, was an interesting place in the nineteenth century, making it worth a special mention at this point.

The harbor of Callao is about six miles in length and breadth, with ample depth of water, and entirely protected—no safer harbor existing on any continent. The barren island of San Lorenzo, which forms this protected harbor, is 1,000 feet in height. The *Beagle* had brought Charles Darwin to this port in 1831, and like many others, he was not impressed with the place, or the inhabitants, about which he wrote, "Callao is a filthy, ill-built, small seaport. The inhabitants, both here and at Lima, present every imaginable shade of mixture, between European, Negro, and Indian blood. They appear a depraved, drunken set of people. The atmosphere is loaded with foul smells, and that peculiar one, which may be perceived in almost every town within the tropics, was here very strong."[28] George Washington Peck, who came to the port about twenty-two years later in 1853, was also not impressed, noting that "The first view of Callao is not imposing." His description of the port is particularly notable:

> You ascend the stairs, and go round the nearest corner that seems to look like a street, and come upon a mud-walled lane, full of sailors and blacks, of all shades of colour, Peruvians and mules. Crossing this and proceeding up half a dozen roads, or not so much, you come to a ship-chandler's shop (Velasquez & Lyons), all open to the street, where there are usually a group of captains sitting on old chairs, as in a Dutch grocery in Western New York. Opposite, on the right hand corner, is another similar

10. The Chincha guano fleet, 1863, lying between North and Middle Islands. *Illustrated London News,* February 21, 1863.

> shop and group of sitters (Bryce's). Directly in front goes down a narrow, ill-paved, dirty-looking lane of one and a half story mud-walled buildings, occupied by clothing shops and the usual retail trumpery of the marine quarters of our cities—only the lane looks infinitely narrower and more dingy and out of repair than Ann or Cherry Street. On the left hand side is the "Marine Hotel," which you set down as being the meanest of sailor taverns, and afterwards discover to be the principal commercial house of the place."[29]

Peck's reference here to the marine store operated by John and Francis Bryce is interesting, for this was the firm where William R. Grace worked as a clerk when he first arrived in Peru. It was also William Grace who was instrumental in setting up the marine store on the Chincha Islands, who, for his substantial contribution to the prosperity of the enterprise, was later to become a full partner, prior to gaining complete control of the firm. As purveyors of naval stores, despite the dingy, unimpressive nature of the their establishment, it was a moneymaking concern, for in the middle years of the nineteenth century Callao literally teemed with ships. Many were engaged in the guano trade, their ships taking this valuable commodity back to Europe and North America, while others were bound for the gold fields of California, refitting and revictualling at Callao after long voyages around Cape Horn from New York, Boston, or Philadelphia. Other vessels brought timber down the West Coast from San Francisco, and the great New England whaling fleet was also extremely active in the Pacific, many on voyages that could last for up to five years. Needless to say, most of these merchant ships would require consumable items and marine stores, such as rope, sails, paint, spars, oakum, and similar items. Therefore, quite apart from drinking, it is almost certain that the master of the *Rimac* would have had to attend to some legitimate business in this or a similar establishment. About the town itself, and the visiting mariners, Peck made further interesting observations:

> I do not recollect whether there were any quarrels of sailors in the street while [——] and myself were speaking together; but if there were none during the space of half an hour, it was rather remarkable. Generally on the principal corner, there is a succession of parties of Jack-tars who are never all sober at once, and are usually discussing or making merry after their fashion ashore. The whole place is little else but a slop-shop, model lodging house and shipping office. The men are nearly all sharks, the women all black-eyed, and black-faced Susans, the houses are mostly low mud walled boxes with a parlour bed-room open to the street, and a kitchen at the back. Half the time as one passes along, he will see in the front apartment a sharp Yankee swinging in a hammock, and smoking a paper cigar, while in a rocking chair sits an Africo-Spanish woman with bright eyes and small hands, dressed in the tawdriest colours possible, but looking old enough to be his mother—so quickly does the life, or the climate, or both, of Callao face them."[30]

Finally, the master of the *Rimac* managed to drag himself away from the dubious attractions of Callao, but not before William Ray had ballasted the ship and they were ready to make their way down the coast to the Chincha Islands for the return cargo of guano. They eventually anchored off the islands, where the captain went ashore to attend to the necessary formalities before commencing to load. Sadly, though, he returned late that night, once more full of liquor, and in such a state that William Ray, assisted by the steward, had a hard time getting him to his bunk. The following day the incorrigible skipper made it clear to all concerned that he intended to get back to Callao and ordered the steward to keep an eye open for the regular steamer that was due to pick up passengers at the Chincha Islands that day. Strenuous efforts were made to prevent this, in his own interests, but they proved futile. Ray then went on to the island and found that his skipper had not entered the ship for loading at all, having done nothing but load himself with liquor. Deeply concerned about the situation, Ray turned to his old friend William Grace, told him about the problem, and he was given sound advice on how to handle this rather delicate situation.[31]

Another Brocklebank mariner, William Ellery, leaves us with an equally graphic description of life on these small oceangoing brigs. Ellery, who came from Cornwall, was bound apprentice at the age of seventeen on December 16, 1856, for a period of four years, and the following day he set sail for Pernambuco, Brazil, in the 266-ton vessel *Hindoo.* After the completion of this voyage, he transferred to the barque *Lanercost,* then being traded to Callao by Captain T. Tully. This vessel had been built in 1842 and was, in fact, to remain in service until 1869, when she was sold and eventually went missing in 1872.[32] When the *Lanercost* set sail from Liverpool bound for Callao on April 14, 1857, she had a crew of fifteen on board—the officers and apprentices of the ship were as listed below.

Name	Situation	Birth place	Remarks
Tully	Master	Carlisle	4th voyage Master the same ship.
T. F. Sumner	Mate	Liverpool	A very well educated young man though some doubts about him being very steady
W. Evans	2nd Mate	London	A stranger in our employ very highly recommended
J. Kirk	3rd Mate	Newton Stewart	Out of his time last voyage in the *Patriot Queen*
M. McKinnon	Carpenter	Liverpool	A Stranger in our employ
D. Raingley	Apprentice	Derbyshire	Bound January 7th 1856 for 5 years
H. B. Lowe	Apprentice	Liverpool	Bound April 13th 1857 for 4 years
W. Ellery	Apprentice	Cornwall	Bound Dec. 16th 1856 for 4 years
J. Madarelle	Apprentice	Liverpool	Out of his time May 1860[33]

Years later, when recalling his adventures at sea, Ellery stated that when they were rounding Cape Horn in the *Lanercost,* his fingers were often so frostbitten that they were black and blue, and the circulation could only be restored by rubbing them with snow, all this due to the fact that the rigging they had to climb was invariably covered with snow and ice. During the frequent storms the decks were often awash with green seas, but everyone was still expected to be at his place when wanted. The work was hard, but Ellery felt this made sailors of them, and he continued his story by stating that he could never forget one experience in this ship that happened in July 1858, the depth of winter in those latitudes. They were bound to Callao with a general cargo, and on nearing the Horn the ship encountered very severe weather, with snow and ice, and the thermometer showing 14 degrees of frost. The jibboom was carried away, and it brought down the fore-topmast:

> I was sent aloft to clear away the wreck, and before obeying the order I took off my oilskin coat and trousers. When I came down from aloft I was literally frozen stiff, but crawled to the lee side of the spars to recover my oilskins. To my intense chagrin they were not there. Afterwards they were found in shreds in the pig house, the animals having drawn them through the iron bars, and gnawed them to pieces. My circulation was restored by persistent rubbing with snow and, after a hard night's work I went on the half deck, got some old canvas and made a jumper, painted it to make it waterproof, the paint freezing as applied, and I again faced the weather. However trying the work, it was always cheerfully done.
>
> The vessels were always extremely well found, but the food was better imagined than described, except by the old salts saying that we "lived on the smell of an oil rag." Hard biscuits—and it was awfully hard in those days—and a weak decoction of cocoa nibs, served for breakfast. One-and-a-half pounds of beef, mahogany coloured and almost as hard, and one-and-a-half quarter pounds of fat pork were served on alternate days, with a pint of pea soup one day and the next "duff" each man being allowed half-a-pound of flour with which to make this delicacy, which was baked flat and stiff, and eaten with molasses. A curious mixture called "dog's body" was made as follows: Half of your pea soup, broken up biscuits, a dab of molasses, and a piece of fat pork saved from dinner. These ingredients were put in the oven by the grace of the cook (alias the doctor). While it was in the oven Jack was always thinking of the savoury treat in store for the meal called tea, with his biscuit and liquid.
>
> We were strangers to milk and butter, but the tea was sweetened with sugar. For supper we had to depend on savings from the earlier meals. On Saturday our dinner consisted of boiled rice, which the sailor dignified with the name of "strike-me-blind." On Sundays the fare was sometimes varied by what the cook called "currant duff," but the difficulty of the eaters was to find the currants. Three quarts of water were served out daily to each of us for all purposes, drinking, cooking, and washing, that is until the supply was exhausted. Our ablutions were generally performed with salt water, and salt-water soap—a thing hardly ever heard of now-a-days. The result was never satisfactory, the salt causing boils, the salt water not cleaning the skin, and it was a genuine pleasure when rain fell so abundantly as to enable us to collect it from the decks and

wash in it. Lime juice was served out once a week in a bottle previous to 1864, after which date, owing to the prevalence of scurvy, lime juice had to be served out daily. I have seen men's teeth drop out and their legs badly swollen from scurvy. No vegetables were carried in those days. I knew an old sailor who suffered from the disease, and whose remedy on landing in Liverpool was to go to Parliament fields (then unbuilt upon) dig a big hole in the earth, and remain there for a few hours with a bottle of rum and his pipe. He persisted in declaring this treatment did him a lot of good."[34]

On the completion of his apprenticeship in the year 1860, William Ellery was appointed third mate of the twenty-eight year-old barque *Patriot King*. Until 1852 this vessel had been traded almost exclusively to Calcutta, until Captain George Wise, the elder brother of Francis Wise, took her on three voyages to Bombay during the years 1852–55.[35] She was then put in the Cape Horn trade, William Ray's old friend, William Lowden, being her commander when Ellery joined her in 1860. Ellery remained with her until the spring of 1862, when he left her, and after a stay of only forty-eight hours ashore, he sailed as third mate of the full-rigged ship *Arachne,* 700 tons register, bound for Calcutta.[36] Ellery then went on to serve as an officer on several other ships before becoming master of the *Bowfell* and the *Baroda*. The last sailing ship he commanded for the company was the great windjammer *Holkar,* 3,009 tons register. He eventually retired from the sea in 1903, when he handed over command of the steamer *Maiwarri* to another commander, bringing to a close forty-seven years in the service.

After his service on the *Rimac,* Francis Wise went on to become, in turn, master of the Indiamen *Harold, Arachne, Cormorin, Cambay,* and *Chinsura*. Due to ill health he left the service on January 22, 1874, and died at his home, 60 Windsor Street, Liverpool, on October 14, 1875. After learning the art of seamanship with Francis Wise, William Ray went on to command the clippers *Mindanao, Maiden Queen,* and *Baroda*. In 1875 he became marine superintendent of the company. Fourteen years later, in 1889, the company sent their first steamer to sea, this being the *Ameer*. In order to facilitate the change over to steam, William Ray and several other captains had been sent on cruises in steam vessels belonging to other firms. Training in this "new technology" continued, for when the *Ameer* first left for Calcutta on October 27, 1889, she was under the command of Captain William Ray, and serving as his first mate was Captain William Ellery! After a long retirement William Ellery died at his home, "Holkar," Orrell Road, Wallasey, in September 1924.[37] William Ray died at his home, "Hallgarth," Brynaston Road, Birkenhead, on April 28, 1926. He was buried at Woodchurch on the Wirral, and among the mourners at his funeral was his grandson, the late Mr. J. H. Ray, who died in 1994 at age ninety-two. William Ray was very highly regarded by the company and his fellow mariners to the extent that as he was laid to rest, the house flag over the company's offices and on all their ships around the coast were lowered to half-mast.

So far as the Cape Horn South Pacific trade was concerned, Thomas & John Brocklebank remained in this trade throughout the 1850s and the 1860s, but this was gradually run down as they developed their Calcutta trade. In 1870 only one sailing was made to the west coast, this being on March 28, when Captain Forsyth took the 482-ton ship *Mindanao* out to Callao. This was the vessel commanded by Captain Ray in 1866. During the late 1860s and the 1870s, after the American Civil War, the Americans sent out many impressive ships to the Chincha Islands, among which were the *Webster* and *Calhoun,* lofty ships of 2,500 tons each.[38]

As Thomas & John Brocklebank moved out of the trade, once-famous American clipper ships moved in and took their place. Reduced to carrying guano, the once-great ships *Webster* and *Calhoun* arrived on the scene. Both had been built for the Patriotic Line established by Spofford & Tileston in 1852 for the Atlantic packet ship trade. One of their other notable ships was the *Orien,* which, on one occasion, had taken $50,000 freight money in one Atlantic voyage out and home, this being capped, on another occasion, by the *Webster,* under Captain Joseph J. Lawrence's command, with a $60,000 voyage.[39] Another great ship that ended her days in the guano trade was the *Intrepid,* one of the last of the clipper ship era, whose beautifully decorated cabin bore witness to the time and money bestowed upon such vessels at this time. At Callao at this time could also be seen the *Harriet Lane,* once-famous revenue cutter, now converted into a barque that was later seized by the Confederates at the outbreak of the Civil War and held by them throughout the struggle.[40]

During the American Civil War, 1861 to 1865, the American Cape Horners, known as "Down Easters," and indeed all merchant ships belonging to the Union, had suffered a severe slump due to the activity of the Confederate commerce raiders, and notably, the infamous Birkenhead-built *Alabama.*[41] However, in 1865, with the ending of the Civil War, the Down East builders started to launch ships again, some of their more notable ones being the *Ivanhoe,* 1,610 tons; the *Seminole,* 1,438 tons; the *Bluejacket,* 1,395 tons; the *Corsica,* 1,336 tons; and the *Pactolus,* 1,204 tons, built at Thomaston, Maine. Then, from 1866 to 1868, the following were among the best-known of the Cape Horners produced by yards at Thomaston, Bath, Kennebunk, and Boston: the *William A. Campbell, Kate Davenport, Arcturas, Highlander, Ringleader, Southern Cross,* and the 1,502-ton *Sovereign of the Seas.*[42] Among the occasional visitor to the Chincha Islands in these post-American Civil War years was the *Nyack,* which had served as a gunboat in this conflict, and saddest of all, the famous *Kearsarge,* which, under the command of Captain Winslow, had been responsible for sinking the *Alabama* on Sunday, July 19, 1864.[43]

After struggling to get their ships around Cape Horn, sailing masters in a later period of the trade had to run the gauntlet of the Peruvian "Guano Ring," then efficiently operated to line the pockets of corrupt local officials. Every guano charter included a clause to the effect that a vessel had to pass an examination by the Board of Surveyors to determine her fitness for this trade. Or, in practice, to pronounce the vessel as being fit, for there appears to be no record of a ship ever being considered unfit, which of course is notable, for some very ancient hulks ended their days in this service! The well-established routine was for the Board of Surveyors, which included an admiral of the Peruvian navy, to visit each ship in turn. Once on board they would take a little luncheon, or a glass or two of wine with the master, while their humble assistants sounded the pump-well and sealed up the pumps, which had to remain unbroken for three days. The next step in this established routine was to automatically state that the vessel needed caulking, no matter what her condition might happen to be.

In the case of the well-known Down Easter the *Lottie Warren,* which had left the graving dock only six months previously when she had been caulked and newly coppered, it required only a bribe of $100 to convince the surveyors that they had made a profound mistake. All then agreed that no caulking was actually required. On the other hand, when a vessel really needed caulking, or when a rather naive captain chanced not to understand the rules of the game, the "fee" could rise as high as several hundred dollars. In some instances a vessel would, in fact, be obliged to caulk merely because the fine floating dock could not be allowed to lie idle. Then again, various devices were sometimes employed by devious skippers to disguise real leaks. An example of this concerns the captain of one American barque, an extremely canny old mariner who ran a hose from his rapidly filling hold to the pump used for washing down decks. For three whole days the crew uninterruptedly washed down decks, showing a truly commendable desire for cleanliness, never before or since developed! Interestingly, the aforementioned admiral subsequently perished bravely during the war between Chile and Peru, going down with his ship when he was inveigled into chasing a Chilean man-of-war into shallow water, where the great *Independencia* struck a rock and was lost.[44]

As already noted, once the Cape Horners had loaded at the Chincha Islands, they were obliged to return to Callao for clearance. As usual with ships on a long voyage, crews were then allowed twenty-four hours' leave. On such occasions some men would take horses to Lima, while others would hire cabs and have a drive in the country, resolved to be gentlemen for one day at least. Unfortunately, most would do as the incorrigible master of the *Rimac* had once done, that is, head straight for the nearest low groggery, where they would spend all their liberty money (generally one month's pay) at one sitting. After this session they would have to be half-carried back to the ship by their more sensible shipmates. On the other hand, sailors who had the sense not to get drunk behaved more sensibly. Such men, who had not forgotten mothers and sisters, wives and sweethearts at home, would spend much of their time and money locating and purchasing curiosities of all kinds to take home as gifts and reminders of their long voyage to distant Peru.[45] Then, in the early 1850s, many men on such leave would never return to their ships at all, their intention being to join another ship and make their way north to the gold fields of California.

So far as the Cape Horn trade itself is concerned, during the seventies and eighties of the nineteenth century, British shipyards were more and more occupied with the construction of iron ships, Messrs. Laird & Company of Birkenhead being foremost in this development. But at the same time the builders of the New England coast clung to their old skills and materials, and continued to produce great wooden square-riggers, many of which were destined for the Cape Horn trade. These Down Easters of New England were the result of more than a century of shipbuilding experience and combined all the attributes of the legendary Yankee clippers—speed and sail power, with large cargo capacity and strength of build.[46]

Among the great clippers produced at this time by one of these yards was the celebrated Down Easter *William R. Grace,* named after the onetime small trader who had come to the rescue of young William Ray on the Chincha Islands in 1856. By this time, though, he was a rich and powerful New York merchant. The vessel named in his honor was a full-rigged ship of 1,799 tons register, which was launched at Bath in 1873 and owned by Flint & Company. The shipbuilding firm of Chapman & Flint were to launch another ship for the Flint Company fleet two years later; this was the 1,928-ton *M. P. Grace,* named after Michael Grace, the younger brother of William. During the seventies Captain Black was the master of the *William R. Grace,* and Captains Wilbar and "Bully" Williams had command of the larger of the two, the *M. P. Grace.* Both ships had interesting careers as Cape Horners. On one occasion, for instance, the latter ship was forty-five days struggling to weather the notorious Cape. The winds were so strong, in fact, that when she was near the Falkland Islands, not a shred of canvas could be raised, and she was hove to under bare poles.[47]

Within a relatively short period of time, however, a great fleet of steamships would be sailing under the house flag of Grace & Company, all of which brings us to the fascinating story of the founder of this notable enterprise, the already mentioned William R. Grace, the "Irish Conquistador." This was the powerful American shipping, trading, and manufacturing conglomerate that was to become known throughout the world as the "Casa Grace."

10
William R. Grace & Company—The Casa Grace

WILLIAM RUSSELL GRACE, THE MAN DESTINED TO PLAY A SIGNIFICANT role in the development of Peru, was born at Riverstown, near the Cove of Cork, Ireland, on May 10, 1832, when his parents, James and Eleanor May Russell, were on holiday. At this time the young couple had been married for three years and already had two daughters. James was the owner of a small estate of about 154 Irish acres, this being about 250 English acres, along with a quarry and limekiln at Ballylinan, Queens County (now Leix), about 100 miles removed from Riverstown.[1] These relatively modest enterprises provided them with a comfortable, lower middle-class existence. However, slowly but surely the Industrial Revolution was undermining the economic and social position of this family, for James's grandfather had operated a cotton mill on the estate, but the development of steam-powered mills in England had undercut this enterprise, as indeed, political and historical developments had been undermining many lines of the proud Grace family for centuries. James Grace's immediate family was a branch of a celebrated family that had descended from the ancient lords of Tuscany and then swept into England with that very notable French conquistador, William the Conqueror.[2]

Facts relating to this period and the Grace family are interesting. Well after the initial conquest, a small force of Norman knights and archers were sent out to establish a beachhead in Ireland. Strongbow, Earl of Pembroke, followed them out in 1170. First, he captured Waterford and then Dublin. On MacMurrough's death, the following year, Strongbow assumed the title of king of Leinster.[3] With Strongbow on this notable expedition was Raymond Fitz-William de Carew, surnamed le Gros, who did much to secure the success of the invasion. For considerable services rendered, le Gros received the hand of Basilia de Clare, sister of that aspiring chieftain, and with it the great district of Kilkenny. In 1176, Raymond le Gros was appointed sole viceroy of Ireland, which he had previously held in conjunction with Earl Strongbow. The name then evolved, first to Grac and then, by English pronunciation, to Grace.[4]

From this point on the fortunes of the Grace family kept improving, and they evolved into firm, powerful, Catholic landlords. By the middle years of the seventeenth century, Baron John Grace of Courtsdown owned an impressive estate of some 32,870 acres. Gerald Grace of Ballylinch and Carney Castle also held a considerable landed inheritance of 17,000 acres in the counties of Kilkenny, Kings, and Tipperary. Both these gentlemen, however, chose to back the losing side in the bloody Civil War of 1641, for which profound error of judgment they forfeited all of their estates.[5] But the various lines of the Grace family survived, although, perhaps understandably, with many contradictory feelings toward the English.

Moving forward to the world of James Grace in the nineteenth century, his already modest estate was then divided into three parts, two of the farms coming down to James by successive inheritance from his great-great-grandfather, yet no Grace had ever owned them. Under a system then common in Ireland, they were held under lease, and an Irish farm lease could last for a thousand years. The third and smallest of the farms, sixty-five English acres, he owned outright and leased to a Mr. Patrick Bolger. The other two, and the limekiln and quarry, he managed himself. Unfortunately, however, the quarry was no longer profitable, due to the fact that a similar one had been opened close to a canal that led directly into the center of Dublin, making it easy for the rival proprietors to undercut the less-well-placed Grace quarry. Despite this problem, James Grace survived, albeit in a modest way.

This small Grace clan, Catholic in religion, and by now predominantly Celtic by blood, was also, in the main, sympathetic to Celtic ideology, and William Grace absorbed these views. The radical nationalist paper, the *Nation,* was launched in 1842. James Grace was among the subscribers, and the indications are that his son William was a regular reader of this influential, nationalist paper. Three years later in 1845, the potato crop failed in the west of Ireland with devastating impact. During the early part of the nineteenth century, the population of Ireland had increased dramatically, with thousands, most notably in the west, becoming totally dependent on this one root crop that was, unfortunately, very susceptible to the blight.

The majority of Irish cultivators held their land by lease, and while the long secure leases, such as the ones held by James Grace, offered security, at the bottom end of the social scale a system of letting and subletting had developed. This resulted in many cultivators of increasingly small plots being tenants at will, who could be turned off the land at a moment's notice. In such an agricultural economy, even a partial failure of the potato crop could bring hunger, sickness, and death. Sadly, the traumatic crop failure of 1845 was to be followed by others, added to which more misery was to be heaped on the shoulders of the hard-pressed Irish peasantry. The policy of evicting them from their diminutive holdings was stepped up. In 1848 the number of holdings in Ireland decreased dramatically. Of the holdings not exceeding one acre, 18,185 vanished; of the holdings exceeding one acre and not exceeding five acres, 24,147 were annihilated; of the holdings exceeding five acres and not exceeding fifteen acres, 28,379 were abolished. Of the larger holdings exceeding fifteen acres and not exceeding thirty acres, 4,274 were swept away: making altogether a total of 74,985 holdings extinguished.[6]

The economy of Ireland began to collapse, and under these conditions many saw emigration as their best, or indeed only, chance of survival. In the eight-year period from 1847–54, it is estimated that one million six hundred thousand Irish people left their native land never to return. These Irish emigrants made their way to many distant places, but the vast majority went to the United States and, to a lesser extent, Canada. Sixty percent of those leaving made their way to the New World via the port of Liverpool.[7] Meanwhile, back in Ireland plans to employ the totally destitute, those too poor to emigrate, were soon in hand, the Board of Public Works being in charge of such schemes. To gain acceptance, proposals put forward had to benefit the community as a whole and not merely one proprietor.[8] One of the proposals that the board accepted under this scheme was a road that ran past James Grace's house. In an attempt to take care of his own men, Grace then employed them to drain ten acres of bog on one of his farms. Eventually, though, he had to give up the struggle. He left an overseer to look after his farms and moved his family to Dublin, where he took a post in the tax administration as supervisor of excises. Young William Grace was then sent to Dr. Cahill's college in Dublin, a Jesuit institution of high scholastic standing.[9]

During the spring of 1846 conditions in Ireland deteriorated rapidly; half a million had died of starvation, and a similar number had fled the country. Among them was thirteen-year-old William Grace, who had decided to run away to sea. This may have had little to do with the famine, for his stated boyhood ambition had been to gain a commission in the Royal Navy, which had been blocked by his Irish nationalist father. During the following two years, according to one account, he apparently made several ocean voyages as a cabin boy on South American traders, then arrived in New York, where he obtained various low-paid jobs, which included a spell as a clerk in a shipping office.[10] Another more detailed and undoubtedly more accurate account states that in the spring of 1846 he had sailed directly to New York, apparently as a passenger, where he found employment with a Jew whose shop was near Franklin Square. He then worked for a cobbler and a printer until late 1847 or early 1848, when he decided to work his passage home. A ship was sailing to Cuba to load with sugar for Liverpool, and young William Grace managed to get signed on as a member of the crew.

From Liverpool he made his way back to Dublin, where he received a warm welcome from his brothers and sisters, but initially a rather cool one from his father. Soon all was forgiven, however, and James Grace saw that William completed his education. He then secured a position as a clerk in a Liverpool office for his adventurous son.[11] By 1850 William had left the countinghouse stool. The ambitious eighteen-year-old boy from Dublin had set himself up as a passage broker in the emigrant trade, with an office at 120 Waterloo Road, Liverpool, working in conjunction with Patrick O'Neil of 6 North Wall, Dublin. From some accounts it would seem that they had a silent partner in this venture, a "man of means" who had put up the money.[12]

Their choice of Waterloo Road, Liverpool, is interesting, for it was here that many of the large well-established commission and forwarding agents had their offices, and the function of a passage broker was to act as a middleman between the prospective emigrant and the owners of the emigrant ships. Clearly they must have thought that proximity to the larger enterprises must have been an advantage, rather than a disadvantage, to them. Among the firms in this road was Harnden Brothers, who also had offices at Philadelphia, Boston, and New York.[13] Young Grace advertised rather extensively in the *Nation,* from which we can gather that he only seems to have dealt with the "White Cross Line of packets" whose ships sailed regularly from Liverpool to Quebec.

While young William Grace had been traveling the world in 1847, the "General Central Relief Committee for all Ireland" had been set up with offices at 36 College Green, Dublin. This attracted wide support in Ireland, England, and indeed internationally. The trustees of the fund were the Marquis of Kildare, D. C. La Touche, Lord Cloncurry, William Murphy, George Roe, Thomas Hutton, and Alexander Boyle. By July 1, 1847, they had collected a total of £59,439 for famine relief work. In addition to the aforementioned trustees, a great many notable people also served on the general committee of this fund, which included the fourth Earl of Donoughmore, who was then acting as the sheriff of County Tipperary.[14] Of particular interest here is the fact that the fourth earl's son was later to work with William Grace, and together they were destined to play a very significant role in the history and economic development of Peru.

John Luke George Hely-Hutchinson, the fifth Earl of Donoughmore, was born at Monkstown, near Dublin, on March 2, 1848, when young William Grace was on his aforementioned travels. He was educated at Eton and Oxford and then served as assistant commissioner in eastern Roumelia. On May 19, 1874, he married Frances Isabella, the daughter of Colonel Frazer Stephens, a colonel in the East India Company.[15] Fourteen years later, in October 1888, he was to sign the famous Grace-Donoughmore Contract, by which means William Grace, and to a lesser extent Donoughmore himself, took over the foreign debts of Peru in return for very substantial and lucrative concessions.[16] Thirteen years later, on December 21, Donoughmore's son, Richard Walter John Hely-Hutchinson, the sixth earl, was to marry Michael Paul Grace, the son of William Russell Grace.[17] However, substantially more mention will be made of all these monumental financial developments, which then lay in the future.

Back in 1850 James Grace and his son William, along with thousands of their fellow Irishmen, were concentrating their attention on survival, mainly through emigration. As already mentioned, by far the most popular destination for departing Irish emigrants was the United States, with Canada a fairly popular second choice; that is, until the disastrous year of 1847, when thousands died en route to British North America, or soon after arrival, due to sickness and neglect.[18] Four years later, in 1851, Edmund Hammond Hargreaves discovered gold at Summerhill Creek near Bathurst, Australia, the formal announcement of this great find being made in the *Sydney Morning Herald* on May 15, 1851. Within one month 10,000 men had made their way to Bathurst, and soon the ships of the Black Ball, White Star, and Eagle lines would be taking tens of thousands of "Gold Rush" emigrants from Liverpool to this distant land, a high percentage of them being from Ireland.[19]

If Gold had been discovered in Australia one year earlier, it could have influenced the thinking of James Grace, for he also got the "emigration fever," but instead of opting for America or Australia, he backed a novel idea, this being to emigrate to Peru. Another notable Irishman, Doctor John Gallagher, who had previously served as a surgeon in the Royal Navy, had, in fact, already emigrated to Peru and invested all his capital in land near the port of Callao. His intention was to develop it into a sugar plantation, but he lacked the labor to work this estate and therefore hit on the idea of employing his fellow countrymen.[20] It is interesting to note that Gallagher did not consider employing slaves for this work, although black slaves still existed in Peru at this time and were normally used for such work. From this we must assume he had an ethical objection to such an option, slaves were not available, at least in sufficient numbers, or he could not afford to buy them.

He must also have known that there was a growing awareness in Peru that the slave system must end, and sooner rather than later. Gallagher would also have been aware of the fact that while there was no formal abolitionist movement in Peru in 1850, the government itself was now beginning to play an important part in new moves against slavery. Then, in 1851, Herrera, the minister of Government and Foreign Relations, asked the Chamber of Deputies to put together a law prohibiting the African slave trade, and argued, "We cannot permit the abuse of enslaving men to continue. Peru cannot remain indifferent any longer in the midst of this censure with which the civilized world wishes to extirpate the monstrous crime of buying and selling men."[21]

Given this situation Gallagher, who was apparently an Irish patriot, got in touch with his friend James Grace, advising him that he had heard of the tragic situation in Ireland and wished to do something for his people. While it is abundantly clear that he was actually looking for hired hands to work his own estate, he presented to Grace the notion of a small Irish Utopia in distant Peru. Unfortunately, details of how he sold this concept to Grace appear to be missing. Therefore, one is left wondering how cutting cane as a hired hand under a burning tropical sun could be presented to emigrants as the "Utopia" of Sir Thomas More's famous book, in which, one will recall, the people lived in great comfort and happiness, with all things being owned in common. However, this rather unique challenge appears to have been met, and late in 1850 James Grace, undoubtedly assisted by his passenger-broker son William, began rounding up prospective emigrants and taking steps to charter a suitable vessel.

By April 1851 they had gathered a party of 180 together, which included women and children. The party was actually led by James Grace and his extremely enterprising young son, William, and with them were Marcella and Eliza Lawler, attractive young cousins of the head of the expedition. Mrs. Grace, however, remained behind, only the second daughter, Ellen, twenty years old, and the baby of the family, Michael, age seven, accompanied William and their father. The Liverpool firm of William Russell Grace & Company was closed, and they all prepared to set sail from London for the fabled land of the Incas and the infamous Pizarro. The ship chosen for this extraordinary expedition was the 1,033-ton *Louisa,* built at New Brunswick in 1845. She was owned by Brooke & Company of London and commanded by Captain Carpenter.[22] As one can understand, the young businessman, William Russell Grace, had no real intention of cutting cane on Doctor Gallagher's estate himself, as his inclinations were for the world of commerce, in which he was now well trained. However, on April 9, 1851, the intrepid band of "colonists" boarded the *Louisa,* dropped down the Thames, and began the long passage to Peru.

News of their arrival did not get back to Ireland until the following October. Then the *Waterford Chronicle* told of the receipt of "letters from some of the emigrants who sailed for Callao, South America under the Superintendence of James Grace, late Supervisor of Inland Revenue." From these we learn that they had "a most pleasant voyage" of 101 days, and the *Louisa* had dropped anchor in Callao harbor on July 20. The news these letters contained was good, with no complaints being made about the usually hazardous passage around Cape Horn or their reception on arrival. They even seemed to like the strange climatic conditions of the Peruvian coastal strip.[23]

One assumes that Doctor John Gallagher would have met the ship and made efforts to take them to the lands he hoped they would convert into a sugar plantation, which were on the fertile, irrigated banks of the river Rimac. Some may have got that far, but the whole venture was doomed to failure. Before any work was actually started, virtually all the emigrants went down with malaria and dysentery, and by the time they had recovered, they had lost all interest in the venture. The sadly disillusioned survivors began to scatter, from which it is clear that unlike the unfortunate Chinese immigrants who were bound to work as indentured labor for a period of years to repay the cost of their passage, these Irish colonists were, fortunately, bound by no such arrangement. Some survivors made their way north to the gold fields of California, while others made their way south to the gold diggings at Summerhill Creek, Australia. Among the few that remained were the attractive Lawler sisters, both of whom did rather well for themselves by marrying prosperous young residents of Lima. James Grace stuck it out for three years, during which time one assumes he was living off his capital, for there is no record of him setting up in business or attempting to find suitable employment in Peru. He set sail for the Emerald Isle in 1854, taking with him his daughter, Ellen, and his young son, Michael, but his elder son, William, remained behind.[24]

According to some accounts, James Grace had actually bought William an interest in a Liverpool firm of ship chandlers, the aforementioned office job, and when in Peru, he helped to place William in a similar firm.[25] While this version may contain some truth, what is certain is that soon after arriving in Callao, William Grace was working as a clerk with a marine store enterprise, namely, John Bryce & Company, whose establishment at Callao has already been mentioned. This firm had actually been in operation since early in the nineteenth century and was formally known as the "Almacén de Artículos Navales de Pablo Romero." John Bryce, a handsome young man from Scotland, had gone out to Peru and obtained work as a clerk with Pablo Romero, married his daughter, and inherited the business. The first partner John Bryce took into the business was his brother Francis; the second, William Russell Grace.[26]

The store itself was built out of old ships' timbers and was rich with the smells of hemp, tar, oakum, turpentine, colza oil, and kerosene. William liked the smells, and he liked talking to the captains of the Cape Horn South Pacific traders who came into the store after making their way around the Horn and up the South American coast.[27] He also mixed well with the local people, studied Spanish, and settled down to life as an employee of John Bryce. Over the next few years, his knowledge of the business increased considerably. As one might expect, it did not take him long to realize that while the Callao business was very profitable even more money was to be made at or near the Chincha Islands. The idea was that from a hulk he would sell marine supplies directly to the guano fleet and a useful range of items to officials, sailors, and soldiers from his store on the main Chincha island.

He was not the only one to identify retailing opportunities at the Chincha Islands. The principal impact of the Chincha laborer on the local economy was through the purchase of foodstuffs and other provisions made on their behalf by the loading contractors. Water, meal, rice, fish, and a minimal amount of clothing and so on, would all have to be brought over to the islands from the mainland, directly opposite the islands, all of which presented an opportunity to local merchants, contractors, and hacendados to make more money; and among them, one can be almost sure, would be Don Domingo Elias, guano contractor and politician, whose estate was close to the Chinchas. Another potential market was the officers and seamen manning the foreign vessels that came to the islands. An account left by an American sailor gives a fair indication of just how substantial that provision market was: "We are supplied twice a week. Wednesday and Saturday, from Pisco City with fresh meat, vegetables and fruits, by boatmen who make quite a business of it. Fresh beef eight and a half cents per pound, fowls $10 per dozen, pigs weighing twenty pounds, $3; sheep $4 each. Vegetables are high, enough for one week's consumption for a crew of fifteen, say £2. Everything in the way of provisions is high."

It is indeed certain that these mariners also offered a bigger market than the poorly paid Chinese guano workers did. Their purchasing power was higher and dietary demands greater, but their numbers would invariably be in excess of those working on the islands. The 200 vessels queuing up at the Chincha Islands in October 1853 probably represented a temporary offshore community of between 3,500 and 4,000.[28] And apart from general provisions, all these ships, as mentioned, clearly required marine stores, which, up till then, were only available in Callao—about 100 miles away to the north.

By 1854 William Russell Grace was working as a full partner of John Bryce & Company.[29] It was also at this time that his father, James Grace, had decided to return to Ireland. One wonders, therefore, if he had been instrumental in procuring this change in his son's status prior to leaving the country. However, notwithstanding this possibility, it was clearly soon after he had become a full partner in the enterprise that he introduced new techniques, new lines, new energy, and new imagination into this small but thriving business. It was, in fact, late in 1855, or early in 1856, that William Grace persuaded John and Francis Bryce to let him take the aforementioned hulk down to the roadstead at the Chinchas, loaded with a similar line of goods as those stocked in their store at Callao. The idea was to take the goods to the buyers rather than wait for buyers to come to the market. This, of course, also ensured that they had a distinct advantage over some of the possibly undercapitalized competitors back in the distant port of Callao. Needless to say, business on this unique floating emporium was exceptionally good, to the extent that it prompted the partners to immediately supplement their hulk with a store on the North Island, which is precisely where Captain Francis Wise had located William Grace on the previously mentioned voyage of the *Rimac* in 1856. Managing the store on the North Island, and the floating store, kept young William Grace exceptionally busy, to the extent that stocks required replenishing with gratifying speed, and this required numerous trips to the main company store in Callao.

By chance, on one of these visits William came across an American captain who was having difficulty finding his way to the United States consulate. He introduced himself as George Gilchrest, commander of the ship *Rochambeau,* just in port after a long voyage around the Cape from Liverpool. The required directions were given, the two men talked for a while, and the conversation concluded with Captain Gilchrest extending an invitation to the young trader to have a meal with him and his family on the *Rochambeau,* as a reward for his considerate and polite behavior.[30]

Captain Gilchrest was a prominent shipmaster and a native of St. George, Maine, whose first occupation was that of a teacher. He later went to sea in small vessels, some of which he commanded. Subsequently, he sailed in ships engaged in foreign trade until he bought and assumed command of the *Rochambeau,* which was registered at Thomaston, Maine.[31] In the fashion of many New England skippers of the time, Captain Gilchrest had his wife and family on board his ship, and when William Grace took up his invitation, he was introduced to Mrs. Mary Jane Gilchrest, and their very beautiful seventeen-year-old daughter, Lillius. Needless to say, young William Grace fell in love with her, and soon after this first meeting, the confident young man advised a friend that he intended to marry her. During the next three months, while the *Rochambeau* was waiting her turn to load with guano, William and Lillius met on many occasions, but eventually they had to part when the ship sailed away, bound for the Cape and the long voyage up the Atlantic to the British Isles.

It was to be three long years before the young lovers met again. Some accounts indicate that they were engaged at this point, while others cast doubt on this assumption, stating that it came later through correspondence. In any event, when the *Rochambeau* sailed away from the Chinchas, Captain and Mrs. Gilchrest were sufficiently confident of the relationship becoming a permanent one that they promised to call on William's parents the next time business took their ship to Dublin. Then, early in 1859, William Grace made the long journey back to Tenants Harbor, near Thomaston, Maine, to claim his bride. They were married there on September 11, when Lillius was twenty years old and William twenty-seven.[32]

The young couple then made their way back to Peru, and on June 11, 1860, their first baby, named Alice Gertrude, was born on the store ship. They were well able to support their child, for by this time William Russell Grace had made a tidy sum for Mr. Bryce, and about $180,000 for himself. A sum, expressed in the monetary values of 2006, would be about $30,000,000.[33] Nevertheless, business on the store ship continued, with five young men working from dawn till dusk to keep on top of the work. These were William Grace, James Lawler, a cousin; Llaguna, the bookkeeper, William Rook, and William's younger brother, Michael, who arrived in 1859 or 1860, to work on board the moneymaking hulk. In 1862 William decided to move to Callao, handing over day-to-day control of the Chincha Islands business to Francis D. Stoneham. It was soon after this move that his doctor advised him that he was suffering from Bright's disease, that rest was urgently required as part of his treatment, and that in any event it was highly unlikely that he would live for very long.

With this depressing scenario dictating events, the Grace family set sail for Ireland, where they duly arrived after the usual trials of a long ocean voyage. Here they attended to some family affairs, then late in 1863, they boarded a ship bound for New York and on arrival stayed for a while with Captain and Mrs. Gilchrest at their home in Brooklyn. The year 1863 had been the crucial year in the American Civil War, and although the Union victory at Gettysburg had turned the tide of battle against the Confederacy, at sea it was a different matter. American merchant vessels were still being destroyed by Confederate commerce raiders, and in particular, the Birkenhead-built *Alabama,* which had spent much of that year destroying American merchant shipping in the Pacific. Insurance rates had gone through the roof, resulting in scores of United States ships being laid-up or sold to foreign owners, and those that did remain under the American flag often had to sail without insurance. Despite all of this, the shipbuilders of New England continued to build and launch fine clipper ships, which included the celebrated Down Easter *Edward O'Brian,* launched at Thomaston, Maine, in November 1863. When Lillius Grace arrived in Brooklyn, her father, Captain George Gilchrest, was waiting to take this great new clipper ship on her maiden voyage around Cape Horn to San Francisco, notwithstanding the risks involved.

The 1,803-ton *Edward O'Brian* was built and owned by the famous New England shipbuilder and shipowner after whom she was named. She was the second ship to sail under this name, the first being the 797-ton *Edward O'Brian,* launched in 1848, which was sold at the outset of the Civil War to a British owner who traded her as the *Arthur.* In 1882 Edward O'Brian was to build yet another ship that was to bear his name, this being a much larger vessel that became known as the *Big Edward* to distinguish her from the vessel launched in 1863.[34] In accordance with his general business policy, O'Brian had no intention of paying the insurance rates quoted by Lloyd's of London. Edward O'Brian intended to let George Gilchrest take this latest addition to his fleet around the Horn and into the Pacific, trusting to luck and the ability of Captain Gilchrest, to outwit Raphael Semmes, commander of the Confederate raider *Alabama.*

Fortunately for O'Brian and Gilchrest, when the *Edward O'Brian* was launched, Semmes had already decided to take the *Alabama* out of the Pacific and make his way back to Europe, although they were not to know this at the time. This notorious Confederate "commerce raider" had actually entered the Straits of Sunda on November 1, 1863, and reentered the Indian Ocean on December 25, on the first stage of her long passage back to Europe. The result of her hunt in the Pacific, though, had been six United States ships caught and destroyed, all of them first-class and very valuable, which had forced up the cost of insurance to astronomical levels.[35] Edward O'Brian was, however, wealthy enough to let his ships sail without insurance and rarely bothered to insure any of his ships. Of Scotch-Irish descent, O'Brian had been born at Warren, Maine, in July 1793. After spending some time at sea, he took to building ships on his own account at Warren before moving his yard to Thomaston. In all he launched over 100 ships, all of which had an enviable reputation for being well built. After 1858 it was his custom to own entirely the vessels he built, and he frequently owned the cargoes carried by his ships, and for years, as noted, acted as his own insurer.[36]

About the close of 1863 William Grace, who had obstinately refused to die and was now much recovered and with Lillius, left the Gilchrest home in Brooklyn and took a steamer to Panama on the first stage of their long journey back to Callao. Some time later Mrs. Gilchrest followed with their daughter Alice, and in March, 1864, they heard that Captain Gilchrest had put to sea in the *Edward O'Brian*. The Graces lived in Callao, but William had to spend much of his time at the Chincha Islands. Lillius found the port an extremely boring place, and it was therefore decided to take up residence on the store ship once more, where she would be able to mix socially with the captains' families in the fleet. To say the least, it was not the most auspicious moment to make this move, for a Spanish naval squadron was then cruising in the Pacific, ostensibly on a scientific mission, but in reality preparing to attack Peru and invade and claim the Chincha Islands. They actually did this on April 14, 1864, when Mrs. Grace was relaxing on the store ship and William was attending to business in Callao. As it happens, the Spanish were soon ousted, and the Grace family survived this international confrontation without injury or loss.[37]

They also survived another traumatic incident off the Chincha Islands that took place just a few months later. In the autumn of 1864, Mrs. Grace and her mother were in Callao when news got through to them that Captain Gilchrest had unloaded his cargo at San Francisco and brought the *Edward O'Brian* down the coast and was then waiting to be loaded at the Chinchas. Accordingly, the Grace family took the steamer down to the islands to meet him. They were in for more excitement, for the vessel moored next to the *Edward O'Brian* caught fire and burned to the water's edge. As it was not possible to move his ship away, Captain Gilchrest and his crew had to work all through the night, pumping water over the *Edward O'Brian* to reduce the chances of the fire spreading to their uninsured ship. If there had been a wind, nothing could have saved O'Brian's new clipper, but fortunately the night was calm and their valuable ship survived unscathed.

At this point in time, though, a "wind of change" was blowing through the corridors of power in Lima. The Peruvian government was now becoming increasingly aware that the guano bonanza would not last forever and was therefore most anxious to develop other

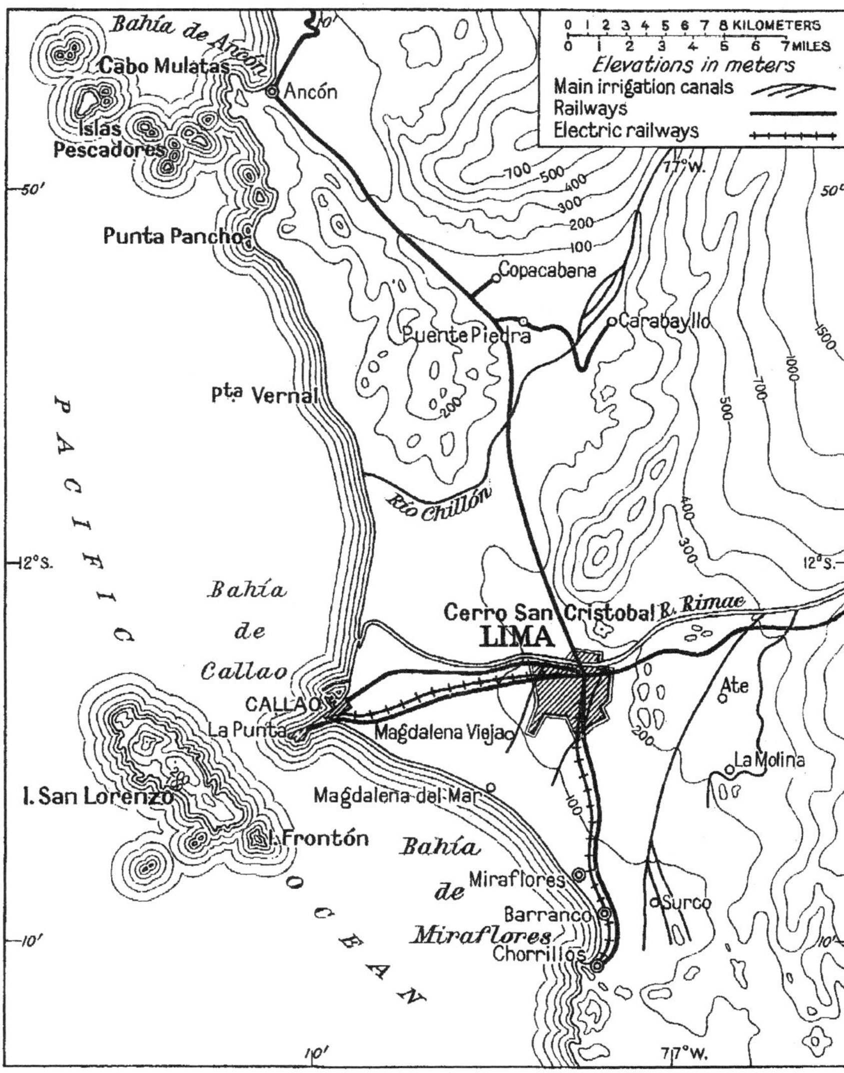

11. Map of the Rimac and Chillon valleys. Beyond the foothills the two valleys unite to form a broad delta plain which extends down to the shore. Lieutenant George Robbins Johnson. *Peru from the Air.* Reproduced by courtesy of the American Geographical Society.

industries before supplies dried up. For this, President Pardo was convinced, Peru required a railroad system, and it was then that an American adventurer by the name of Henry Meiggs made his appearance. A fugitive from American justice, Meiggs had already established himself as a competent railroad contractor in Chile, and he was destined to win many of the contracts to develop the Peruvian rail system. William Russell and Michael Grace, in turn, then secured contracts with Meiggs for practically all the required supplies on these vast guano-funded projects—the most notable of which was the Oroya Line, the highest in the world.[38] Unfortunately, while the construction of these lines brought profits to Messrs. Meiggs and Grace, they did not bring prosperity to Peru, having the adverse effect of plunging this badly managed nation even deeper into debt.

The American Civil War dragged on during the first part of the 1860s, but, as noted, United States ships such as the *Edward O'Brian* were still being traded to Peru, and the Grace family mixed socially with the masters of these ships and their families. This, linked to the fact that William Grace was now married to an American citizen, made him increasingly pro-American and sympathetic to the Union side in their war against the Confederate rebellion, a political outlook that was not held by many people at Callao and Lima. Early in this war of rebellion, the English and Peruvian business houses at Callao decided to refuse credit to vessels of the United States Navy, which then called frequently at the port, the main base for naval supplies on the west coast of South America. Although not at the time an American citizen, William Grace immediately placed the resources of Bryce & Company at the disposal of the Union ships, and his action was subsequently recognized as having relieved the Lincoln administration from an exceedingly difficult situation.[39] As will be noted, this policy was to stand in his favor at a later date when he entered politics in New York.

William Grace, who had left Peru when deemed terminally ill, was still not as fit as he would have wished. He worked too hard, once again, until his old complaint returned, and he also went down with dysentery. His health was now seriously impaired to the extent that he had no option other than to quit Peru for good. In March 1865, the family, including Mary Jane Gilchrest, sailed away for Ireland by way of New York. Here it should be mentioned that he left Bryce & Company on his own terms, leaving his younger brother Michael as managing clerk of the enterprise, who, thus placed, would later be in a position to manage affairs for William in Peru.

Once back in the Emerald Isle, William Grace acquired an estate in the northern part of Queen's County, placing another younger brother, John W. Grace, in charge, as he clearly had no intention of managing the land himself. Here the Grace brothers found in existence a tyrannical combination of landlords lined up against the local working people, which they decided to undermine by refusing to be parties to what they considered were unjust and arbitrary agreements. They established on their property the higher wage prevalent in the more prosperous southern part of the country from whence they had come and where their family had been prominent for several hundred years. This independent action completely destroyed the other landlords' schemes against laboring men throughout the county, making them extremely popular with the local workers but considerably less so with their fellow landowners.[40]

With his health fully restored, William Grace then decided to go to New York. On arrival the family moved into a house in the village of Parkville, near Brooklyn, prior to moving to Brooklyn Heights, an area then popular with prosperous master mariners and others with maritime interests. It was here that Captain Gilchrest lived, by then retired from the sea, and Benjamin Flint, of Chapman & Flint, the largest shipbuilders on the Maine coast, whose company was soon to build the already mentioned clippers *William R. Grace* and *M. P. Grace*. Further links were soon to develop between the Flint and Grace families. Originally J. W. Elwell & Company had been the New York agents for the Chapman & Flint fleet. Charles R. Flint, son of Benjamin Flint, then became a partner in W. R. Grace & Company, at which point the Grace Company succeeded to this valuable agency.[41]

The Chapmans also had other links with the Grace family and company. Captain James F. Chapman, born in 1830 to the second wife of Robert Chapman, was therefore a half-brother to Isaac F. and Benjamin Flint Chapman. After serving in the family yard as a ship caulker, he went to sea and subsequently became master of the celebrated clipper ship *St. John,* one of many ships built by Chapman & Flint. Under his command this ship made record-breaking runs on three round voyages between San Francisco and Australia, in times that were never to be matched by any other sailing ship. After serving as master of this ship for four years, in 1873 Captain Chapman went to San Francisco and, as a partner in the enterprise, established the firm of William R. Grace & Company in California.[42]

Although Captain Gilchrest had given up the sea by 1865, he had not retired from business. Despite the postwar shipping depression, he had set himself up in a ship chandlers store at 110 Wall Street, where he was only a few yards away from South Street, close to the East River, with its busy wharves, lined with the ships of many nations. As William Grace's plan was also to establish himself as a maritime trader, he took office space in his father-in-law's establishment. From this base he began chartering ships and then ordered them to be built for his own account. However, as his correspondence prior to 1867 has not been preserved, much detail about just how he launched this international trading enterprise has been lost. It was in this year that William Grace acquired a full partnership in Messrs. Bryce & Company at Callao at the cost of $50,000 dollars, the Bryce brothers both leaving a similar amount in the company, with Michael Grace remaining as junior partner and manager.

The firm was now trading under the style of Bryce, Grace & Company. Michael put in no capital, but for his invaluable services as manager, it was agreed he was to have 25 percent of the profits. Francis Bryce was now to get more deeply involved in work on his Peruvian sugar plantations, while John was developing his considerable interests in London and Paris. In the former capital John Bryce had set himself up as an international banker under the impressive style of the General South American Company, and in Paris he bought himself a large hotel. He also decided to rebuild "Marley," his palatial country estate in Devonshire. Naturally, all of these projects required funding, for which he continued to rely heavily on a constant flow of profits from Peru.

In the year when he acquired a share in the Bryce enterprise in Callao, William Grace also appeared in the records as the part owner of a ship named after his wife—the *Lillius*. That same year another daughter, Agnes Isadora, was born to the Graces. Two years later a ship was launched at Thomaston, Maine, and she was christened the *Agnes I. Grace*. The man appointed to commandeer her was Captain George C. Smalley, a cousin of William's mother-in-law. Things were clearly on the move. In 1869 the records also indicate that William Grace held a part-interest in an old clipper, the *Nereus,* which he used to carry coal, guano, cotton, or whatever cargo could be obtained. At this time he was also buying cargoes that he shipped out for sale on his own account, usually in vessels that he part-owned

12. New York and the Brooklyn Bridge in the 1880s when William R. Grace was Mayor of New York. "The Metropolis Today." New York: the International Publishing Company, 1888.

or was managing, and he made many purchases on commission for foreign dealers, principally in South America. He also developed links with representatives in California, Europe, and the British Isles. In Callao, he naturally began to work very closely with his younger brother Michael, after his investment in Messrs. Bryce & Company, for it was in this part of the world that the main future development of his ever-expanding trading empire lay. The company would soon become known throughout the world as the "Casa Grace."[43]

Primarily merchants, and prepared to take a merchant's risk for a merchant's profit, William Grace in New York and Michael in Callao, sought to fill the holds of their ships with merchandise. William took note of all that was available in the United States that could be purchased, shipped out to Peru, and pay him a trading profit as well as furnish cargo for the ships he owned or controlled. Among the various items he shipped out were stoves, lamps, furniture, wallpaper, tacks, glassware, grindstones, medicines, tools, cutlery and machinery of every kind, and then, when the Peruvian railroad construction was under way, everything from tracks to railroad cars and locomotives.[44] The Bryce-Grace partnership lasted until 1876, when the Graces bought out the Bryces and the firm became known as Grace Brothers & Company.

By 1880 the Graces were bankers, naval contractors, operators of several ships of their own, and agents for other shippers in three strategic ports. John W. Grace had left the family estate in Ireland in 1873 and made his way to California, where he worked with Captain Chapman to develop the interests of the company on the West Coast. After several years working with Chapman in San Francisco, John went to join Michael Grace in Peru, and George L. Duval went out to San Francisco from New York to replace him. Chapman withdrew in 1880 to establish himself as a very successful shipping agent, but the Casa Grace continued to expand. In 1889 Grace Brothers & Company of Lima, Peru, were the registered owners of the 1,574-ton ship *Lancashire Witch,*[45] and soon more ships were to be added to their ever-expanding fleet. Grace ships were now carrying cargoes of goods manufactured in the eastern United States through the Straits of Magellan to California, loading wheat there and taking it back to New York for shipment to Europe, but invariably touching at Callao, outward and homeward bound. The Chilean government then had a monopoly in the nitrate fields of southern Peru, and Grace Brothers were shippers in Peru and consignees in New York—and there was also guano, still being shipped in great quantities from various deposits off and around the coast of Peru. The Casa Grace was well and truly in business and on its way to becoming a vast international conglomerate.

So important had W. R. Grace become in New York that the Democratic Party ran him for mayor in 1880. Things weren't going well until a Grace campaign manager made shrewd use of the Republican contention that he was an Irishman who had lived most of his life in Peru and was therefore not a proper United States citizen. Unfortunately for the Republicans, this tactic backfired on them, for a Mr. Eldridge, senior paymaster in the United States Navy, then came forward, stating that he remembered William Grace from his Civil War days. Voters were then told about the 1862 affair when, as mentioned, two Union cruisers had put into Callao with empty bunkers and a crew that had not been paid for months. At this time the war news reaching Callao looked bad for Lincoln and the Union forces, and consequently no bank in Peru would honor Mr. Eldridge's drafts. Finally he was directed to the office of William R. Grace, who, Eldridge reported, had leaned back in his chair and said, "I have faith in the Union and I will give you all the money you need." Due to this timely intervention, William Russell Grace won the election with ease, becoming the first Roman Catholic mayor of New York City. Opposing the corrupt "Tammany Ring," he conducted a reform administration, attacking patronage, police scandals, and organized vice, breaking up the Louisiana lottery in New York, and reducing the tax rate. He was elected a second time in 1884, on an independent ticket.[46]

During the period when William Grace was serving as mayor of New York, the enterprise he had created went through its most difficult period. Between 1879 and 1883 Peru and Bolivia were lined up against Chile in the War of the Pacific, out of which victorious Chile acquired the Peruvian province of Tarapacá, and all of Peru's valuable nitrate fields. At one stroke Casa Grace lost their profitable traffic in Peruvian nitrates. Also lost was the Peruvian navy, and the Grace profits, as outfitters to this navy, went down with the fleet. The cost of the war had left Peru even deeper in debt, and the House of Grace found its investment in Peruvian bonds frozen. Michael P. Grace rushed from New York, where he had been running the firm during his brother's term as mayor, only to find affairs in Peru in a sorry state. The first move he made to save the company was to extend the Casa Grace into Chile, as a bid for what had now become the Chilean nitrate trade.

Michael Grace then settled down to the unenviable task of collecting, or rather attempting to collect, some of the money that Peru owed for this disastrous war and the funding of Henry Meiggs's famous, but expensive, railroads. Mainly due to these two factors, Peru had to declare itself bankrupt in 1886, when it owed its English bondholders alone around $250,000,000—most of which was secured by the nitrate fields that Chile had taken. It was at this point that Michael Grace stepped in as a negotiator between the Peruvian government and the bondholders, the result of which was the famed Grace-Donoughmore Contract.[47]

11

Peru Moves into the Twentieth Century

THE YEAR OF 1890 WAS A VERY DECISIVE ONE IN THE LONG AND TURbulent history of Peru, for it was early in this year that Michael Grace, with others, brought to a conclusion a deal that finally settled the Peruvian debt problems. In fact, from the ending of the war with Chile, Michael Grace in particular, and W. R. Grace & Company —the Casa Grace, as they liked to be known—were to play an ever-increasing role in the economic and political affairs of Peru. The unsuccessful outcome of the war with Chile had left Peru with an unstable government and a national debt of some $250,000,000. Fortune had indeed declared against this nation, for at the end of this bitter struggle the republic also found itself despoiled of one of the principal sources of its fiscal wealth, the southern nitrate fields, which had all been lost in this struggle with her belligerent southern neighbor, Chile.

The economy was wrecked, and nothing remained in the way of assets except its own 100,000 soles of paper money, which circulated with difficulty at 10 percent of the face value. Under these conditions, from 1884 onward, various political parties, Civilist, Constitutionalist, Liberal, and Democratic presented themselves as political forces. Out of all this chaos General Andes A. Caceras emerged as leader. Although claiming to be a Constitutionalist, Caceras chose to seize the reigns of power by unconstitutional means. On December 2, 1885, he entered Lima and deposed Iglesias by a coup d'état, although it has to be conceded that eight months later, on August 10, 1886, he did hold elections, and "amid the acclamations of the people" managed to get himself installed as the constitutional president of the republic.

Caceras was to remain in power until 1894 when he was replaced by the administration of Colonel Remigio Morales Bermudez, who in turn was replaced when Caceras returned to serve a second term as president. It was, however, Pierola who captured the limelight during these turbulent years. Imprisoned in 1890, when he campaigned for the presidency, he became a symbol of opposition to oppression. Authoritarian though he was, his courage through all adversity and his personal charm won the people's support, and in 1895 he organized a revolution that brought him, at last, the real power he had coveted for so long.[1] Nicolas de Pierola's regime, which lasted until 1899, was to greatly change Peru.

Such was the political situation in postwar Peru, under which Michael Paul Grace, together with his aristocratic colleague, John Luke George (Hely-Hutchinson), fifth Earl of Donoughmore (1848–1900), were to broker, then introduce, the celebrated Peruvian financial "contract" that was to bear their names. United at this point by an involvement in the affairs of Peru, it is interesting to note that the Grace and Donoughmore families were, just eleven years after the signing of this contract, to be united by marriage. In 1901 Michael Grace's daughter Elena Maria and Donoughmore's son, Richard Walter John (Hely-Hutchinson), the sixth Earl of Donoughmore, married. Both the fifth and the sixth earls were active in business. In 1883, just prior to the family involvement with the affairs of Peru, the family estates consisted of 4,711 acres in County Tipperary; 2,878 in County Waterford; 1,972 in County Cork; 1,307 in County Wexford; and 1,082 in Counties Kilkenny, Monaghan, Dublin, and Louth, valued at £10,424 a year.[2] Like the Grace family, the earls of Donoughmore had also been active in Irish relief work during the ever-recurring potato crop failures, and the fourth earl served on the "General Central Relief Committee for all Ireland" during the terrible famine year of 1847.[3]

Michael Grace, more than many others, fully understood that in the aftermath of the War of the Pacific, the crux of Peru's climb to some semblance of short-term recovery lay in her ability to borrow on foreign capital markets. While an influx of capital would obviously have eased the way to economic recovery, Peru clearly could not go to American or European capital markets because of the continuing burden of foreign debt on which the government had defaulted in 1876. The war, of course, had exacerbated all the republic's economic and social problems. Therefore, in 1885, the prospects of agreeing on a settlement concerning the massive debts with the bondholders, which would allow Peru to borrow again on the foreign capital markets, seemed further away than ever. The position of the Chilean government also complicated the issue, their prime concern being to ensure that they were not held responsible for any portion of the debt that might have been secured by the guano and nitrates of Tarapaca. Although, it is worth noting, they did actually authorize the sale of a million tons of guano from the Lobos Islands, half the net proceeds of which, it was agreed, would go to creditors holding a lien on Peruvian guano.[4]

It was this situation, under which the bondholders, especially in London, were growing ever more restive, that gave Michael Grace a chance for his "masterstroke." The idea was that he, with Donoughmore acting as a prestigious figurehead, would broker a deal between the Peruvian government and its foreign bondholders. The end result of their negotiations, which lasted several years, was via the famous Grace-Donoughmore Contract and the establishment of the Peruvian Corporation Limited. This enterprise was nominally directed by Lord Donoughmore, with a board largely composed of British bondholders, but Michael Grace was undoubtedly the real negotiator, "the power behind the scenes" who, at a very early stage in the establishment of the corporation, made the true position abundantly clear; this, in particular, being when he advised the bondholders that "His Lordship [Donoughmore] must be given to understand that we are the men commissioned to handle the situation & that matters will be put before him for signature.".[5]

The gist of the final agreement, at last concluded on January 11, 1890, after years of negotiating, was that the corporation would completely extinguish the huge foreign debt, but only in return for massive and extremely unpopular concessions to the foreign corporation, namely, that in return for assuming two bond issues, the government would be obliged to turn over to the Peruvian Corporation all (769 miles) of the state railroads for sixty-six years (soon to be extended another seventeen years and finally granted in perpetuity) and the exclusive right to export two million tons of guano from the islands. It also granted the former bondholders an annuity of £80,000, later reduced to £60,000, for thirty-three years; 500,000 hectares of land in the Perene Valley (land that contained valuable oil and mineral deposits); and the valuable franchise to run steamships on Lake Titicaca.[6]

Michael Grace did not undertake all of this as a work of pure altruism, for he was the first to recognize that the considerable Grace holdings in Peru, which included a substantial stake in the Cerro de Pasco silver mines, would be enhanced by the recovery of the country. On top of that, Michael Grace intended to be well paid for organizing this rescue package, although he was well aware that before the Graces received anything, they would have to spend a great deal of their own money. Nevertheless, to be fair, there was more to it than this, as just one incident will illustrate. When, after four years of unceasing toil, negotiations looked like they were breaking down, a London attorney sought privately to console William Grace by saying that, after all, "the business to you is purely a mercantile venture." Grace corrected the Englishman at once, and in no uncertain terms: "The business to us has not been purely a mercantile venture; for, as such, I would never have touched it. My brother has had the natural and praiseworthy ambition of making for himself a great record in settling the Foreign Debt of Peru & re-establishing her in a position of prosperity, and it was the influence of this feeling in his mind and my desire to forward his wishes in that direction that induced us to spend so very large an amount of money & time, and I personally don't regret it."[7]

The Peruvian Corporation, initially set up in January 1890, became a going concern in April, and Peru's credit in the money markets of the world was reestablished overnight. The long-suffering republic was back in business and this was, in the main, due to the negotiating skill of one man, Michael P. Grace. He had spent five years working on this contract and more than the $250,000 that had been his limit in the beginning.[8] On the other hand, the contract had been personally very profitable for Michael Grace and the other concessionaires. First, Grace received £150,000 in cash plus a 3 percent commission on the shares or cash distributed among the bondholders' agent. He was also granted a contract, worth about £100,000, to extend the Oroya Railroad. Therefore, taken together, it is estimated that he earned between a half million and a million dollars, provided one took the future profit on the Oroya Railroad into account.[9]

The progress of the Peruvian Corporation during the following twenty-odd years may be gauged from the figures that are available. From 1890 to 1891, for instance, the net receipts in sterling amounted to £91,771 11s. 3d., while for 1891–92, the receipts went up to £137,816 214s. 8d. In the next three years they slid back, however, mounting again in 1895–96, only to fall back once more in 1897; but from that time onward the receipts seemed to have shown a steady, if not sensational, increase until 1908, when they amounted to £263,203 19s. 5d. For the years 1908–9 there was, however, a slight fall in receipts due to a decrease in the guano income, and partly to increased fixed charges, which had to an extent been counterbalanced by an increase in net receipts from the railroads. With the exception of their land colony, which showed a small debit of a little more than £5,000, the whole of the undertakings in the hands of the Peruvian Corporation proved remunerative for the year ending June 30, 1910; a profit for the twelve months of £285,177 was shown. It is interesting to compare statistics of this corporation since it was established in 1890, to those twenty years later, in 1909–1910. From 1890–91 receipts amounted to £9,771, while for 1909–10 they figured at £333,559, or more than a 200 percent increase.[10]

Writing in 1976, the British historian Rory Miller stated that "Peruvians have almost without fail denigrated the Grace Contract. Mariategui considers that, in delivering the railways to British bankers, the Peruvian Government managed slowly to stimulate the investment of foreign capital in other sectors of the economy, reemphasizing its colonial condition."[11] He continued, "More recently Virgilio Roel has written that these railways were the most important in the country. For this reason their foreign ownership put our country into a typically colonial category even though it kept a facade of political autonomy. Jorge Basadre, on the other hand, appreciates the fact that the debts of the past were liquidated by the contract, though he declines to answer the question as to whether Peru paid too much."[12]

Sadly though, these Peruvian attitudes, although understandable, do tend to draw attention away from several crucial and unpalatable aspects of the issue. The first of these is the postcolonial social structure of Peru. Independence from Spain, to a large extent, merely meant that the Peruvian ruling elite, the descendants of the conquistadors, no longer needed to pay colonial tribute to Spain. However, they themselves remained, to all intents and purposes, as "colonial" oppressors of the indigenous people and the imported, bonded workforce, who they continued to exploit ruthlessly. Peru, to these wealthy hacendados, merchants, and government officials, was still a geographical entity to be exploited for short-term gain. Such attitudes inevitably surfaced in bad strategic long-term planning, which resulted in the squandering of the guano revenues, then the unbalanced, overzealous investments in railroads, and finally a total lack of foresight in failing to strengthen Peru's naval and military defenses. The Chilean ruling class clearly learned something from the Spanish naval attacks of 1863–66, while the Peruvian establishment obviously did not. Several more orders placed for ships, such as the *Huascar,* rather than for yet another railroad would, undoubtedly, have saved Peru from the Chilean attack. It would clearly have prevented the loss of the southern nitrate fields and the subsequent loss of her railroads and other major assets to the control of the Peruvian corporation and other foreign interests. Above all else, this mortgaging to foreigners of Peru's most valued resources struck a very serious blow at national pride.

As Miller has pointed out, first, the dividend record of the Peruvian Corporation was exceptionally poor, for it never paid a dividend on its ordinary stock, except during a very brief period in the 1920s.[13] Second, only during the same period, in the 1920s, did the rate of return on the railroads exceed 5 percent, confirming the view that holdings here could hardly be considered a profitable investment. Third, to answer the charge that the real profit from the Grace-Donoughmore Contract came to those who had bought Peruvian bonds when they were at their lowest price in the 1880s, Miller states that a calculation was made to see how such a speculator would have gained, and he concluded: "An investment of £1,000 in Peruvian bonds in 1885, in fact, would have earned less than $300 in dividends over the next twenty-five years. In no sense, therefore, could the Peruvian Corporation be considered to have fulfilled its original function—the servicing of a bondholder debt in perpetual default. The major profits were, in fact, only to be made by speculation in short-term sale and purchase of the bonds, and any capitalist who bought depreciating Peruvian bonds in the 1880s in the hope of seeing a secure income from the bondholders' concessions must have been highly disappointed."[14]

The railroads, it appears, managed to cut freight rates in the Peruvian sierra to about 35 percent of the rates charged by animal transport. This, however, did not advance agriculture in the sierra much because rural development in these areas was still being held back, to an appreciable extent, by the lack of capital and oppressive land tenure practices. However, in connecting the highlands of the central sierra to the markets of Lima, exports of agricultural produce to Lima at last became practical. The real impact of the railways on the Peruvian economy came in mining. It took place not on the basis of silver mining in Cerro de Pasco, but in copper, as prices rose after 1897.

Not surprisingly, the years around 1890 also saw extensive investments by the House of Grace in Peru. The Casa Grace actually bought the Hacienda Cartavio in the Chicama Valley from Guillermo Alzamora in 1882, but did not really begin to develop it until Michael

Grace formed the Cartavio Sugar Company in 1891. In the same year both Michael Grace and the Peruvian Corporation also began to take an interest in the cotton industry by setting up the Peruvian Manufacturing Company in Lima. This enterprise was established with the main aim of gaining control of the Vitarte Cotton Mill. However, Grace interests did not actually get outright control of this enterprise until many years later in 1917.[15]

Here one should note, however, Grace's partner in the Peruvian Corporation, John Luke George, the fifth Lord Donoughmore, did not live to see this development. He died at the early age of fifty-two, on December 5, 1900, at his London residence, 84 Sloane Street, after a few days' illness. Interestingly, this notable aristocrat, chosen to front the Peruvian Corporation by Grace because of his wealth, charm, and influence, had been a prominent Freemason. In fact, the year following that on which the Prince of Wales was first installed as Grand Master of the Masonic Brotherhood, he appointed Lord Donoughmore as Senior Grand Warden, which is the fourth-highest office in the Grand Lodge. A week afterward his lordship received the appointment of Scribe N. in the Supreme Grand Chapter of Royal Arch Masons.[16]

William Russell Grace, twice mayor of New York and founder of the dynasty now known as the Casa Grace, survived Donoughmore by more than three years. The millionaire succumbed to pneumonia at the age of seventy-two at his home, 31 East Seventy-ninth Street, New York, on March 21, 1904. When news of the ex-mayor's death arrived at city hall, John H. O'Brien, the mayor's secretary in the absence of Mr. McClellan, ordered the flag on the cupola to be lowered at half-mast. Word of the event then spread along the waterfront, and flags were seen everywhere flying at half-mast from ships and sailing craft large and small. Acting mayor Fornes, on hearing the news, said, "In the death of William R. Grace the city has lost one of its most distinguished and valuable citizens and a man who was one of the best and ablest Mayors New York ever had. He was a born diplomat and impressed his views upon his associates in business and government affairs in a kindly and persuasive way, but with a force and intelligence which carried conviction."

At the time of his death the New York press reported that Messrs. W. R. Grace & Company had been responsible for establishing the pioneer direct steamship service between New York and the west coast of South America in 1892. The New York and Pacific Steamship Company, the press noted, was also owned and operated by the

13. The United States frigate *Constellation* with relief stores for Irish Distress, off Haulbowline, in Cork Harbour, 1880. This voyage being part-funded by William R. Grace, Mayor of New York. *The Illustrated London News*, May, 1880.

House of Grace, adding that its fleet of seven large steamers had been constructed especially for their trade, which then plied between New York and Guayaquil in Equador via the Straits of Magellan. The *New York Times* also drew attention to the fact that the firm owned or controlled important nitrate and soda properties in Chile, a sugar and cotton mill in Peru, and was closely identified with railroad developments in both countries.

William Russell Grace had indeed come a long way since his early days as a marine store proprietor on the Chincha Islands. In his last years he had been president of W. R. Grace & Company. In addition to this he had held an interest in the Ingersoll-Sergeant Drill Company and Haesler-Ingersoll Pneumatic Tool Company. Grace had been a trustee of the New York Life Assurance Company and the Lincoln Safe Deposit Company. He had also been a director of the Central and South American Telegraph Company, City Trust Company, Lincoln National Bank, Northern Insurance Company, Terminal Warehouse Company, Terminal Improvement Company, Grace Brothers & Company Limited, and the Evergreens Cemetery. At the time of his death it is estimated that he left a fortune of nearly $10,000,000. A widow and five children survived him. Each of William Grace's brothers had also had successful careers. In 1904 Dr. Morgan S. Grace was serving as a member of the Upper House of the New Zealand Legislature. The other brothers, Michael P. and John W. Grace, were then residing with their families in England, the former being chairman of the English business house, the latter having retired. Very appropriately, considering the families' Norman origins, Michael Grace was then residing in the historic Battle Abbey, which he was holding under lease, and which was constructed by William the Conqueror to commemorate his victory over Harold in the Battle of Hastings.[17]

Meanwhile, on the coast, the labor system in post-1890 Peru continued to be run on colonial lines. Increasingly, however, the large landowners such as the Casa Grace began to utilize advanced capitalist technology. In short, a sort of feudalistic system developed, which ran from the patriarchal charitable system of the Larco brothers in Chiclin to establishments utterly devoid of social vision, where the workers were paid exceptionally poor wages. Labor, in many cases, was obtained by the notorious enganche system by which debts were artificially created, which held the workers in virtual serfdom. These unfortunates were Indians rounded up from the Sierra, or imported Chinese and Japanese bonded workers. There can be no doubt that the real cost of Peruvian policy was now being paid for by these poor workers.

The enormous social downside of the Grace-Donoughmore Contract was that a large proportion of the best coastal land had passed to foreign ownership, and wages paid on these establishments certainly did not conform to profits. The workers, at least according to the historian Carleton Beals, were invariably housed in dark, windowless huts with dirt-floored rooms, walls full of vermin, and completely without plumbing or sanitation. The largest Chicama Valley estate, covering an area larger than the smaller European nations, was owned by the powerful German Gildermeister family, the second largest being the aforementioned Cartavio, owned by William R. Grace & Company, although it has to be said that Beals did not make it clear if these particular enterprises were operated badly or under a more humane patriarchal system as adopted by the Larco brothers.

Nevertheless, it is certain that the majority of the vast foreign-owned coastal estates soon became independent kingdoms devoid of any real interest in the internal affairs of Peru. To them the republic had virtually ceded its sovereignty. Their power became so great that they could appoint resident government officials, enforce law and order, and in some cases evade taxes. Under European feudalism the local cities did at least become the first markets for goods, but in Peru the products of all these great estates went directly to foreign markets. With their tremendous importing advantages they also bought most of their requirements from abroad. They in fact carried on substantially more trade with the outside world than they did with Peru. Consequently, their local and national influence tended to be negative and destructive. Apart from these new, post-1890, foreign-owned estates, much of the best land still remained under Spanish ownership, a remaining legacy of the Spanish colonial period. Thus, from former Jesuit estates in Arequipa (which passed into the hands of the Goyeneche family, relatives of the famous bishop), it is estimated that even as late as the 1930s, 300,000 soles went annually across the sea to the absentee owners in Spain.[18]

As for the shipping interests linking the Peruvian "export economy" with the international community, these continued to develop during the first decade of this century. Among the steamship companies that were doing business with the west coast at this time was the notable enterprise established by Wheelwright, the Pacific Steam Navigation Company of Liverpool, although this was then amalgamated with the Royal Mail Steam Packet Company. Working with this company was the Compania Sud-America de Vapores of Valparaiso. These concerns arranged their sailings in such a way as to make alternative calls at the ports between Panama and Callao, and between Callao and Valparaiso, while the vessels of the first-named company continued to make their way to Europe through the Straits of Magellan.

Another west coast line was the German Kosmos Company. Unfortunately, it had by then gained a reputation for not sailing in accordance with its published sailing schedules. There was also another line of German steamships known as the Roland, which, like those of the Kosmos Company, made monthly voyages to European ports via the Straits of Magellan. These steamers also made runs along the whole western coast of the Pacific Ocean, proceeding northward as far as San Francisco, calling at Panama and the principal Central American and Mexican ports. Two well-known

British enterprises, the Booth Line and the Red Cross Steamship Company were also operating services up the Amazon to the Peruvian region of the Amazon rain forests, the practice being to dispatch one of their steamers monthly from Liverpool and another from New York to the Peruvian port of Iquitos.

The Japanese Steamship Company Toyo Kison Kaisha and a Chinese company both ran services from Callao to the principal ports of Japan and China, carrying mails for the East. The Lamport and Holt and Gulf Line steamers also called regularly at Callao from Liverpool and Cardiff, proceeding with cargo to Guayaquil in Ecuador. Of particular interest is the fact that the Merchants' Line (or New York and Pacific Steamship Company), owned by Grace Brothers was by then operating a regular service from Chilean and Peruvian ports to New York and other eastern ports of the United States. At this time the Barber Line was also operating a regular service from Chilean and Peruvian ports to New York. In 1911 sailing vessels, which still arrived regularly at Callao, generally brought grain or coal from Australia, grain and lumber from Puget Sound, and general cargo from Europe, but even then, this class of craft was diminishing, and Callao was gradually ceasing to be a sailing ship port.[19]

Of particular interest is the fact that from June 1928 to January 1930, U.S. Navy Lt. George R. Johnson, in his capacity as chief photographer of the Peruvian Naval Air Service, pioneered aerial photography in Peru. One of his most remarkable shots, published in 1930 by the American Geographical Society, shows four sailing ships of the guano fleet at anchor in Callao Bay, indicating that this trade was still operating well into the twentieth century, although, of course, not on the same spectacular scale as it was during the second part of the previous century.[20]

It would now be appropriate to take a glance at the part of Peru that lies to the east of the great Cordilleras, the "Green Hell" of Amazonia where, in the 1880s, Michael Grace and many others had invested in the rubber business.[21] When he was writing in 1911, the historian Percy F. Martin stated that plans were being discussed for the construction of a railroad to run from Iquitos in the Amazon jungle to the Pacific coast by way of a tunnel through the northern Andes, to Iquitos, the Peruvian port situated some 2,600 miles up the Amazon River from the coast. In 1911 this inland port had a population of about 30,000, and its chief export was rubber. Steamers, drawing up to twenty-three feet, then made monthly trips to Iquitos from the Para end, occupying nearly thirty days between

Para and that port. One of the most notable fleets on the river belonged to the British concern known as the Amazon Steam Navigation Company Limited. However, in July 1910, this enterprise was disbanded, and a new concern, called the Amazon River Steam Navigation Company, was registered with a capital of £300,000, which purchased from the old company a great part of its flotilla.

The whole of the commerce of the important Department of Loreto passed through Iquitos Customs. A thriving trade was also carried on between the small river steamers bringing up consignments of rubber from, and taking back supplies to, ports as far away as Para, Brazil, and a distance of nearly 2,650 miles. British shipping on the river during 1909 amounted to 15,104 registered tons, as compared with 11,927 tons in 1908. There were twelve steamers of 13,868 tons for Liverpool and other European ports and two steamers of 1,236 tons for New York. The exports from Iquitos at this time consisted of hides, tobacco, Panama hats, a commodity described as "Vegetable Ivory," and par excellence rubber.[22]

It was at this time that the collecting of rubber on the Putumayo River, one of the main tributaries of the Amazon, was in the hands of J. C. Arana. Sadly, once again, the brutal treatment of workers was to feature in Peruvian history. What became known as the "Putumayo Affair" was first brought to the attention of the international community in September 1909 by the editor of the outspoken British magazine *Truth*. The course of the Putumayo, the scene of terrible atrocities, now marks the boundary between Peru and Columbia, except for a short stretch where Columbia has access to the main river, but until the start of the rubber boom neither countries showed much interest in the area. The indigenous people who lived there were allowed to continue their simple way of life, without much outside interference, until Arana arrived on the scene looking for cheap labor to exploit.

Julio Arana arrived in Iquitos in the 1880s penniless, but with a determination to make money. At first he earned a meager living hawking hats, but he soon acquired a few small boats with which he began to trade with the Amazonian rubber gatherers. After he had built up a monopoly in supplying Colombians, he started entering into partnership with them, buying them out when they showed a desire to leave and forcing them out when they did not. In 1903 his growing enterprise, known as J. C. Arana Hermanos, entered the Putumayo area. Backed by a small but effective band of armed thugs, Arana was soon in control of a large part of Amazonia. Then, in October 1907, a new company was incorporated and set up in London under the name of the Peruvian Amazon Rubber Company Limited, with a capital of £1,000,000, to take over the business and possessions of the J. C. Arana and Hermanos Company. The directors were seven in number, three of them being Englishmen, three Spaniards or of Spanish extraction, the remaining member being a French banker who soon resigned, his place being taken by another gentleman with a Spanish name.

The company's registered office was at Salisbury House, London Wall. On July 8, 1908, it dropped the word "rubber" from its title, and became known to the public as the Peruvian Amazon Company. On December 6, 1908, shares in Arana's company were offered to the British public. The issue was, however, a failure, 90 percent of the stock remaining in the underwriters' hands. The prospectus was actually fraudulent, for the profits declared had never been made, and the enterprise had no legal title to any of its so-called "rubber estates." Nevertheless, a handful of gullible speculators were found, and three suitably dim-witted Englishmen were coopted onto the board. This company, now masquerading as a respectable London-based English enterprise, thus inherited from its predecessors their disgraceful methods of dealing with the rubber gatherers. Some inkling of what was going on in their names should have reached the ears of the local English directors, although they consistently denied this, despite the fact that at least two of the members of the original Arana Company were directors of the London company that succeeded it.

Evidence against Arana soon reached the editor of *Truth* magazine. The persons responsible were a young engineer, W. E. Hardenburg, and his companion Perkins. However, their own observations were supplemented by a large number of statements substantiated by declarations before a notary. In addition to this, they had already been referred to, in no ambiguous terms, in at least three newspapers, *La Felpa* and *La Sancón,* both published at Iquitos, and *O Jornal do Commercio,* published at Manaos, Brazil. They were terrible indictments and, as set forth by *La Sanción,* the charges were that the agents of the company:

> Force the pacific Indians of the Putumayo to work day and night at the extraction of rubber without the slightest remuneration; that they give them nothing to eat; that they rob them of their crops, their women, and their children, to satisfy the voracity, lasciviousness, and avarice of them-

> selves and their employees, for they live on the Indians food, keep harems of concubines, and sell these people wholesale and retail at Iquitos; that they flog them inhumanely until their bones are laid bare; that they do not give them any medical treatment, but let them linger, eaten by maggots, till they die, to serve afterwards as food for the chiefs' dogs; that they mutilate them cut off their ears, fingers, arms, and legs; that they torture them by means of fire, of water, and by tying them up, crucified head down; that they burn and destroy their houses and crops; that they cut them to pieces with machetes; that they grasp children by their feet and dash out their brains against walls and trees; that they have their old folk killed when they can work no longer; finally, that to amuse themselves, to practice shooting, or to celebrate the Sabado de gloria, as Fonseca and Macedo have done, they discharge their weapons at men, women, and children, or in preference to this, they souse them with kerosene and set fire to them, to enjoy their desperate agony.

The considerable evidence collected by Hardenburg and Perkins, and the other newspapers mentioned, confirmed that all of the forgoing was true and in no way an exaggeration. More horror stories emerged, among which was Perkins's experience of life at the Peruvian Amazon Company's headquarters, where he stayed for some time. While there he states that he suffered in various ways, namely, sickness without medicine or even drinking water, daily threats of death, and so on, but, he conceded, he fared better than any other prisoner in that he was the only one not murdered after his arrival at this base! While he was there he reported that he saw many things that shocked him, brutal acts that not only gave him an insight into the ways of the Peruvian Amazon Company, but also, significantly, the Peruvian army, who were working hand-in-glove with Arana's thugs.

After he had been there about three weeks, Perkins states that twenty-nine Colombians were captured by a large force of Peruvians after being tricked into laying down their arms. These prisoners, unarmed and tied, were then butchered with pistols and machetes. Some of the Peruvians, being "braver" than the others, mutilated the dead bodies by cutting them about the face, and some were decapitated. The men who did this were regarded as "heroes" and went unpunished. Perkins then stated, "One morning while a company of soldiers was lined up in the yard for inspection a party started from the house to a camp in the woods carrying provisions on the backs of Indian porters. All these Indians were in a state of starvation, and one poor devil was too weak to carry his load, about 70lb. After falling repeatedly he was told to fall no more, and as he staggered and looked as if he was going to fall, one of the Peruvians shot him in the back and he died."[23]

After reports of these atrocities reached Britain, a question was tabled in the House of Commons asking whether the foreign secretary's attention had been "called to the proceedings of an English company called the Peruvian Amazon Company." Few parliamentarians seemed to know where the Putumayo was. Nevertheless, British MP's were shocked by what they heard. The upshot of this was that Roger David Casement, then in the British Consular Service, who had already exposed similar atrocities in the Congo, was sent out to the Putumayo to make a full inquiry. His notable report on the Putumayo atrocities soon confirmed the truth of the first reports to a horrified world. Public opinion was then influenced by the Anti-Slavery Society. Unfortunately, the "Putumayo Affair" dragged on for many years before it was finally resolved.

The report produced by Casement then brought to light abuses of labor in other parts of Peru. Knighted in 1911, before he became hostile to England, Sir Roger wrote in his "Blue Book" (page 158), "The crimes of the Putumayo, horrible as they are, have their counterparts, I am assured, in other remote regions of the same lawless forests—although possibly not to the same extent." However, abuses, and even cruelties, in the exploitation of native laborers were, as Casement had been informed, not just confined to the Peruvian "Green Hell" to the east of the Andes. For example, on July 24, 1912, the *Comercio* of Lima, putting forward the views of the Asociación Pro-Indígena of Lima, commenced a leading article with these words: "Although we now account for ninety years autocratic life, we have not yet wholly shaken off certain abuses and corrupt practices which were the current coin, that is to say, during the arbitrary administration of the Colonial period. The encomiendas of Indians, the Mita, and other irritating acts of injustice of that epoch threaten from time to time to break out again in our Serranias under distinct forms, having always as their basis the abuses, the immorality and the lack of humane sentiments which characterised the odious exploitation by which the authorities of those times victimised the aboriginal element of Peru."

Here it should be noted that these observations, and the larger number of cases dealt with at this time by the Asociacióon Pro-Indígena of Lima, related not to the savage Indians of the Putumayo in eastern Peru, but to the nominally civilized Roman Catholic Indians descended from the Inca Empire. Of these indignities Senor

Pedro S. Zulen, the secretary, wrote that his association received or obtained information of almost all the cruelties daily practiced on the Indians in the various parts of the Peruvian republic. Of a somewhat different order were the atrocities brought to the notice of the Asociación by Senor Francisco Mostajo, their delegate from Arequipa. In a letter of June 17, 1912, he dealt with what he rightly called alarming iniquities practiced in the Montanas of the Yavero, belonging to the district of Lares of the province of Calca (not far from Cuzco). The details of these atrocities were vouched for by Father Eliserio Martinez, who in a letter from Cuzco of May 1912 stated: "A thousand acts of ill-treatment are being committed against the savages; some are killed, others are sold and carried off to be exploited as simple slaves. The authorities have received information of all this, and I hope they will take suitable measures."

Senor Mostajo commented as follows: "We are confronted by an attack on humanity as nameless as that of the Putumayo, which has echoed round the world in a manner so shameful to Peru. In view of the gravity of the matter and the fact that the labourers who are victims of this ill-treatment are natives, and that the press of Cuzco appears satisfied by the explanations already alluded to, and that the newspapers of Lima have overlooked the serious charges made, I have deemed it my duty to call the attention of our humane Society to the unspeakable deeds being committed in the Montanas region of Cuzco."

The following day, July 2, 1912, the *Comercio* of Lima in a strong and courageous leading article entitled "The Crimes in the Montanas of Cuzco," asked: "How long shall we permit the economic rapacity of soulless traffickers to pile up riches by scattering death and grief amongst the very men who secure them? How long will part of the money accumulated in our Montanas be the transformation of the blood of the savages of the unexplored regions of Peru? This situation cannot be prolonged indefinitely."[24]

Roger David Casement had indeed rendered a service to humanity by exposing the abuses in the Congo and on the Putumayo in Peru. In 1912 Casement retired from the case, and leaving public life became a popular hero. But before his death his name was to become almost a term of execration in England, and after it millions of Irish were to elevate him to the status of a martyr. Born in Dublin, on September 1, 1864, he subsequently entered the British consular service and served in equatorial Africa and then Brazil, prior to being asked to produce his famous report on the Putumayo Affair.

Then, becoming hostile to England, he was in Berlin in November 1914, urging Irish war prisoners to form a brigade for service against the allies. In April 1916 he landed at Tralee from a German ship and was arrested on a charge of high treason. The police then found in his lodgings a number of typewritten journals that showed Casement to be a homosexual and, even worse, a compulsive writer. A truly dreadful combination! Needless to say, these startling developments and revelations brought a degree of solace to the rogues he had worked so hard to expose in Peru.

As it happens, before these interesting developments occurred, in October 1912, a new government had come to power in Peru, under a leader with the reassuringly English, middle-class name of Billinghurst, who was hostile to Arana's party in Loreto. Consequently, in December, Judge Valcarcel issued warrants for the arrest of Arana and two of his partners-in-crime, Zumaeta and Vega. Unfortunately, on February 2, 1913, the high court in Iquitos annulled this order. Six days later, however, another archvillain in this scandal, Armando Normand, was arrested in Bolivia and held for extradition. Little of any real importance concerning this sad affair happened in Peru for the remainder of the year, but in England a parliamentary select committee was set up to examine the involvement of the directors of the Peruvian Amazon Company, the conclusion reached being that the English directors had been negligent, greedy, and exceptionally stupid, but were found not to have had prior knowledge of the atrocities.

To the amazement of all who had followed this distressing case, on January 4, 1914, Zumaeta was elected mayor of Iquitos, but was forced to resign under pressure from the president. Arana managed to get out of the country before he could be brought to trial, but others responsible for these crimes were eventually tried. On May 29, 1915, just before a verdict was expected, nine men, including Normand, Homero, and Rodriguez, with obvious help from inside, escaped from the jail in Iquitos. They made good their escape, and with them went the last chance of punishing any of those responsible for these terrible crimes against humanity.[25]

Meanwhile, back on the west coast of Peru business was booming. Glancing at available statistics that were provided for 1905 and 1906, it seems that Great Britain was at that time far ahead of all other countries in regard to the tonnage of steamers coming to Callao. In the latter year, the arrivals showed for Great Britain 507,309 tons, and the sailings 502,876 tons, her nearest competitor being Germany, with 172,063 tons arrivals and 182,608 tons sailings. Chile, Peru's old archenemy, came in third with 168,272 tons arrivals and 170,070 tons sailings. Interestingly, both France and Norway showed considerably higher results than the United States, which, indeed, marked a most astonishing falling off in both arrivals and sailings. In 1905 the United States recorded 9,450 tons arrivals and 8,708 tons sailings, while in 1906 these fell away to 3,420 tons and sailings to 2,678 tons.[26]

Just a few years later in 1909 statistics regarding Peruvian imports and exports tell a different story. In this year Peru imported goods to the value of £1,567,898 from Britain, this being 36.47 percent of the total, while the value of imports from the United States stood at £846,127, or 19.73 percent of the total. Only Germany came anywhere near these figures at £687,233, representing 15.98 percent of the total. Imports from Chile then stood at just 4.23 percent of the total.[27] A glance at the shipping statistics for 1909 is quite revealing. These show that for this year there were 224 British vessels out of a total of 496, which represents an aggregate of 618,953 out of the total tonnage of 1,161,732. At this time, according to Martin, Callao received, on average, some 400 steamers and 1,020 sailing ships in the course of each year, this standing in contradiction to some reports that stated sailing ship trade at this time was in a marked decline. In addition to this, there was also an immense number of locally owned smaller craft using the port of Callao that were engaged in the local coastal trade.

Next to Callao, the most important port for British vessels was at this time Mollendo, and here, out of a total of 460 steam vessels representing a tonnage of 275,339, the British claimed 74,547 tons. In regard to sailing vessels with cargo, Britain and the United States stood on a par so far as the number of vessels was concerned, but the former represented a total tonnage of 10,549, as against 4,137 for the United States. The customs receipts at this port in 1910 amounted to £797,867, the largest sums collected in one month being £84,343 in June. It is also interesting to note that at this time practically all of the Peruvian rubber was being shipped from the Pacific side, despite the fact that a very substantial maritime trade was then being conducted by Peru via the Amazon. For the year 1910 the shipments in this product alone via Mollendo were as follows: Peruvian rubber, fine, 1,680 quintals (1 quintal = 100 pounds), say, about 84 tons; Concho, 4,164 quintals, or about 208 tons; Bolivian rubber, of all classes, 280 tons. The export trade from Mollendo had, in fact, been worked up, with much effort in opposition to the shipments via Iquitos and Para to Europe.[28] The following résumé of Peru's international commerce for the three years 1908–10 inclusive give an interesting insight into the economic condition of the republic at this time:

	1910	1909	1908
Exports	£6,408,282	£6,492,670	£5,478,941
Imports	£4,631,280	£4,298,627	£5,311,973

	Imports	
Year	Via the Amazon	Via the Pacific
1902	£250,928	£3,816,615
1903	£298,285	£4,940,698
1904	£570,683	£4,803,954
1905	£560,027	£4,370,772
1906	£639,724	£3,797,669
1907	£715,797	£3,786,655
1908	£371,275	£3,485,096
1909	£482,012	£3,177,355[29]

With this growth in trade came an intensification of industrial action by the workers of Peru, particularly those at Lima and Callao. An indication of the growing militancy of the labor movement after 1895 was the increasing frequency and intensity of strikes. The agitation was an understandable reaction to the worker's poor wages and harsh living conditions. Anarchist influence was also a factor in these disputes, but the main aim of the strikers during the 1895–1912 period was to achieve better wages to offset the ever-rising cost of living. This continued growth in the militancy and consciousness of the workers culminated in April 1911 when Lima's workers staged their first general strike, which clearly showed the advances that had been made by the local labor movement. In the port of Callao the most militant workers continued to be those employed by the Central Railroad and the Dock Company. Both being central to Peru's export-oriented economy, they enjoyed a certain amount of power. Of these the workers on the docks showed more cohesion and as a result enjoyed greater success. Nevertheless, both groups were at the mercy of international trade, and when the commercial crisis of 1908 hit, both suffered considerably.

14. Sailing ships of the guano fleet [ca 1930] at anchor in Callao Bay with the irrigated fields of the delta of the Rimac river in the background. Reproduced by courtesy of the American Geographical Society.

United, the men working on the docks had shown they could confront their employers successfully, but new factors arising in 1907 soon began to undermine their hard-won unity. A register of regular dock laborers was scrapped, which meant that the various commercial enterprises using Callao were free to hire whoever they wished, and many of the former dock laborers found themselves out of a job. This situation was exacerbated with the arrival of hundreds of refugees from Iquique following the December 1907 nitrate workers' strike. The Pacific Steam Navigation Company tried to take advantage of the situation by hiring some of the ex-nitrate workers at lower rates. This led to a strike in February 1908, which brought the port of Callao to a halt. Sailors, soldiers, and the unemployed nitrate workers were brought in, but only managed to move a proportion of the goods. Subject to much criticism from the local workers, the refugees then claimed they had not really intended to cause trouble. However, the dock laborers of Callao were not impressed with this claim. They remained on strike until the company agreed to terminate the refugees' contract after a month. The government minister, German Arenas, then ordered the arrest of the strike leaders and suspended all the dock workers' hard-won rights. Fortunately, the unions, and Augusto Leguia, the presidential candidate, managed to get Arenas's order repealed, and the strike was settled, but from this point on, dock worker's conditions continued to be eroded.

The Pacific Steam Navigation Company continued to hire outside workers and managed to pay them fixed wages, rather than the Callao dock worker's tariff rate. On the other hand, cargoes on Kosmos and Grace Company ships were being unloaded by the ships' crews. Without the protection of the register, the workers had little real defense, and efforts to get it reintroduced failed. Unemployment on the docks then rose so much that agitation became too great a risk to take, and further attempts at unity were undermined by the 1908 trade depression. In 1909 the Peruvian Corporation was still operating the railroads, the manager in charge being a Mr. William Morkill. Assisted by the depression in world trade, which reduced the amount of goods being carried and the number of workers the railroads required, he was unsympathetic when the men began making new demands in June 1909. They were protesting against the hours of work, the treatment they received from one of the foremen, and company regulations that made them responsible for any damage done to the trains, but conveniently denied them the right to compensation for work-related injuries. As might be expected, Morkill considered these demands "exorbitant" and opposed all concessions, claiming that he would lose all control over the workers if he acceded. Despite assistance from several mutual aid societies and the Dock Workers' Union, Morkill eventually won and forced them back to work.

In addition to this, working conditions in the textile industry also continued to be a cause for great concern. Starting in December 1906, the industry was hit by a series of strikes. The Vitarte workers were first, demanding the same wages as Lima's other textile workers and better food. This company was actually owned by the London-based Peruvian Cotton Manufacturing Company, William R. Grace & Company providing the management services for this enterprise in Peru. The wages were very low; according to one report, they amounted to just thirty centavos for a workday of sixteen hours, and it was for higher pay, fewer hours, and better food that the workers went on strike. The strikers hoped that President Pierola would support them since the workers had supported his revolution and election the previous year.

A mysterious fire then occurred on the night of August 27. Only minor damage was done, and the workers helped extinguish it, but Pierola used this as an excuse not to intervene. Congressional deputy Rosendo Vidaurre, who had been involved in all the negotiations, then attempted to convince his fellow deputies that far from being responsible for the fire, the strikers had opposed the arson attempt. Most of the deputies, however, were not impressed by this argument and charged that the strike indicated a new and dangerous militancy among Peru's workers, and a very dangerous spread of socialism, and, even worse, "Proudhonian Communism." Feigning great concern about these imaginary threats to life, as they knew it, they made public their fears that this would soon lead to greater violence, with dynamite and gasoline bomb attacks being made by the revolutionary workers. Without external support by September 5, work at Vitarte was virtually back to normal. Four workers were then arrested, found guilty of arson, and sentenced to six years in prison.[30] Another notable strike took place at this mill in the early months of 1911, when at 8:00 AM on April 10, the first general strike in Peruvian history began. Peru, at long last, was, it would seem, on the long road to social reform—but she still had a long way to go.

The year of 1912 marked a new milestone in the development of the Peruvian labor movement with the election of Guillermo E. Billinghurst as president. His electoral success was mainly due to support from Lima's workers. Although very wealthy Billinghurst, as his name might suggest, was not a typical member of the Peruvian upper class. Born in 1851 in the southern province of Arica, he was the grandson of a British hero of the independence wars and the son of a wealthy businessman. Of great significance is the fact that his money came from the nitrate industry of Tarapacá, in contrast to the estate-based wealth of Peru's traditional elite. The subsequent loss of Tarapacá to Chile during the War of the Pacific set Billinghurst further apart, for his wealth was now based in the country that had been Peru's archenemy. Billinghurst had little or no affection for the Peruvian aristocracy. He was a member of the Democratic Party and, initially, a loyal supporter of Pierola. He financed and participated in several of Pierola's rebellions and, following the successful revolution of 1895, was rewarded for his generosity and loyalty by being named first vice president.

Under difficult circumstances Billinghurst did what he could to support the Peruvian workers, but this generated opposition from the business community and the ruling elite, who worked against him and traded on his links with Chile to undermine his credibility. There was, it was suggested, some question about Billinghurst's loyalty because of his contacts with the archenemy, Chile. Rumors were spread that he intended to sell the captive provinces of Tacna and Arica to Chile, and his postponement of a plebiscite designed to decide the ultimate future of the provinces antagonized all the nationalist elements in the republic. Nevertheless, the Billinghurst period was a profitable one for the Peruvian working class. Oscar R. Benavides, representing the perceived interests of the ruling elite, mounted a successful coup d'état against Billinghurst in February 1914. Six months later, war broke out in Europe when Austria attacked Serbia in July following the murder of Archduke Ferdinand at Sarajevo.

Exiled to Chile, following the coup, Billinghurst died there on June 28, 1915. On hearing the news, the workers' societies in Lima declared a period of mourning. The following year, when his remains were returned to Peru, his supporters once more filled the streets of Lima. Thousands of workers then accompanied the coffin to the cemetery in a final demonstration of respect for a man who had claimed that his constant desire had been to ameliorate the lot of Peru's working class.[31]

12

The Casa Grace Sails On

FROM 1908 TO 1912, AND AGAIN FROM 1919 TO 1930, THE RULER OF PERU was President Augusto B. Leguia, who was a small man physically, tactful and adroit with visitors, and with a great flair for administration and finance. In his second term of office these "flairs" led to history repeating itself, for during this period some £19,000,000 in American and British loans poured into the republic, which, once again, was far too much for the Peruvian economy to stand. Some startling testimony regarding these loans surfaced in the United States Senate. For instance, officers of one New York banking house paid £83,000 to Juan Leguia, the son of the President, for helping "arrange" three bond issues. Not surprisingly, revolution came in 1930, and Leguia was forced out by a soldier of humble origin, Sanchez Cerro, who was notable for his dedication to force rather than democracy. Just three years later, in 1933, this forceful president was assassinated, much to the delight of the majority of Peruvians. Sanchez Cerro was replaced by General Oscar Benavides, yet another military officer who ruled until 1939.[1]

During these years Peru continued as the classic example in South America of a colonial or "export economy." While local Peruvian capital did control a percentage of the republic's cotton, sugar, and wool industries, almost everything else continued to be controlled by foreigners. Understandably, this situation did not meet with the approval of patriotic Peruvians. Just how bad was the situation? At this time the British were mainly represented by the aforementioned Peruvian Corporation, which then owned the spectacular Central Railroad, created by Henry Meiggs. This line led to the fully operational Cerro de Pasco mines. The British also controlled the Southern Railroad and the shipping on Lake Titicaca. Other British investments accounted for 18 percent of the Republic's oil production, 33 percent of Peruvian cotton, the nation's largest brewery, and a large flour mill.

A powerful Italian company gave Lima and Callao electricity and power, and the Banco Italiano Lima did about half of Peru's banking business. The Italians also fully controlled the Peruvian postal service. German interests were, in the main, represented by the powerful Gildemeister family, who were, however, Peruvian citizens. They owned Casa Grande, one of the largest sugar-producing estates in the world and in total were responsible for 43 percent of Peruvian sugar production. The Japanese also owned much sugar and cotton land. One Japanese company, Nikumatzu Okada, was the biggest single cotton producer in the republic. Sadly, at this time, foreign interests still dominated the Peruvian guano industry through a contract system, although this commodity then featured to a much less appreciable extent as a factor in the national economy, this despite the fact that since 1936 the actual collection of this fertilizer had been a national government monopoly, strictly administered, so that the annual deposit was not wasted.

At this time the United States controlled no less than 80 percent of Peruvian oil production, through a subsidiary of Standard Oil of New Jersey. United States interests controlled almost 100 percent of the mineral output; the Cerro de Pasco Corporation exporting 95 percent of Peru's copper, 75 percent of its silver, and 50 percent of its gold. Other powerful American interests accounted for the rest—the Guggenheims in copper and the Vanadium Corporation in vanadium, of which Peru then produced 80 percent of the world's supply. Last but not least, William R. Grace & Company—the "Casa Grace"—were then growing 24 percent of the Republic's sugar, they had big textile interests, ran a dominant shipping business, had control of Lima's telephone service, and were half-owners of Pan-American–Grace-Airways.[2]

William R. Grace & Co. had indeed come a long way in 70 short years. The founder's younger brother, Michael Paul Grace, had actually brought this ever-expanding enterprise through the days of the Cape Horn sailing ships and the pioneering age of steamship development to the early days of twentieth-century air travel. Yet, strange to say, in the 1920s and 1930s these three forms of international transportation were simultaneously extending a service to Peru and the entire west coast of South America. The death of Michael Paul Grace in 1920, the decade in which air transportation

15. A Grace Line Steamer [ca 1930] at anchor in Callao harbor unloading freight into launches for transfer to the piers. Reproduced by courtesy of the American Geographical Society.

first made its appearance on the west coast puts all of this into historical perspective.

Michael Paul Grace, of W. E. Grace & Company of New York, and of Grace Brothers, London, died suddenly on Monday morning September 20, 1920 at the house of his son-in-law, Lord Donoughmore, 5 Chesterfield Gardens. His American address at the time was "Westbury House," Westbury, Nassau, Long Island, New York. He was buried at Battle, and his son, Joseph P. Grace, who was destined to head the family enterprise, was among those present at the funeral. Strange to say, Michael Grace, the man who had virtually arranged a mortgage on Peru, did not leave an exceptionally large fortune, at least in Great Britain—his total effects being subsequently listed in the British Calendar of Probate at just £35,201.[3]

By coincidence, 1921 was the year in which Michael Paul Grace's will was published, and it was also the year in which the Peruvian government first published regulations governing civil aviation. This took place on November 15, but it was not until September 20, 1926, that a commercial service was specifically authorized. The route operated by the Peruvian Naval Air Service was entirely inland, following the course of the rivers and using waterborne aircraft. The objective was to provide mail and passenger service between the capital, Lima, and Iquitos, in the remote Amazonian province of Peru. A route was finally established on January 3, 1928, which started at San Ramon, on the Ucayali River, a major tributary of the mighty Amazon, and terminated at La Oroya, which in turn was linked directly to Lima by both road and rail. Six Keystone aircraft were supplied from the United States—two land aircraft and four seaplanes to operate this route.

Air travel in Peru was pioneered by Elmer J. Faucett, a citizen of the United States. He arrived in the republic on June 28, 1920, as a representative of the Curtiss Aviation Corporation. Just over two years later, on October 15, 1922, young "Slim" Faucett made aviation history by taking his light plane from Chiclayo to the Amazon River in a Curtiss Oriole. For this pioneering achievement he was rightly hailed as a hero when he finally arrived at Iquitos. Six years later, on May 1, 1928, a group of Peruvian citizens, headed by Faucett, applied to the government to operate a regular passenger and cargo air service. The following month the group received the necessary operating permission and on September 15 regular flights of Compãñia de Aviación Faucett started a coastal service from Lima to Chiclayo, which was then extended to Talara in the north and Arequipa in the south. The aircraft used were Stinson Detroiter six-seat monoplanes.[4]

Meanwhile, back in the United States the desirability of encouraging United States airline services in Latin America by financial support had been studied intensively by an interdepartmental committee in 1927. In 1928 President Coolidge, in his message to Congress, recommended the establishment of such a service, and the "granting of liberal long-term contracts for carrying our mail." The "Foreign Air Mail Act" authorizing such contracts was signed by the president on March 8, 1928. Advertisements were then placed for seven foreign airmail contracts pursuant to the Act. Bids came in from about seventeen companies, fourteen of which were from enterprises that were considered "speculative and irresponsible." However, the remaining three bids came from well-financed and competent organizations, namely Pan-American–Airways, Inc., Pan-

American–Grace-Airways, Inc. and New York, Rio and Buenos Aires Line, Inc. Pan-American-Airways was, in fact, established in 1927 with the backing of leading American aircraft manufacturing enterprises and a number of steamship lines.[5]

At this time the Casa Grace was in effective control of the West Coast shipping lines, and they were, not surprisingly, anxious to keep competitors out of what they considered to be their "transport territory." Accordingly, negotiations took place and on January 25, 1929, Pan American-Grace Airways Inc. (PANAGRA) was formed, with William R Grace & Company, with Aviation Corporation of the Americas each holding a half-share of the stock valued at $1,000,000. Peruvian Airways, a local venture, was absorbed on the same day and therefore ceased to exist as a separate entity.[6] In two years, 1929–30, Pan-American–Grace-Airways inaugurated or acquired control over about 18,000 miles of routes, one third more than the 14,000 miles opened by European interests in the entire period of 1921–31, during which they had been operating in South America. In May 1930, Pan-American introduced a service from Curacao to Venezuela. Pan-American-Grace then became the successful bidder on the route from Cristobal to Mollendo, Peru (2,300 miles), which was later extended to Santiago and Buenos Aires (2,300 additional miles).[7]

During these great pioneering days of air transportation, yet another American based in Peru was making aviation and photographic history. This man was United States Navy lieutenant George R. Johnson. He was the chief photographer of the Peruvian Naval Air Service, and an instructor in aerial photography at Ancon, the Naval Air Station of Peru. From June 1928 to January 1930, he effectively pioneered aerial photography in Peru with numerous photographic flights, mainly over the coast, but also over the Andes, and the Amazon River basin.[8] These surveys led to the production of an American Geographical Society publication, by Johnson, with text and notes by Raye R. Platt, the head of the department of Hispanic American Research, American Geographical Society. Their Book, *Peru from the Air*, was issued by the Society in 1930. This venture paid particular attention to the coastal strip of Peru, the main subject of this work. In a few well-chosen words Johnson's colleague Raye Platt tells us much about this strange, geographically divided land:

> There are thirty of these ports on the coast of Peru. A few, Salavery, Chimbote, Callao, and Mollendo are ports not only for the coastal val-

leys but for the mining districts in the Andes as well. The majority, however, have but a single function, to connect a nearby irrigated valley or group of valleys with the sea. Valley, railway or road, and port together form a complete independent economic unit. There is no continuous railway running from valley to valley across the desert to connect them with a common center of distribution and supply. Their great transportation trunk line is the sea. To each it seeks an outlet by the shortest possible route to the nearest point where a pier can be built. Each sends its products to the foreign markets and imports its manufactured supplies from abroad.

A third of the people of Peru live in these irrigated valleys and their ports. Yet, seen on a map of the coastal region they seem insignificant as compared with the wide stretches of desert that surround them and isolate them from each other. In a flight along the coast they are only incidents of the journey - occasional oases in the desert, ribbons of green along the banks of widely separated rivers, broader patches of green on alluvial fans and deltas-pleasant and restful to the eyes after the glare of the desert but soon passed. The larger of them, like the Rimac delta and the famous group of valleys in the Department of Lambayeque, are impressive, dotted with haciendas and towns, criss-crossed by roads and railways. But even these are, at the most, only a few hundred square miles in extent.

All the valleys together occupy not more than three per cent of the whole coastal region between the crests of the western border of the Andes and the sea. Yet they contain a sixth of the 4,000,000 acres estimated to be under cultivation in the whole of Peru, and such is their fertility and productiveness that the value of the annual crop is nearly equal to that of all the other agricultural areas of the country combined, while the exports of sugar and cotton alone from them are now about equal in value to the country's total exports of copper, silver, and petroleum.[9]

Meanwhile, the creation of a network of trunk air routes brought about the involuntary entrance of Pan -American and, to a lesser extent, Pan-American-Grace, into local operations in several Latin American states. The two parent companies had been organized to provide international services, and the contracts let under the Foreign Air Mail Act of 1928 provided subsidies only for such services. It soon became evident, however, that the acquisition or formation of local nationally incorporated air transport companies was required in order to secure operating rights. Nevertheless, the only local company acquired by Pan-American-Grace during the 1928–32 period was Huff-Daland Inc., an enterprise started by United States pilots who had gone to Peru in 1927 on a crop-dusting expedition, which later operated local scheduled services in Peru. PANAGRA also operated local Peruvian services through its subsidiary, Aerovias Peruanas. During these early years the Pan American system expanded dramatically, but almost all of the basic system of routes that had been established were covered by United States mail contracts, paying the companies $1.80 to $2.00 per mile flown with mail. Under these terms there was little real incentive to open new routes without such contracts.[10]

Many years earlier the British had gained the upper hand on the transatlantic liner routes, through granting Samuel Cunard generous subsidies to carry the mails. It was now becoming apparent that the United States was not going to allow history to repeat itself with the carriage of airmail. Government policy was now lined up solidly behind American enterprises developing these services. However, the extremely generous system of subsidizing the Pan American and the Pan-American-Grace system in Latin America was to cost the United States government exceptionally large sums, in relation to the total volume of traffic handled. For example, during the eleven fiscal years July 1, 1929–June 30, 1940, net government mail payments to Pan-American and Pan-American-Grace totaled $47,202,000. To put this figure into perspective, net Government payments to all United States domestic lines in the same period only totaled $59,852,000, although they flew eight times as many passenger miles as Pan-American and Pan-American-Grace put together. In 1941 this system resulted in Pan-American-Grace Airways showing a healthy operating profit of $1,461,159, and Pan-American Airways, on their Latin American services, $3,419,000."[11]

Looking back, however, it must be acknowledged that W. R. Grace had pioneered the direct steamship service between New York and the West Coast of South America. In 1895 the Grace companies had united under a Virginia charter as William R. Grace & Company.[12] Further developments followed rapidly, as in 1889 Grace Brothers & Company of Lima, Peru owned and was operating the *Lancashire Witch,* a vessel of 1574 tons.[13] At the time of his death in March 1904, however, his New York and Pacific Steamship Company was operating a fleet of seven large steamers constructed specially for this trade. These were now sailing on a regular basis from New York, via Guayaquil in Ecuador, and by way of the Straits of Magellan, to the West Coast of South America.[14]

To put this in historical perspective it must also be recognized that William R. Grace was far from being the first to pioneer steamship services on the West Coast of Latin America. In fact, soon after the diminutive sailing ships of the Brocklebank fleet began trading on this coast, and well before Darwin made his celebrated voyage to this part of the Pacific in the *Beagle* in the 1830s, in 1825 a small steamer named the *Telicia* was operating in these waters. She was, as already noted, owned and commanded by a Spaniard bearing a Russian name, Mitrovich, who, in a serious fit of despair, decided to relieve the tension by attacking his own ship![15]

As already noted, the next person to attempt to establish steamship communications along the Pacific coast was an American citizen, William Wheelwright of Newbury Port. Born in 1798, he began his long and successful career as a printer. Bored with life in a printing works Wheelwright decided to make his way to the Pacific Coast of South America. In 1824 he was appointed United States Consul at Guayaquil, and three years later he was also owner and master of a small barque. Undisturbed by the fate of Captain Mitrovitch and the *Telicia,* Wainwright was convinced that, properly planned, work could be found on this coast for not just one steamer, but many. He began in a very well considered way by first assuring his trade before getting the steamers for it. His foresight was justified when, after six years of intensive effort he managed to obtain the exclusive rights of steam navigation along the coasts of Chile, Boliviar, and Peru for a period of ten years.

Armed with these concessions he proceeded to raise capital for the venture. Unfortunately, he found he could obtain no support from his own country, so he turned to England for help. Lord Abinger became the first English shareholder.On February 17, 1840, a Royal Charter was obtained and the P.S.N.C. came into being. Two steamers, the *Chile* and *Peru,* each of about 700 tons gross, were ordered and toward the close of 1840 left the United Kingdom for South America to take up a service between Valparaiso and Panama. Though formed in and originally operated from London, the majority of the shareholders were Liverpool residents and because of this in 1846 the offices of the company were transferred to Liverpool. In 1850 four new steamers, *Bogota, Lima, Quito,* and *Santiago* were built at a cost of £140,000. From this point on the rise of the company was phenomenal and by 1874 the company owned fifty-four steamers.[16]

At this point in time the company became the largest firm of shipowners in the world, their fleet exceeding the tonnage of the entire United States navy. So frequently were their vessels seen in the Mersey that they became known as the "Birkenhead Navy," due to the fact that the firm's loading berths, repair shops, laundry etc., were situated on that side of the Mersey.[17] The official opening of the Panama Canal took place on June 12, 1920. This meant that by the mid-1920s the P.S.N.C. mail steamers were now able to maintain a fortnightly service to the west coast via the Panama Canal. In 1925 the fleet was comprised of ships fitted with the most modern and economical appliances. Their mail vessels were practically all oil fuel burners, while the majority of their cargo carriers were fitted with diesel engines.[18]

As mentioned, Michael Paul Grace, the brother of William R. Grace, the late mayor of New York, died in his sleep on September 20, 1920. At this time he was chairman of the board of directors of William R. Grace and Company of London. He was survived by his wife and three daughters—Mrs. J. S. Phipps of London, the Countess of Donoughmore, and Mrs Joseph Benskin (also of London).[19] At this point the Pacific Steam Navigation Company of Liverpool had thirty-three ships in their impressive fleet. Nevertheless, W. R. Grace and Company of 7 Hanover Square, New York, with their subsidiary enterprises, The Atlantic & Pacific Steam Ship Company, and The Grace Steamship Company, were running a substantial number of ships. The combined fleet lists for the year 1920 were as follows, with the 1934 Grace fleets listed for comparison

The W.R. Grace & Company Fleet, 1920

Ship	Year built	Tons	Ship	Year Built	Tons
Cacique	1910	6202	*Santa Flavia*	1917	2113
Colusa	1913	6003	*Santa Inez*	1909	1742
Coquimbano	1901	114	*Santa Rita*	1912	1600
Santa Elicia	1912	2244	*W.J. Pirrie*	1883	2583
Santa Clara	1913	6462			

The Grace owned Atlantic & Pacific Steam Ship Company Fleet, 1920

Ship	Year built	Tons	Ship	Year built	Tons
Santa Ana	1918	4942	*Santa Paula*	1917	6415
Santa Barbara	1916	6621	*Santa Rosa*	1917	6415
Santa Luisa	1918	4944[20]			

The Grace Steamship Company Fleets, 1935

Ship	Year Built	Tons	Ship	Year Built	Tons
Cacique	1910	6,245	*Santa Clara*	1930	9,502
Capac	1919	5,586	*Santa Elena*	1932	11,201
Charcas	1919	5,555	*Santa Inez*	1929	4,691
Condor	1920	4,747	*Santa Isabel*	1915	5,641
Coya	1919	4,954	*Santa Lucia*	1933	11,200
Cuzco	1919	5,498	*Santa Maria*	1928	8,060
Nora	1920	9,621	*Santa Olivia*	1915	5,544
Santa Barbara	1928	8,060	*Santa Rita*	1929	4,577

Panama Mail S.S. Co., Inc.

Ship	Year built	Tons	Ship	Year built	Tons
Corinto	1905	1,973	*Santa Monica*	1924	2,433
Santa Ana	1918	4,847	*Santa Paula*	1932	11,200
Santa Catalina	1924	2,434	*Santa Rosa*	1932	11,200
Santa Cecilia	1918	4,870	*Santa Teresa*	1918	4,858
Santa Elisa	1919	5,004			

W.R. Grace & Co., 10 Hanover Square, New York City

Ship	Year built	Tons
Coquimbana	1901	114[21]

However, as this long story about the Peruvian guano trade began with Messrs. Thomas and John Brocklebank and their mariners, it would seem appropriate to end it by providing the following details about the company and their men. Like William R. Grace and Company and the Pacific Steam Navigation Company the Brocklebank Line also built up a fleet of steamships during the twentieth century, but unlike the two former enterprises this was mainly based on the Liverpool-Calcutta trade. Their final link with South America was made in 1872 by a lone voyage of the *Mindanao.*

The effect of the opening of the Suez Canal in 1870 was to transfer most of this trade to the East to steamers. Nevertheless, for some time after the opening of the canal, the ever-increasing traffic to India, Australia, and New Zealand was carried on to a limited extent in sailing ships and the old keen rivalry as to the best passages continued. Notwithstanding these profound changes, Brocklebanks continued to place orders for larger and larger sailing ships up until 1888.[22]

THE BROCKLEBANK CAPE HORN SOUTH PACIFIC TRADERS

Vessel	Tons	Date built	Built by	Years in which the vessel traded in the South Pacific	
Ariel 3	154	1820	Brocklebanks	1822, 1823	1828–31
Crown	297	1821	Brocklebanks	1821–24	
Globe 1	212	1822	Brocklebanks	1822–24	1828–32
Swallow 2	141	1822	Brocklebanks	1823–29	1823–29
Andes	216	1823	Brocklebanks	1823–30	1840
Manchester	163	1824	Brocklebanks	1825–30	1825–30
Courier 1	142	1826	Brocklebanks	1827–40	1843
Oberon	150	1827	Brocklebanks	1828–35	1839, 1840, 1842
Irt	215	1828	Brocklebanks	1828, 1834	
Esk	217	1828	Brocklebanks	1828–31	1833, 1836, 1837
Maypo	173	1829	Brocklebanks	1829–35	1838–42 1844–46
Bonanza	176	1830	Brocklebanks	1830–36	1845–56
Tampico	129	1830	Brocklebanks	1836	
Patriot King	338	1832	Brocklebanks	1856–1862	1866
Lord Althorp	233	1832	Brocklebanks	1841, 1843	1847–54, 1856, 1857
Rimac	214	1834	Brocklebanks	1834–62	
Earl Grey	242	1834	Brocklebanks	1846–55	
Globe 2	252	1836	Brocklebanks	1836–60	
Dryad 4	251	1837	Brocklebanks	1837–40	1846, 1847, 1849–58
Horsburgh	320	1838	Brocklebanks	1839–55	
Aden	339	1839	Brocklebanks	1862–68	
Swallow 3	236	1839	Brocklebanks	1840	Missing on maiden voyage
Kestrel	231	1840	Brocklebanks	1840–59	
Valparaiso	317	1841	Brocklebanks	1841–68	
Callao	170	1842	Brocklebanks	1842–59	
Lanercost	318	1842	Brocklebanks	1842–69	
Camana	185	1842	Brocklebanks	1843–59	
Courier 2	135	1845	Brocklebanks	1846–55	
Sir H. Pottinger	334	1845	Brocklebanks	1855–59	

(*continued*)

Vessel	Tons	Date built	Built by	Years in which the vessel traded in the South Pacific	
Petchelee	393	1850	Brocklebanks	1855–59	1863, 1864
Mindanao	482	1854	Williamson	1854–72[23]	

THE BROCKLEBANK SAILING FLEET, 1899

Vessel	Tons	Date	Built by
Belfast	1865	1874	(Harland & Woolff)
Zemindar	2053	1885	(Harland & Woolff)
Sindia	3007	1887	(Harland & Woolff)
Holkar	3009	1888	(Harland & Woolff)[24]

THOMAS & JOHN BROCKLEBANK/ANCHOR FLEET, 1934

Vessel	Tons	Date built	Vessel	Tons	Date built
Anchoria	6112	1911	*Malakand*	7649	1919
D.W. Williams	177	1920	*Malakuta*	7205	1914
Magdapur	9265	1921	*Manaar*	7242	1917
Mahanada	7181	1914	*Mandasor*	5144	1920
Mahout	7880	1925	*Mangalore*	9784	1920
Mahronda	7880	1925	*Manipur*	9279	1920
Mahratta	6690	1917	*Markhor*	7821	1929
Mahseer	7864	1925	*Masirah*	6578	1919
Mahsud	7540	1917	*Matheran*	7653	1919
Maiden	7861	1925	*Mathura*	9775	1920
Mathar	7563	1917	*Matra*	7911	1926
Maimyo	5819	1918	*Media*	5437	1911
Makalla	6677	1918	*Stockwell*	5757	1914[25]

SIR THOMAS BROCKLEBANK. Sir Thomas died on June 8, 1906. He was laid to rest in the picturesque rural churchyard of Halewood, near Liverpool. Among those present were many members of the Brocklebank family, including Ralph Brocklebank of Houghton Hall Cheshire and Mr. Thomas Brocklebank of the Roscote Heswall, both cousins of the deceased. Mr Stamper represented the office staff and Mr Pinchin represented the Domestic staff. Significantly, Captain W. Ray, once a young apprentice on the *Rimac,* was present in his new role as the firm's Marine Superintend. Also present on this sad occasion was Captain William Ellery, once an apprentice on the barque *Lanercost* then, in 1888, the first commander of Brocklebank's last sailing vessel, the great 'windjammer' *Holkar.* It was, however, Mr J.H. Ray, Captain William Ray's grandson, who was to provide me with a unique living link between the distant past and the closing decades of the twentieth century. It is also worth noting here that many of the firm's South Pacific traders, built and owned by the firm and as listed, also participated in the East Indies trade. In fact, Brocklebank ships were among the first to enter this trade when Indian ports were made free. This trade increased dramatically over the years until, at the time of Sir Thomas Brocklebank's death, almost all the company business was with Indian and, to a lesser extent, China. Sir Thomas was for forty-nine years a director of the Liverpool, London and Globe Insurance Company, and in 1864 was High Sheriff of Cumberland.[26]

CAPTAIN WILLIAM RAY. Captain William Ray died at his home, "Hallgarth" Brynaston Road, Prenton, Wirral on April 28, 1926, at the age of eighty-eight. He had served for fifty-seven years with the Anchor-Brocklebank Line, and was marine superintendent of the firm from 1875 until his retirement in 1911. He began his life at sea in 1854 as an apprentice on the *Rimac,* then went on to command other Brocklebank sailing ships. Providing a link between the old and the new, the first Brocklebank steamer, the *Ameer,* was taken on its maiden voyage to Calcutta by Captain Ray in 1889. Captain Ray was held in such special regard by the company that to mark the occasion the house flag over the company's offices and on their ships round the coast were lowered to half-mast when news of his death was received. The funeral took place at Woodchurch Parish Church. Many master mariners were present and these included Captains Wheeler, Connell, Peterkin, Guthrie, Hickes. Jones, Woodcock, Legg, and Jefferson. Also present was young Mr. J. H Ray, William Ray's grandson. Related to my maritime research work, I spoke to him on the telephone in 1981, corresponded with him, and received his last letter on May 6, 1981.[27]

CAPTAIN SIR JAMES ANDERSON. Sir James Anderson died at his London home on May 7, 1893. As was the case with Sir Thomas Brocklebank, his life had spanned the greater part of the nineteenth century. During this period his life in particular had marked, in a most dramatic manner, the transition from the old days at sea in small sailing brigs to the new era of steam navigation on board the early Cunarders and then Isambard Kingdom Brunel's *Great Eastern*. As noted, his days at sea with Brocklebanks began in 1840 as an apprentice on the *London,* under a genial old skipper, Joe Benn of Whitehaven, and closed after serving as chief officer to Captain Abraham Vaux Wise on the *Kestrel.* Soon after this he left Brocklebanks when he was appointed captain of the *Aliwal* which sailed from London to Natal with emigrants. For two years Captain Anderson sailed in the Far East, in 1851, he entered into the service of the Cunard Steamship Company, beginning life again as it were, as third officer on the *Africa.* It was, however, in this year that he obtained his "Extra Master Certificate" at Liverpool. In 1855 he was back as a commander once more, but this time as master of a passenger liner, the *Melita.* Anderson went on to command many ships in the Cunard fleet that were employed in the trans-atlantic emigrant service.

In 1856 the Atlantic Telegraph Company was formed. Some years later Captain Anderson received a letter from Sir Samuel Cunard, in which he said: "The directors of the Telegraph Company have made a request to us to lend you to them to take command of the *Great Eastern* while engaged in laying the cable across the Atlantic." Anderson took up the offer, serving as commander of the great ship during the crucial years of 1865–67. It was during this period when, after monumental setbacks and misfortunes, the cable was eventually completed. To mark this historic occasion, on September 10, 1866 Captain Anderson sent a brief message to his mother, Mrs John Anderson of Dumfries, Scotland: "It is with great pleasure that I have to report to you the successful completion of the Atlantic Cable of 1865."

After serving as commander of the *Great Eastern* Anderson never went to sea again. His later career as a businessman, based on his cable-laying experience at sea, was equally impressive. This to the extent that at the time of his death, Sir James was chairman of the Eastern and South African Telegraph Companies. He was chairman of the Brazilian Submarine, and Direct Spanish, and a Director of the Anglo-American, the African Direct, the Eastern Extension, the West India and Panama Telegraph Companies, the Globe Telegraph and Trust, and the Metropolitan Electric Supply Companies. He was also a Trustee of the Submarine Cable Trust. Collectively, these Companies represented a gross capital of twenty-one million pounds sterling, and possessed eighty thousand miles of "wire." A "submarine network," as it was put at the time, "of the greatest utility and advantage to the human race."[28]

CAPTAIN WILLIAM ELLERY. William Ellery was the son of a Cornish farmer. He was born in 1838 in the village of St. Columb Minor, near Penzance—the family itself being a long-established one in this part of England. Unfortunately, in 1846 things went irretrievably wrong on the farm so the family decided to move to Liverpool. Inspired by the beautiful sight of the great sailing ships entering and leaving the port under full sail, young Ellery soon decided on a life at sea. When he was seventeen he was apprenticed for four years with Messrs T & J Brocklebank, which even then was considered to be the oldest shipping firm in the world. He began his apprenticeship on the barque *Hindoo,* bound for Pernambuco, Brazil, then moved to the Cape Horn trader *Lanercost.* On the completion of his apprenticeship he was appointed third mate of the barque *Patriot King.* On shore for just forty-eight hours, he then sailed out of Liverpool, once more as third mate of the full-rigged ship *Arachne,* 700 ton register, bound for Calcutta. Ellery then served on other ships in the Brocklebank sailing fleet. But the days of serving in wooden sailing ships was drawing to a close. After building and launching the 1,003 ton *Mahanada 1* in 1865 the Brocklebank building yard at Whitehaven was closed and the firm now turned to other builders.

In 1866 they placed their first order with Harland & Woolff of Belfast, this being for the 1,418 ton iron ship *Candahar.* In the same year her sister ship the 1,419 ton iron ship *Tenasserim 11* was also launched at Belfast and, in 1877, Ellery was appointed master of this vessel. The next iron ship ordered by the firm was the 1,266 ton *Chinsura,* built by G. R. Clover of Mersesyside. She was launched in 1868 and between the August 25, 1871 and January 22, 1874 she was commanded by Captain Francis Wise, under whom William Ray had served his time on the old Cape Horn Trader *Rimac* back in the 1850s. Due to poor health Francis Wise then came ashore. He died the following year on October 11. However, the *Chinsura* stayed afloat and after various changes of ownership about 1921 she was bought by the Polish government and converted into the training ship *Lwow.* She was hulked in 1929.

The iron-built sister ships *Belfast* and *Majestic* were then built for the firm by Harland & Woolf. The former was launched in 1874, the latter, of 1,884 tons, the following year. She carried a crew of forty and was commanded by William Ellery from about 1879–83. The iron built ships *Khyber, Bolan,* and *Bactria* were then added to the fleet. In 1885 Brocklebank returned to Harland & Woolff, with whom they placed their final orders for steel-built sailing ships. The 2,053 ton *Zemindar* was launched in 1885, and her sister ship, the 2,053 ton *Talookdar,* later in the same year. Ellery was given command of this vessel, taking her on her maiden voyage to Calcutta in 1866, and he took her out to the same port once more the following year.

The great 3,007 ton four-masted steel barque *Sindia* was launched at Belfast in 1887. She was traded to Calcutta by the firm until she was sold to the Anglo-American Oil Company in 1901. Her sister ship, the 3,009 ton *Holkar,* was launched the following year. The last of the Brocklebank sailing ships, her first master was Captain William Ellery (1888), followed by Captains Russell, Peterkin, Graham, Nicholson, Frederickson, and Dunning. She was sold to Germany in 1901, and renamed *Adelaide*. In 1913 she was re-named *Odessa*. Captured as a prize of war in 1914 she was sold to Norwegian owners in 1923, then re-named *Hippalos*. She was eventually broken up in 1925. Ellery left a graphic account of the conclusion of his last voyage as commander of this great "Windjammer" that was published in the *Wallasey and Wirral Chronicle* on June 29, 1912:

> The sailor always finds it a pleasure to see the British shore rising above the horizon after a long voyage, and I felt this genuine thrill in the good ship Holkar, as, under a press of canvas in a stiff Nor' wester, she bounded up channel in February, 1889, at her best speed, the Tuskar Lighthouse meanwhile flashing her welcome from the Irish coast. Passing the Skerries the following morning, it is also delightful to take the bearings of the old familiar landmarks leading to the Pilot Station at Point Lynas. Then, with home flag, ensign and signals hoisted and fluttering in the breeze, we rounded to the wind, and with the sails on mizzen aback, and the ship stopped, the pilot climbs on board. With a broad smile, a hearty handshake and a cheery welcome home, he hauls out the inevitable pocketful of crumpled newspapers, probably about a week old, but none the less precious as conveying tidings of the dear Homeland. "Up helm" is then the word, and we square away and head for the North West Lightship. Sail is gradually reduced, and with a crisp northerly breeze and the tide two hours ebb, we pass New Brighton, and proceed to the Sloyne where we anchor. Soon afterwards the tug comes alongside with the docking order and at night we are safely berthed at the Herculanean Dock after a pleasant voyage of precisely 100 days from Calcutta.

It was then that William Ellery heard that Messrs T & J. Brocklebank were, at long last, placing orders for steamers and, once again they had turned to Harland & Woolff of Belfast to meet their requirements. The magnificent fleet of four-masted steamers built from

1889 to 1891 were the *Ameer, Gaekwar, Pindari,* and *Mobratta.* The *Ameer* was launched in October 1889; gross tonnage 4,100 tons, length 401 feet, breadth 45 feet, depth 28 feet; and she was fitted and equipped with the most modern improvements. Captain Ray, once master of the diminutive, 214 ton *Rimac,* commanded on her maiden voyage, with a navigation staff consisting of senior captains and chief officers, the firm being intent on giving them all a thorough training in their transference from sail to steam.

On September 16, 1924 the *Liverpool Echo* carried the following notice in their obituary columns. "September 15th at 5 Orrel Road, Wallasey, in his 86th year, William Ellery late master mariner, funeral at Anfield Cemetary tomorrow 2 pm." In 1984 I received a telephone call from the occupants of this house who advised me that they had just found a photograph of the old skipper in their loft. Unfortunately, it was quite inadvertently exposed to the light and the image faded away. Sad indeed, but in a way this, perhaps, very graphically symbolized the fading away of an old era and the establishment of a new, more technologically advanced one.[29] A large painting of the *Holkar* by W.S. Beesley, a well-known marine artist, was presented to me as a gift in 1985 from two friends. This was to be Beezley's last work, for he died shortly after this beautiful painting was completed.

William R. Grace, William Wheelwright, and the Brocklebank mariners arrived in Peru in the early part of the nineteenth century and left their marks on that troubled land as firmly as Francisco Pizarro and his fellow conquistadors had when they first entered the country in the sixteenth century. Unlike these original conquistadors, however, these men fought no bloody battles, but undoubtedly gained more from their commercial ventures than those who had wielded the sword before them. Nevertheless, Pizarro and his ruthless band had, unwittingly, laid the foundations on which the Grace and Wheelwright enterprises totally rested. The same, of course, applies to Brocklebanks, but because of their varied, global interests, proportionately to a lesser extent. The ships of the Casa Grace, Brocklebanks, and the Pacific Steam Navigation Company have long since gone. Unfortunately, in the opening years of the twenty-first century the nation of Peru, like so many other ex-colonial nations in Latin America, remains as troubled and socially divided as ever.

Notes

Chapter 1. Peru

1. A. J. Duffield, *Peru in the Guano Age,* (London: Richard Bently, 1897), 1.
2. *New Encyclopaedia Britannica,* vol. 25, 515.
3. Carleton Beals, *Fire in the Andes,* (London: J. P. Lippincott & Company, 1934), 11.
4. R. E. Coker, "*Peru's Wealth Producing Birds,*" *National Geographical Magazine,* vol. 37, 537.
5. Ibid.
6. C. Reginald Enock, *The Republics of Central and South America* (London: J.M. Dent, 1913), 193.
7. Beals, *Fire in the Andes,* 12.
8. Enock, *Republics of Central and South America,* 8.
9. *Britannica,* vol. 25, 515.
10. J. R. Owen, *Peru,* (Oxford: Oxford University Press, 1963), 3.
11. "A Railroad in the Sky," *Scribner's Magazine* August 1877, 461–62.
12. Beals, *Fire in the Andes,* 20.
13. Sir Robert Marett, *Peru,* (London: Ernest Benn, 1969), 21. 22.
14. Ibid., 31.
15. Beals, *Fire in the Andes,* 25.
16. Alan Samagalski, *Chile and Easter Island,* (Berkeley CA: Lonely Planet Publications, 1978), 240–41.
17. David P. Werlich, *Peru, a Short History,* (Carbondale: Southern Illinois University Press; Feffer & Simons, 1978), 30.
18. Enock. *Republics of Central and South America,* 245.
19. Preston E. James, *Latin America.* (Indianapolis: Bobbs-Merrill, 1976), 452.
20. Enock, *The Republics of Central and South America,* 17.
21. William Hickling Prescott, *History of the Conquest of Peru,* (New York: Dent & Company, 1968), 24–25.
22. Ibid., 30.
23. Enock, *The Republics of Central and South America,* 20.
24. Beals, *Fire in the Andes,* 35.
25. Ibid., 38.
26. Prescott, *History of the Conquest of Peru,* 36.
27. Ibid., 70.
28. Marrett, *Peru,* 36.
29. Prescott, *History of the Conquest of Peru,* 72–73.

30. Ibid., 46.
31. Enock, *The Republics of Central and South America,* 29.

Chapter 2. The Conquest

1. Covering this period of Spanish and Peruvian history, general reference has been made to the previously listed works by Duffield, Enock, Marrett, Werlick, Prescott, James, and the following: *Mexico before Cortes,* by J. E. Thompson, published by Scribners. *The Life of Ferdinand Magellan,* by F. Guillemard, published by Philip, 1890; *Ferdinand Magellan,* by E. F. Benson, published by John Lane, 1929; *Two Years in Peru,* by Thomas J. Hutchinson (British consul–general, Peru), published by Sampson Low, Marston, Low, and Searle, London, 1873; and *The Exploration of the Pacific,* by J. C. Beaglehole, published by Adam and Charles Black, in London, 1934.
2. Beals, *Fire in the Andes,* 51.
3. Clifford Collinson, *Explorers All,* (London: Hutchinson, 1933), 127–60.
4. Prescott, *History of the Conquest of Peru, 1933* 321–22.
5. William Goodell, *Slavery and Antislavery* (1853; repr., New York: Augustus M. Kelly, 1970), 4–5.

Chapter 3. From Colony to Guano Republic

1. Salvador De Madariaga, *The Rise of the Spanish American Empire* (London: Hollis & Carter, 1947), 12–13.
2. Werlich, *Peru, a Short History,* 42.
3. Marrett, *Peru,* 54.
4. Enock, *The Republics of Central and South America,* 56–58.
5. Werlich, *Peru, a Short History,* 43–44.
6. Beals, *Fire on the Andes,* 70–71.
7. Werlich, *Peru, a Short History,* 49–50.
8. C. H. Haring, *Trade and Navigation between Spain and the Indies,* (Cambridge, Massachusetts: 1918, XXiii.
9. Ibid., 20.
10. Sir Julian Corbett, *Drake and the Tudor Navy,* (London: Longmans, 1898), 1:208.
11. Enock, *The Republics of Central and South America,* 60.
12. Trevor R. Davies, *The Golden Century of Spain,* (London: Macmillan, 1964), 263–65.
13. Enock, *The Republics of Central and South America,* 60–61.
14. Beals, *Fire in the Andes,* 72.
15. Clements R. Markham, *Travels in Peru and India,* (London: John Murray, 1862), 129–30.
16. *Letter from General del Ville to two Friends at Lima,* October 3, 1781, cited by Markham, 128.
17. J. H. Parry, *The Spanish Seaborne Empire,* (London: Hutchinson, 1966), 341.

18. Markham, *Travels in Peru and India,* 154–55.
19. Ibid., 130–31.
20. Enock, *The Republics of Central and South America,* 64.
21. John Harris, *A Century of Emancipation,* (London: J. M. Dent & Sons, 1933), 3.
22. J. Holland Rose, *Man and the Sea* (Cambridge: Heffer & Sons, 1933), 244.
23. Enock, *The Republics of Central and South America,* 65.
24. *New Encyclopaedia Britannica,* vol. 25 (Peru), 520.
25. Beals, *Fire in the Andes,* 177.
26. Enock, *The Republics of Central and South America,* 69.
27. Jonathon V. Levin, *The Export Economies: Their Pattern of Development in Historical Perspective,* (Cambridge, MA: Harvard University Press, 1960), 30.

Chapter 4. Dawn of a New Age

1. *Illustrated London News,* February 21, 1863, 200.
2. Henry F. Dobyns, and Paul L. Doughty, *Peru, a Cultural History* (New York: Oxford University Press, 1976), 160.
3. R.E. Coker, "*Peru's Wealth Producing Birds,*" *National Geographical Magazine,* vol. 37, 1920, 538.
4. R.E. Coker, *Habits and Economic Relations of the Guano Birds of Peru,* Smithsonian Institution Proceedings of the United States Museums, vol. 56, published by the Government Printing Office, 1920, 454.
5. *National Geographical Magazine,* 1920, 552.
6. "*The Chincha Guano Islands,*" Illustrated London News, August 17, 1850, 120.
7. Hutchinson, *Two Years in Peru,* 104–5.
8. Coker, *Habits and Economic Relations,* 506.
9. Levin, *The Export Economies,* 28.
10. *New Standard Encyclopaedia,* (London: Odhams Press, 1932), 663.
11. Frederic William Wallace, *In the Wake of the Windships,* (London: Hodder and Stoughton, 1927), 54; and Rosemary Burton, Richard Cavendish, and Bernard Stonehouse, *Journals of the Great Explorers,* (ed. Helen Douglas Cooper, (London: Automobile Association, 1992), 104–5.
12. W. M. Mathew, *The House of Gibbs and the Peruvian Guano Monopoly* (London: The Royal Historical Society, 1981), 23.
13. Hutchinson, *Two Years in Peru,* 109.
14. *Times,* November 26, 1853.
15. Shane J. Hunt, "Growth and Guano in 19th Century Peru," in *The Latin American Economies,* by Robert Cortes Conde (Liverpool Undergraduate Collection, Document 15097, Liverpool University Library), 258.
16. Charles Darwin, *Journal of Researches into the Natural History and Geology of the Countries Visited During the Voyage of the Beagle.* (New York: Ward Locke, 1845), 23.
17. *Dictionary of American Biography,* (London: H. Milford; New York: Scribner's Sons, 1904).

18. John Kennedy, *The History of Steam Navigation,* (Liverpool: Charles Birchall, 1903), 58–59.
19. Acting Consul Sealy, at Lima, to Viscount Palmerston, London, January 1, 1842, British Foreign Office, General Correspondence and Embassy and Consular Archives relating to Peru. (PRO FO 61/087).
20. "The Chincha Islands," *Illustrated London News,* February 21, 1863.
21. Levin, *The Export Economies,* 37–38.
22. Ibid., 50.
23. Probate Register, 1872.
24. David Hollett, *From Cumberland to Cape Horn, the Sailing Fleet of Thomas and John Brocklebank of Whitehaven and Liverpool, 1770–1900* (London: Fairplay Publications, 1984), 11.
25. Ibid., 151–59.
26. Lloyd's Register, 1841.
27. Acting Consul, Sealy to Viscount Palmerston, January 1842. (Peru Archives, PRO FO/087).
28. Mathew, *The House of Gibbs,* 22.
29. W. M. Mathew, "Antony Gibbs & Sons: The Guano Trade and the Peruvian Government," chapter 9 in *Business Imperialism, 1840–1930: An Inquiry Based on British Experience in Latin America,* by D. C. M. Platt, 338.
30. Mathew, *The House of Gibbs,* 78.
31. Gibbs, *The History of Antony and Dorothea Gibbs,* 184.
32. David Hollett, *Fast Passage to Australia,* (London: Fairplay Publications, 1986), 5.
33. Gibbs, *The History of Antony and Dorothea Gibbs,* appendix 7A, 452.
34. Ibid., 394–95.
35. Ibid., 399–400.
36. Ibid., 407.
37. Ibid., 414.
38. Ibid., Partners and Chief Managers of A. Gibbs & Sons' Branch Firms, appendix 7C, 455.
39. Mathew, *The House of Gibbs,* 10–11.
40. Ibid.

Chapter 5. Guano

1. *Treaty of Amity, Britain—Peru-Colombian Confederation, 1837–1838,* British Parliamentary Papers, vol. 52, 288–385.
2. Mathew, *The House of Gibbs,* 51–52.
3. *Correspondence with the Peruvian Government respecting the importation of Guano, 1852–1853.* Papers by J. Thomas Way Esq., consulting chemist to the Royal Agricultural Society, British Parliamentary Papers, 1854, vol. 71, 582–679.
4. Mathew, "Antony Gibbs & Sons." (Chapter 9).
5. *Times,* July 30, 1841.
6. *Liverpool Mercury,* February, 3, 1843.
7. Ibid.

8. Ibid.
9. Ibid.
10. *Times,* (December 28, 1843, citing *John O' Groats Journal.*
11. *Liverpool Mercury,* May 24, 1844.
12. *Times,* July 20, 1844, citing *Agricultural Gazette.*
13. *Times,* November 4, 1844.
14. *Liverpool Mail,* November 30, 1844.
15. George Townsend Warner, *Landmarks in English Industrial History* (London: Blackie & Sons, 1930), 317.
16. David Hollett, *Passage to the New World* (Abergavenny: P. M. Heaton, 1995), 62–64.
17. Crew list of the ship *Princess Royal,* voyage from Liverpool to Calcutta, December 1845 (Public Record Office, Ref. BT 98/697).
18. Crew list of the ship *Rimac,* voyage from Liverpool to Lima, December 1856 (Public Record Office, Ref. BT 98/4553).
19. *Illustrated London News,* January 24, 1891.
20. Markham, *Travels in Peru,* 306.
21. Maria Robinson Wright, *The Old and the New Peru,* (Philadelphia: George Barrie & Sons, 1908), 286–287.
22. British Parliamentary Papers, 1852; vol. 52, 215; 1860, vol. 66, 10–11; 1865, vol. 52, 314; 1870; vol. 63, 305.
23. Alexander Garland, *Peru in 1906 and After,* trans. G.R. Gepp (Lima: La Industria Printing Office, 1908), 319–21.
24. British Parliamentary Papers (135) 1846, vol. 45, 377.
25. James E. Thorold Rogers, MP, *Six Centuries of Work and Wages* (London: Swan, Sonnenschen Le Bas & Lowry, 1886), 510.
26. Warner, *Landmarks in English Industrial History,* 318.
27. Levin, *The Export Economies,* 74–75.
28. Jasper Ridley, *Lord Palmerston,* (London: Constable, 1970), 445–46.
29. Werlich, *Peru, a Short History,* 81.
30. *Times,* November 26, 1853.
31. *Times,* (January 9, 1857.
32. *Illustrated London News,* February 21, 1863.
33. Mathew, *House of Gibbs,* 220–21.
34. Sir Llewellyn Woodward, *The Age of Reform 1815–1870,* (Oxford: Oxford University Press, 1990), 382.
35. *Times,* May 6, 1862, citing the *Liverpool Albion.*
36. Garland, *Peru in 1906 and After,* 322–23.
37. *Geographical Magazine,* April 1, 1876.

Chapter 6. Cape Horn

1. Duffield, *Peru in the Guano Age,* 77–78.
2. Levin, *The Export Economies,* 36.
3. W. M. Mathew "A Primitive Export Sector: Guano Production in Mid-Nineteenth Century Peru," *Journal of Latin American Studies,* 9 (1977): 35–57.
4. Levin, *The Export Economies,* 87.

5. Clements R. Markham, *Cuzco: A Journey to the Ancient Capital of Peru,* (London: Chapman & Hall, 1856), 35.
6. Hutchinson, *Two Years in Peru,* 245.
7. Levin, *The Export Economies,* 88.
8. S. H. Sullivan, British Legation, Lima, September 4, 1854, to Samuel Went, Lima, PRO FO 61/147.
9. David Cowan, *Anecdotes of Life on the Ocean, being a Report of the Experiences of Twenty-Seven Years Service in Many Parts of the World* (Montreal, Canada: John Lovell, 1871), 55–72.
10. Markham, *Cuzco: A Journey,* 36–38.
11. *Dictionary of American Biography,* (Oxford: Humphrey Milford, Oxford University Press, 1931.
12. *Chronicle of America,* (Mount Kisco, N.Y: Chronicle Publications, 1989), 340–42.
13. George Washington Peck, *Melbourne and the Chincha Islands, with Sketches of Lima and a Voyage Round the World,* (New York: Charles Scribner, 1854), 160–67, 205–8.
14. *Nautical Magazine,* (April 1856, citing the *Daily News* of January and February, 1856.
15. *Household Words,* September 25, 1852, 42–44.
16. *Times,* January 12, 1855, citing the *New Orleans Picayune.*
17. *Times,* January 18, 1855.
18. Ibid., January 20, 1855.
19. Ibid., October 17, 1853.
20. *New York Daily Times,* January 7, 1854.
21. Ibid.
22. Thomas Fowell Buxton, *The African Slave Trade and its Remedy* (London: John Murray, 1840), 1.
23. *Times,* December 1, 1853.
24. Ibid., December 23, 1853.
25. Peruvian Government Respecting the Importation of Guano, British Parliamentary Papers, 1854, vol. 72:582ff.

Chapter 7. Chinese Bondage in Peru

1. Clements R.Markham, "From China to Peru, The Emigration Question," 14.
2. *Geographical Magazine,* December 1, 1874, 367.
3. Peter Blanchard, *Slavery and Abolition in Early Republican Peru: The Emigration Question* (Wilmington, DE: Scholarly Resources, 1992), 19.
4. Ibid., 79.
5. Ibid., 114.
6. Ibid., 119–20.
7. Ibid., 171.
8. Harris, *A Century of Emancipation,* 1–3.
9. Ibid., 7.
10. David Hollett, *The Conquest of the Niger by Land and Sea* (Abergavenny: P.M. Heaton Publishing, 1995), 170–71.

11. Christopher Lloyd, *The Royal Navy and the Slave Trade* (New York: Longman, Green, 1949), 24.
12. Buxton, *The Remedy,* 15.
13. Blanchard, *Slavery and Abolition in Early Republican Peru,* 182–83.
14. Treaty of Friendship, Commerce, and Navigation between Her Majesty and the Republic of Peru, 1850, British Parliamentary Papers, 1852–53, vol. 103, 413.
15. Mathew, *The House of Gibbs,* 101.
16. Rev. L. Crookall, *British Guiana or Work and Wanderings among the Creoles and Coolies,* (London: T. Fisher Unwin, 1898), 169.
17. Ibid., 170.
18. Basil Lubbock, *The Coolie Ships and Oil Traders,* (Glasgow: Brown, Son & Ferguson, repr. 1981), 26.
19. Captain W. H. Angel, *The Clipper Ship Sheila—Angel Master,* (London: Heath Cranton, 1920), 161.
20. E. J. Eitel, (Inspector of Schools, Hong Kong), *Europe in China: The History of Hong Kong From the beginning to the Year 1882* (London: Luzac; Hong Kong: Kelly & Walsh 1895), 273.
21. Franklin J. Jameson, *Dictionary of United States History,* (Boston, MA: Puritan Publishing, 1898), 106.
22. Eitel, *Europe in China,* 273.
23. Harley Farnsworth MacNair, *The Chinese Abroad, their Position and Protection: A Study in International Law and Relations* (Shanghai, China: Commercial Press, 1933), 210–11.
24. Ibid., 211.
25. Watt Strewart, *Chinese Bondage in Peru,* (Durham, NC: Duke University Press Press, 1951) 72.
26. Hutchinson, *Two Years in Peru,* 250.
27. Eitel, *Europe in China,* 344.
28. Stewart, *Chinese Bondage in Peru,* 72–73.
29. Hutchinson, *Two Years in Peru,* 246–47.
30. *Illustrated London News,* July 3, 1852.
31. Correspondence upon the subject of Emigration from China, British Parliamentary Papers, 1854–55, vol. 39, 187–89.
32. British Parliamentary Papers, 1854–55. vol. 39, 187–89, Chargé Sulivan to Jose Gomez Sanchez, Lima, September 2, 1854.
33. Ibid., Chargé Sulivan to Samuel Went, Lima, September 4, 1854.
34. Ibid., Samuel Went to Chargé Sulivan, Lima, September 4, 1854.
35. Ibid., Chargé Sulivan to Lord Clarendon, Lima, September 11, 1854.
36. Ibid., Samuel Went to Chargé Sulivan, Lima, September 21, 1854.
37. Ibid., Don Hose Sanchez to Samuel Went, Lima, December 12, 1854.
38. Levin, *The Export Economies,* 88.
39. Chargé Sulivan to Lord Clarendon, Lima, July 11, 1855, PRO FO 61/155.
40. Ibid., August 1, 1857, PRO FO 61/174.
41. Mathew, *Primitive Export Sector,* 46–48.
42. Lawrence A. Clayton, *W. R. Grace & Co: The Formative Years, 1850–1930* (Ottawa, IL: Jameson Books, 1985, [caption to illustration of shackled Chinese worker], 108.
43. "A Railroad in the Clouds," *Scribner's Monthly,* August 1877, 461.
44. Mathew, *House of Gibbs,* 108.
45. Eitel, *Europe in China,* 344–45.

46. Papers relating to Coolie Emigration, Smale & Whittall to MacDonnel, Hong Kong, June 27, 1867, British Parliamentary Papers, 1867–68, vol. 48, 8.
47. Ibid., Acting Colonial Secretary Henry John Ball to the Hon. Chief Justice Smale and the Hon. James Whittall, July 4, 1867.
48. Macnair, *The Chinese Abroad,* 213.
49. Clements R. Markham, *Geographical Magazine,* December 1, 1874, 368.
50. Stewart, *Chinese Bondage in Peru,* 71.
51. Lubbock, *Coolie Ships and Oil Traders,* (Glasgow: Brown, Son & Ferguson, 1981), 43.
52. Hutchinson, *Two Years in Peru,* 245.
53. Stewart, *Chinese Bondage in Peru,* 71.
54. Markham, *Geographical Magazine,* December 1, 1874, 369.
55. Hutchinson, *Two Yeas in Peru,* 246–47.
56. MacNair, *The Chinese Abroad,* 217.

Chapter 8. The Lobos Islands Adventure

1. Marquis James, with introduction by Lawrence A. Clayton, *Merchant Adventurer: The Story of W. R. Grace,* (Wilmington DE: Scholarly Resources, 1993), 150.
2. Mathew, *The House of Gibbs,* 150.
3. *Times,* April 17, 1852.
4. Correspondence respecting the Guano Islands of De Tierra and Lobos de Fuera, British Parliamentary Papers, 1852, vol. 51, 309.
5. Ibid., Rankin to the Lords Commissioners of the Admiralty, Liverpool, April 13, 1852.
6. Ibid., Allan Edward to the Earl of Malmesbury, Dundee, April 20, 1852.
7. *Times,* April 22, 1852.
8. Correspondence respecting the Guano Islands, Rankin to Derby, April 21, 1852, British Parliamentary Papers, 1852, vol. 51, 309.
9. Hamond to Malmesbury, April 20, 1852, British Parliamentary Papers, 1852, vol. 51, 309.
10. Correspondence re Guano Islands, Dempsey to William Pitt Adams, British Chargé in Lima, February 14, 1845, and statement of G. F. Seymour, rear admiral and commander-in-chief, ca. March 1845, British Parliamentary Papers, 1852, (1514) vol. 54, 123.
11. *Times,* May 4, 1852.
12. Mathew, *The House of Gibbs,* 162–63.
13. *Times,* June 11, 1852.
14. James, *The Merchant Adventurer,* 28.
15. Ibid., 29.
16. *Times,* October 27, 1852, citing the *New York Herald.*

Chapter 9. The Brocklebank Line

1. Liverpool Customs Register, 1847.
2. David Hollett, *From Cumberland to Cape Horn,* (London: Fairplay Publications, 1984), 11, 20–26.

3. John Frederick Gibson, *Brocklebanks, 1770–1950,* (Liverpool: Henry Young, 1953), 1:88–90.
4. Hollett, *Cumberland to Cape Horn,* 155.
5. Lloyd's Register, 1841.
6. Gibson, *Brocklebanks,* 1:114.
7. Hollett, *Cumberland to Cape Horn,* 156–57.
8. PRO FO 61/087.
9. Hollett, *Cumberland to Cape Horn,* 185.
10. *Gallovidian: An Illustrated Southern Counties Quarterly Magazine,* no. 22, vol. 6, Summer 1904.
11. Gibson, *Brocklebanks,* 1:204, and Hollett, *Cumberland,* 147.
12. Gibson, *Brocklebanks,* 1:251.
13. Brocklebank Apprentice Book, 1840–42, Ref. B/1370c, Maritime Archives and Library, Liverpool (re: James Anderson).
14. Crew list of the *Kestrel,* 1842–43, wages taken from crew list of the *Princess Royal,* voyage of 1844, voyage to Calcutta, which shows wages paid. PRO BT/697 Crew Lists and Agreements.
15. *Gallovidian,* Summer 1904.
16. Captain's register of Lloyd's of London, held by the Guildhall Library, London, re James Anderson, Extra Masters' Certificate, No. 5,677, taken at Liverpool in 1851.
17. Brocklebank Records, Document No. 387.MD 26, the Maritime Museum, Liverpool.
18. Ibid., Voyage of the *Bonanza,* 18/4/1852.
19. Ibid., Voyage of the *Rimac,* October 1854. Also, Crew Lists and Agreements, PRO BT 98/4208, Crew Lists and Agreements Voyage of the *Rimac* to Lima, October 1854.
20. Yves Le Scal, *The Great Days of the Cape Horners,* trans. Len Ortzen (London: Souvenir Press, 1966), 151.
21. Ibid., 152.
22. Captain William Ray, (late Marine Superintendent of the Brocklebank Line), "Fifty-seven Years in the Merchant Service," *Liverpool Journal of Commerce,* October 22, 1921.
23. Lubbock, Basil, *The Down Easters,* (Glasgow: Brown, Son & Ferguson, 1981), 40.
24. Hollett, *From Cumberland to Cape Horn,* 186.
25. PRO. BT 98/3818, Crew Lists and Agreements, Voyage of the *Courier* to Lima, October 5, 1853.
26. PRO. BT 98/3818. Crew Lists and Agreements, Voyage of the *Rimac,* (Liverpool to Lima, December 8, 1856.
27. Ray, *Fifty-seven Years in the Merchant Service.*
28. Darwin, *Journal of Researches,* 351.
29. Peck, *Melbourne and the Chincha Islands,* 351.
30. Ibid., 143–44.
31. Ray, *Journal of Commerce,* October 22, 1921.
32. Hollett, *Cumberland to Cape Horn,* 159–60.
33. Brocklebank Records, the Maritime Museum, Liverpool, 387.MD 26.
34. William Ellery, *Incidents of Life at Sea for nearly Fifty Years: The Wallasey and Wirral Chronicle,* March 4, and other dates, 1912.

35. Hollett, *Cumberland to Cape Horn,* 156.
36. Ellery, *Incidents of Life at Sea,* March 16, 1924.
37. Ibid., March 20, 1924.
38. Cushman, *Bird Islands of Peru,* 100.
39. Basil Lubbock, *The Western Ocean Packets,* (Glasgow: Brown, Son & Ferguson, 1977), 23.
40. Murphy, *Bird Islands of Peru,* 101.
41. David Hollett, *The Alabama Affair,* (Wilmslow, Cheshire: Sigma Leisure, 1993).
42. Lubbock, *The Down Easters,* 59.
43. Hollett, *The Alabama Affair,* 100–107.
44. Murphy, *Bird Islands of Peru,* 103–104.
45. Cowan, *Anecdotes of a Life on the Ocean,* 66–67.
46. Lubbock, *The Down Easters,* 61.
47. Ibid., 89.254–255.

Chapter 10. Wiliam R. Grace & Company

1. James, *Merchant Adventurer,* 7.
2. Grace, *Memoirs of the Family of Grace,* (London, 1823), 105.
3. Brian Inglis, *The Story of Ireland,* (London, Faber & Faber, 1956), 39.
4. Grace, *Memoirs of the Family of Grace,* 9.
5. Ibid., 25.
6. David Hollett, *Passage to the New World: Packet Ships and Famine Emigrants 1845–1851,* (Abergavenny, Gwent: P. M. Heaton, 1995), 35.
7. Ibid., 11.
8. Ibid., 17.
9. James, *Merchant Adventurer,* 13.
10. *Dictionary of American Biography,* (Oxford: Humphrey Milford, Oxford University Press, 1931).
11. Clayton, *W. R. Grace and Co.,* 8–9.
12. *New York Daily News,* March 21, 1904.
13. Hollett, *Passage to the New World,* 88.
14. *Freeman's Journal,* July 2, 1847.
15. The Hon. Vicary Gibbs, ed., *The Complete Peerage,* vol. 4, (London: Burkes, 1916), 404–5.
16. Rory Miller, "The Making of the Grace Contracts, British Bondholders and The Peruvian Government 1885–1890," *Journal of Latin American Studies,* vol. 8 (1976): 88.
17. Gibbs, *The Complete Peerage,* (London: Burkes, vol. 4, 1916), 404–405.
18. Hollett, *Passage to the New World,* 165–90.
19. David Hollett, *Fast Passage to Australia,* (London: Fairplay Publications, 1986), 7.
20. James, *Merchant Adventurer,* 17.
21. Blanchard, *Slavery and Abolition in Early Republican Peru,* 163.
22. Lloyd's Register, 1851.
23. James, *Merchant Adventurer,* 18–19.

24. Ibid., 20.
25. *Dictionary of American Biography,* (see "W. R. Grace.")
26. James, *Merchant Adventurer,* 23.
27. "Casa Grace," *Fortune Magazine,* December 1935, 158.
28. Mathew, *Primitive Export Sector,* 55.
29. *New York Herald* and *New York Times* March 22, 1904.
30. James, *Merchant Adventurer,* 33.
31. Frederick C. Mathews, *American Merchant Ships, 1850–1900,* Series 11 (New York: Dover Publications, 1987). Originally published as publications 21 (1930) and 23 (1931) by the Marine Research Society, Salem, MA), 95.
32. James, *Merchant Adventurer,* 36.
33. "Casa Grace," *Fortune Magazine,* December 1935, 158.
34. Mathews, *American Merchant Ships,* 93.
35. Hollett, *The Alabama Affair,* 91.
36. Mathews, *American Merchant Ships,* 94.
37. James, *Merchant Adventurer,* 41.
38. Mary Robinson Wright, *The Old and the New Peru,* (Philadelphia: George Barrie & Sons; London: Cazenove & Sons, 1908), 367.
39. *New York Times,* March 22, 1904.
40. Ibid.
41. Mathews, *American Merchant Ships,* 183.
42. Ibid., 293–94.
43. James, *Merchant Adventurer,* 47–52.
44. Clayton, *W. R. Grace and Co.,* 14.
45. Lloyd's Register, 1889–90.
46. *Dictionary of American Biography,* see "W. R. Grace."
47. "Casa Grace" *Fortune Magazine,* December 1935, 158–61.

Chapter 11. The Twentieth Century

1. Owen, *Peru,* 50.
2. Vicary Gibbs, ed., *The Complete Peerage,* vol. 4 (London: Burkes, 1916), 405–406.
3. *Freeman's Journal* (Dublin), July 2, 1847.
4. Clayton, *W. R. Grace and Co.,* 140.
5. Ibid., 153.
6. Levin, *The Export Economies,* 111; also *Dictionary of American Biography,* (1931), see "William R. Grace."
7. James, *Merchant Adventurers,* 226.
8. Ibid., 243.
9. Clayton, *W. R. Grace and Co.,* 173.
10. Martin, *Peru in the 20th Century,* 308–9.
11. Miller, "The Making of the Grace Contract," Journal of Latin American Studies, 8(1976):97.
12. Ibid., 91.
13. Ibid., 97.
14. Ibid., 99.

15. Ibid., 100.
16. *Times,* December 6, 1900.
17. *New York Times* and *New York Herald Tribune,* March 22, 1904.
18. Beals, *Fire in the Andes,* 299–300.
19. Martin, *Peru in the 20th Century,* 241–42.
20. Lieutenant George R. Johnson and Raye R. Platt (texts and notes), *Peru from the Air,* (American Geographical Society, Special Publication No. 12, published by the Society at New York in 1930.
21. James, *Merchant Adventurer,* 138.
22. Martin, *Peru in the 20th Century,* 243–45.
23. *Truth,* September 22, 1909; *The Devil's Paradise,* 663–66.
24. *The Anti-Slavery Reporter and the Aborigines Friend,* October 1912.
25. Ibid. Also see Series 5, vol. 1, no. 2, (January 1910), *Rubber Slavery in South America,* 54–56; Series 5, vol. 3, no. 1. (April 1913): 7, *Aboriginese Protection in S. America;* Series 5, vol. 3, no. 2 (July 1913) 73–79, *The Putamayo Slavery;* ibid., *Native Labour in Peru,* 156–57; *El Comercio* (Lima), January 4, 1913; *Times,* February 25, 1913, South American Supplement; Robin Furneaux, *The Amazon: Story of a Great River,* (London: Hamish Hamilton, 1969), 167–95; and for further reading, Richard Collier, *The River that God Forgot* (London: Collins, 1968).
26. Martin, *Peru in the 20th Century,* 247–48.
27. Ibid., 335.
28. Ibid., 251.
29. Ibid., 334.
30. Blanchard, *The Origins of the Peruvian Labour Movement,* 65–78.
31. Ibid., 101.

Chapter 12. The Casa Grace Sails On

1. Gunther, *Inside Latin America,* (New York: Harper Brothers, 1940), 166.
2. Ibid., 170–171.
3. *Times,* September, 23–25, 1920, and The Calender of Probate, 1921.
4. R. E. G. Davies, *Airlines of Latin America since 1919,* (London: Putnam, 1984), 288–89.
5. William A. Burden, *The Struggle for Airways in Latin America,* (New York: Council on Foreign Relations, 1943), 24.
6. Davies, *Airlines of Latin America since 1919,* 291.
7. Burden, *The Struggle for Airways,* 27.
8. William M. Denevan, *The 1931 Shippee–Johnson Aerial Photography Expedition to Peru,* (New York: the American Geographical Society. 1930), 238–251.
9. Johnson and Platt, *Peru from the Air,* 2–3.
10. Burden, *The Struggle for Airways* 27–28.
11. Ibid., Citing data furnished by Pan American Airways, Civil Aeronautics Board, Docket no. 716, Appendix C., 59.
12. *New York Tribune,* January 11, 1895.
13. *Lloyd's Registers,* 1889/1890.
14. *New York Times,* March 22, 1904.
15. John Kennedy, *The History of Steam Navigation,* (Liverpool: Charles Birchall, 1903), 58.

16. *The Mersey Magazine,* April, 1925.
17. *The Journal of Commerce and Shipping Telegraph Annual Review,* 1940.
18. *The Mersey Magazine,* April, 1925.
19. *The New York Times,* September 21, 1920.
20. *Lloyd's Registers,* 1919/1920.
21. *Lloyd's Registers,* 1933/1934.
22. William Ellery, in *Wallasey and Wirral Chronicle,* June 6, 1912.
23. Hollett, *From Cumberland to Cape Horn,* 139–67. John Frederick Gibson, *Brocklebanks 1770–1953,* vol. 1, 176–287.
24. *Lloyd's Registers of Shipping,* 1865–1888.
25. *Lloyd's Register of Shipping,* 1934.
26. W. Burnett Tracy, *Lancashire at the Opening of the Twentieth Century, The Liverpool Courier,* June 12, 1906, 20.
27. Correspondence between Mr. J. H. Ray and the author.
28. *The Gallovidian,* Summer, 1904. Captains' Registers of Lloyd's of London. F.E. Baines, *Forty Years at the Post Office* (London: Richard Bently & Sons, 1895), 1:334–37.
29. William Ellery, "Incidents of Life at Sea for Nearly Fifty Years," in the *Wallasey and Wirral Chronicle,* March 4, 1912–July 6, 1912. Hollett, *From Cumberland to Cape Horn,* 134–38 and 163–66. *Lloyd's Registers of Shipping.*

Bibliography

Primary

387. MD 26	Maritime Archives & Library, Liverpool Maritime Museum. *The Brocklebank Records*
PRO. BT 98/697	*Crew List of the Ship 'Princess Royal'- Voyage from Liverpool to Calcutta, December, 1845.*
PRO. BT 98/4553	*Crew List of the Ship 'Rimac'—voyage from Liverpool to Lima, December 1856.*
PRO. F.O. 61/147	*S.H. Sullivan, British Legation, Lima, 4 September 1854 to Samuel Went, Lima.*
PRO. F061/087	*Acting Consul Sealy, at Lima, to Viscount Palmerston, London, 1st January 1842.* (British Foreign Office, General Correspondence and Embassy and Consular Archives relating to Peru).
PRO. FO 61/148	*Samuel Went to Charge' Sullivan,Lima, 21st September, 1854 Don Hose Sanchez to Charge' Went, Lima, 12th Dec. 1854.*
PRO. FO 61/155	*Charge' Sullivan to Lord Clarendon, Lima, 11th July, 1855*
PRO. BT98/4208	*Crew Lists & Agreements, Voyage of the 'Rimac'to Lima, October, 1854.*
PRO. BT98/3818	*Crew Lists & Agreements, Voyage of the 'Courier', Liverpool To Lima, 5th October, 1853.*
PRO	(Public Record Office)

British Paliamentary Papers

Irish University Press Series of British Parliamentary Papers

Vol. L11, 1838.	*Treaty of Amity, Britain-Peru-Columbian Confederation, 1837–1838*
Vol. LXX1, 1854.	*Correspondence with the Peruvian Government Respecting the Importation of Guano.*
Vol. LXX11, 1854	*Peruvian Government Respecting the Importation of Guano.*

Vol. C111. 1852/53 *Treaty of Friendship, Commerce and Navigation between Her Majesty and the Republic of Peru, 1850.*

Vol. XXX1X

1854–1855 *Correspondence upon the subject of Emigration from China. Charge' Sullivan to Jose Gomez Sanchez, Lima 2nd September, 1854. Samuel Went to Charge' Sullivan, Lima, 4th September, 1854. Charge Sullivan to Lord Clarendon, 11th September, 1854.*

VOL. XLV111

1867–1868 *Papers Relating to Coolie Emigration, Smale & Whittall to MacDonnell, Hong Kong, 27th June, 1867–1868. Acting Colonial Secretary Henry John Ball, to the Hon. Chief Justice Smale, and the Hon. James Whittall, 4th July, 1867.*

VOL. L1 309 *Correspondence Respecting the Guano Islands of De Tierra and Lobos De Fuera, 1852. Rankin to the Lords Commissioners of the Admiralty, Liverpool, 13th April, 1852. Allan Edward to the Earl of Malmesbury, Dundee, 20th April, 1852. Correspondence regarding Guano Islands, Rankin to Derby, 21st April, 1852. Hamond to Malmesbury, 20th April, 1852.*

VOL. LIV 123 *Correspondence Respecting the Guano Islands, Dempsey to William Pitt Adams, British Charge' in Lima, 14th February, 1845. Statement of G.F. Seymour, Rear Admiral and Commander-In-Chief, c March, 1845.*

Newspapers, Periodicals and Registers

Dictionary of American Biography
El Commercio, (Lima)
Fortune Magazine
Household Words
Lloyd's Captain's Registers
Lloyd's Registers
Scribners Magazine
Truth
The Anti-Slavery Reporter and the Aborigines Friend
The Calendar of Probate.
The Complete Peerage Vol. 1V
The Daily News
The Freeman's Journal
The Gallovidian, an Illustrated Southern Counties Quarterly Magazine
The Geographical Magazine
The Illustrated London News
The Journal of Latin American Studies
The Journal of Commerce and Shipping Telegraph Annual Review,1940
The Liverpool Courier

The Liverpool Journal of Commerce
The Liverpool Mail
The Liverpool Mercury
The Mersey Magazine
The National Geographical Magazine
The Nautical Magazine
The New York Daily News
The New York Daily Times
The New York Herald
The New York Herald Tribune
The New York Times
The New York Tribune
The Times
The Wallasey and Wirral Chronicle

Secondary

Angel, Captain William H. *The Clipper Ship Sheila—Angel Master.* London: Heath Cranton, 1920.

Baines, F.E. *Forty Years at the Post Office* London: Richard Bently & Sons, 1895.

Beaglehole, J.C. *The Exploration of the Pacific.* London: Adam & Charles Black, 1934.

Beals, Carleton. *Fire in the Andes.* London: J.P. Lippincott & Company, 1934.

Beson, E.F. *Ferdinand Magellan.* London: John Lane, 1929.

Blanchard, Peter. *The Origins of the Peruvian Labour Movement.* Wilmington DE: University of Pittsburgh Press, 1982.

Blanchard, Peter. *Slavery and Abolition in Early Republican Peru.* Wilmington De: Scholarly Resources Inc., 1992.

Burden, A.M. *The Struggle for Airways in Latin America.* New York: Council on Foreign Relations, 1943.

Buxton, Thomas Fowell. *The African Slave Trade and its Remedy.* London: John Murray, 1840.

Clayton, Lawrence A. *W.R. Grace and Company, the Formative Years, 1850–1930.* Ottawa IL: Jameson Books, 1985.

Coker, R.E. "Peru's Wealth Producing Bird." *The National Geographical Magazine.* vol. 37, 1920.

Coker, R.E. *Habits and Economic Relations of the Guano Birds of Peru.* Smithsonian Institution Proceedings of the United States Museums, vol. 56, Washington, D.C.: Government Printing Office, 1920.

Collinson, Clifford. *Explorers All.* London: Hutchinson, 1933.

Corbett, Sir Julian Stafford. *Drake and the Tudor Navy.* London: Longmans, 1898.

Cowan, David. *Anecdotes of Life on the Ocean, being a Report of the Experiences of Twenty Seven Years Service in Many Parts of the World.* Montreal: John Lovell, 1871.

Crookall, Rev. L. *British Guiana or Work and Wanderings among the Creoles and Coolies.* London: T. Fisher Unwin, 1898.

Darwin, Charles. *Journal of Researches into the Natural History and Geology of the Countries Visited during the Voyage of the 'Beagle.'* New York: Ward Locke & Co. Ltd., 1845.

Davies, R. E. G. *Airlines of Latin America.* London: Putnam, 1984.

Davies, Trevor R. *The Golden Century of Spain.* London: Macmillan & Company, 1964.

Denivan, William M. "The 1931 Shippee-Johnson Aerial Photography Expedition to Peru." *The Geographical Review, 1933.* New York: The American Geographical Society, 1933.

Dobyns, Henry F. and Paul Doughty. *Peru, a Cultural History.* New York: Oxford University Press, 1976.

Duffield, A. J. *Peru in the Guano Age.* London: Richard Bently, 1877.

Eitel, E.J. (Inspector of Schools, Hong Kong). *Europe in China, the History of Hong Kong, from the beginning of the year 1882.* London: Luzac & Co., 1895.

Enock, C. Reginald. *The Republics of Central and South America.* London: J.M. Dent, 1913.

Furneaux, Robin. *The Amazon—the Story of a Great River.* London: Hamish Hamilton, 1969.

Garland, Alexander. *Peru in 1906 and After.* Translated by G.R. Gepp. Lima: La Industria Printing Office, 1908.

Gibson, John Frederick. *Brocklebanks, 1770–1950.* vol.1. Liverpool: Henry Young & Sons, 1953.

Goodsell, William. *Slavery and Anti-Slavery.* 1853. Reprinted. New York: Augustus M. Kelly, 1970.

Grace, Sheffield. *Memoirs of the Family of Grace.* London, 1823.

Guillemard, F. *The Life of Ferdinald Magellan.* Phillip & Company, 1890

Gunther, John. *Inside Latin America.* New York: Harper Brothers, 1940.

Haring, C. H. *Trade and Navigation between Spain and the Indies.* Cambridge, Mass: 1918.

Harris, John. *A Century of Emancipation.* London: J. M. Dent & Sons, 1933.

Hollett, David. *From Cumberland to Cape Horn.* London: Fairplay Publications,1984.

———. *The Alabama Affair.* Wilmslow: Sigma Leisure, 1993.

———. *Fast Passage to Australia.* London: Fairplay Publications, 1986.

———. *Passage to the New World.* Abergavenny, Gwent: P.M. Heaton, 1995.

———. *The Conquest of the Niger by Land and Sea.* Abergavenny, Gwent: P. M. Heaton, 1995.

Hunt, Shane J. *Growth and Guano in 19th Century Peru. The Latin American Economies.* by Robert Cortes Conde. Liverpool undergraduate collection, Document 15097, Liverpool University Library.

Hutchinson, Thomas J. (British Consul in Peru) *Two Years in Peru*. London: Sampson Low, Marston, Low and Searle, 1873.

Inglis, Brian. *The Story of Ireland*. London: Faber & Faber, 1956.

James, Preston E. *Latin America*. Indianapolis: Bobbs-Merril Co.1976.

Jameson, J. Franklin. *Dictionary of United States History*. Boston, Ma: Puritan Publishing Company, 1898.

Johnson, Lieutenant George R. and Platt, Raye R. "*Peru From the Air,*" American Geographical Society special publication, New York, 1930.

Kennedy, John. *The History of Steam Navigation*. Liverpool: Charles Birchall, 1903.

Levin, Jonathan V. *The Export Economies—Pattern of Development in Historical Perspective*. Cambridge Ma: Harvard University Press, 1960.

Lloyd, Christopher. *The Royal Navy and the Slave Trade*. London: Longman, Green & Company, 1949.

Lubbock, Basil. *The Coolie Ships and Oil Traders*. Glasgow: Brown, Son & Ferguson, 1981.

Lubbock, Basil. *The Down Easters*. Glasgow: Brown, Son & Ferguson, 1981.

Lubbock, Basil. *The Western Ocean Packets*. Glasgow: Brown, Son & Ferguson, 1977.

MacNair, Harley Farnsworth. *The Chinese Abroad, Their Position and Protection, a Study in International Law and Relations*. Shanghai: The Commercial Press, 1933.

Madariaga, Salvador De. *The Rise of the Spanish American Empire*. London: Hollis & Carter, 1947.

Markham, Clements R. *Cuzco, a Journey to the Ancient Capital of Peru*. London: Chapman & Hall, 1856.

———. *Travels in Peru and India*. London: John Murray, 1862.

Marquis, James. With an Introduction by Lawrence A. Clayton, *Merchant Adventurer, the Story of W.R. Grace*. Wilmington DE: Scholarly Resources, 1933.

Marrett, Sir Robert. Peru. London: Ernest Benn, 1969.

Martin, Percy F. *Peru in the 20th Century*. London: Edward Arnold, 1911.

Mathew, W.M. *The House of Gibbs and the Peruvian Guano Monopoly*. London: The London Historical Society, 1981.

Mathew, W.M. "A Primitive Export Sector: Guano Production in mid-Nineteenth Century Peru." *Journal of Latin American Studies*. Chapter 9, vol. 9, 1977.

Mathews, Frederic C. *American Merchant Ships 1850–1900*. Series 11. New York: Dover Publications Inc. 1987. Originally published as Publication 21 (1930) and (1931) by The Marine Research Society, Salem, MA.

Miller, Rory. "The Making of the Grace Contracts, British Bondholders and The Peruvian Government 1885–1890." *The Journal of Latin American Studies*. 8: 1976.

Murphy, Robert Cushman. *Bird Islands of Peru,The Record of a Sojourn on the West Coast*. New York: G. P. Putnam's Sons, 1925. London, 1925.

Owen, J. R. *Peru*. Oxford: Oxford University Press, 1963.

Parry J. H. *The Spanish Seaborne Empire*. London: Hutchinson, 1966.

Peck, George Washington. *Melbourne and the Chincha Islands, with Sketches of Lima and a Voyage Round the World.* New York: Charles Scribner & Sons, 1854.

Prescott, William Hickling. *History of the Conquest of Peru.* New York: Dent & Company, 1908.

Ridley, Jasper. *Lord Palmerston.* London: Constable & Company, 1970.

Rogers, James E.Thorald, MP. *Six Centuries of Work and Wages.* London: Swan, Sonnenschen Le Bas & Lowry, 1886.

Rose, J. Holland. *Man and the Sea.* Cambridge, UK: Heffer & Sons Ltd., 1933.

Samagalski, Alan. *Chile and Easter Island.* Berkeley, Ca: Lonely Planet Publications, 1978.

Scal, Yves Le. Translated by Len Orten, *The Great Days of the Cape Horners.* London: Sovenir Press, 1966.

Stewart, Watt. *Chinese Bondage in Peru.* Durham NC: Duke University Press, 1951.

Thompson, J.E. *Mexico before Cortes.* New York: Scribners, 1933.

Tracy, W. Burnett. *Lancashire at the Opening of the Twentieth Century.* Liverpool: 1903.

Wallace, Frederick William. *In the Wake of the Wind Ships.* London: Hodder and Stoughton, 1927.

Warner, George Townsend. *Landmarks in English Industrial History.* London: Blackie & Sons, 1930.

Werlich, David P. *Peru, a Short History.* Carbondale: Southern Illinois University Press, 1978.

Woodward, Sir Llewellyn. *The Age of Reform.* Oxford: Oxford University Press, 1990.

Wright, Maria Robinson. *The Old and the New Peru.* Philadelphia: George Barrie and Sons, 1908.

Index